FROM THE TOP DOWN

from the top down

THE EXECUTIVE ROLE IN SUCCESSFUL VOLUNTEER INVOLVEMENT

Susan J. Ellis

Third Edition

ENERG!ZE INC

Copyright © 2010 by Energize, Inc.
5450 Wissahickon Avenue
Philadelphia, PA 19144
www.energizeinc.com

Paperback ISBN-13: 978-0-940576-59-9
E-book   ISBN-13: 978-0-940576-60-5

Library of Congress Cataloging-in-Publications Data

Ellis, Susan J.
  From the top down : the executive role in successful volunteer involvement /
Susan J. Ellis.—3rd ed.
    p. cm.
  Includes bibliographical references and index.
  ISBN 978-0-940576-59-9 (pbk.) — ISBN 978-0-940576-60-5 (e-book) 1.
Voluntarism—Management. 2. Personnel management. 3. Volunteers. I. Title.
  HN49.V64E44 2010
  361.3'7068—dc22   2009053598

This is a fully revised third edition, 2010

Second edition: Energize, Inc., 1996

First edition: Energize, Inc., 1986

Printed in the United States of America

Contents

Preface

I wrote the first edition of *From the Top Down* in 1986. Revisiting it ten years later for the second edition, I was struck by the continued relevance of the words I had chosen so carefully a decade previously. A dozen more years (and a new century) later, the continuing relevance of most of the material in this book is both comforting and disturbing. Of course, much has changed both in the world and in volunteerism, which is why I am producing this third edition (Internet-related developments alone required edits and additions). But the basic *rationale* for executive involvement in successful volunteer engagement is as clear and constant as ever.

In fact, the profession of "volunteer administration" has made great strides in the training of leaders of volunteer involvement. The number of books on how to work effectively with volunteers has more than quadrupled since the first books of the 1970s. (The resources in appendix B are almost completely new to this edition.) Volunteerism conferences attract several thousand at the international or national level and hundreds at the state or provincial level. It is increasingly possible for someone to learn about volunteer program development and management at the local level through regular workshops, some college courses and certificate programs, and professional societies. And, of course, the Web has brought an inconceivable wealth of materials to everyone's fingertips and has made international professional exchange a daily occurrence.

Most books and articles about involving volunteers are designed for the person designated to implement an organization's volunteer resources strategy and who has direct contact with volunteers on a daily basis. Such frontline managers are the usual audience in the thousands of training workshops my company, Energize, Inc., has conducted since 1977. Our workshops (as well as individualized consultations) deal with all aspects of how to start, maintain, or expand the engagement of volunteers in organizations that range from hospitals to courts to museums to schools. The skills of volunteer administration are generic and apply to all settings. They are also amazingly universal. We have presented sessions in twenty-six countries on six continents; the context varies from culture to culture, but the principles always apply.

However, not much progress has been made in the training of executives and other agency staff who interface daily with volunteers but who do not carry major responsibility for the organization's overall volunteer involvement strategy. That's the gap this book tries to fill.

The great news is that today, *From the Top Down* has company in two important new companion publications:

- Sarah Jane Rehnborg's *Strategic Volunteer Engagement: A Guide for Nonprofit and Public Sector Leaders* distills research conducted through the University of Texas at Austin with actual executives of agencies to make a very strong case for what is needed to invest in volunteer effectiveness. I quote from this report throughout the book.

- Betty Stallings has created a unique resource, *Leading the Way to Successful Volunteer Involvement: Practical Tips for Busy Executives*. It offers guides, worksheets, checklists, and templates specifically selected or created to assist readers of *From the Top Down* to put the recommendations here to work. At the end of each chapter, I note the sections of *Leading the Way* that provide tools to implement the ideas in that part of *From the Top Down*.

Acknowledgments

There is no way I can thank all the many colleagues who have expanded my knowledge of volunteer involvement over the last three decades, but their collective influence is reflected in these pages—as are anecdotes and examples they have shared publicly and individually.

Special and huge amounts of gratitude go to the people who reviewed this manuscript at various stages and generously offered solid feedback, worthwhile critiques, and additional content: Betty Stallings, Colleen Kelly, Sarah Jane Rehnborg, Linda Graff, Jeff Kahn, Janine Bovatsek, and Keith Skillman. You are all wonderful! This group represents the United States and Canada, and I also appreciate the constant support from Rob

Jackson in England and Andy Fryar in Australia. We are truly an international field, and I hope readers from around the globe will recognize the universality of much of what I try to convey in this book.

Thanks, too, to Jenn Kepler at Scribe for her thorough copyediting.

Finally, my sincerest gratitude to Cara Thenot, director of online publishing at my company, Energize, Inc., for her unflagging commitment to helping me produce the highest-quality publication, on schedule, and still in my right mind.

Needed: Executive Attention

Picture the following:

> *Two dutiful volunteers assemble patient information kits at a card table in the outpatient waiting room of the just-renovated hospital. When asked about the temporary-looking workspace, they explain their prior workspace had been eliminated from the new floor plan without anyone noticing.*

> *Two snow-covered volunteers brave a major blizzard to come in to meet with their assigned clients, only to find that the agency was closed because of the weather conditions and that only the paid staff had been notified.*

> *Surprised museum volunteers displaced after ten years of service when the institution hires a part-time information desk staff member—and then asks those volunteers to train the new hire and keep the desk staffed for the other hours—all without prior notice or discussion.*

> *Actively engaged civic association members stopped in their tracks after their national board eliminated the local clubs' favorite,*

well-established service project because a new attorney felt it had too much risk potential, even though there had not been a single lawsuit for fifteen years.

The common problem in all these real-life scenarios is that no one was envisioning volunteers when making decisions. Each organization in which these situations took place considers itself welcoming to volunteers, and its executive leader speaks of community involvement in glowing terms. But, in day-to-day practice, the volunteers were, in effect, *invisible*, limited from contributing their full range of talents because they were not seen as important to the organization's mission-driven work and not integrated into the *full scope* of strategic planning.

Too many volunteer involvement efforts suffer from "benign neglect." Top executives consider volunteers nice but not essential, and so they rarely monitor the accomplishments of volunteers or give the director of volunteer involvement the benefit of ongoing input from the administrative perspective. CEOs may want to engage volunteers but do not necessarily see this strategy as requiring vision or much management attention.

If only senior leaders could see what they are missing! Because volunteer initiatives languish from a lack of high expectations, volunteers are stopped from having substantial impact and from achieving their fullest productivity. The unfortunate fact is that more volunteers are *underutilized* than are overburdened.

Over and over—and still as often in 2009 as in 1986 when I wrote the first edition of *From the Top Down*—colleagues say, with frustration, "I just wish my *boss* would understand this!" The person responsible for volunteer engagement cannot do it alone. If your organization has a human resources department head or a development officer, it's a sure bet that you, as executive, still get involved with situations involving employees or fundraising. The same must be true to assure success with volunteers.

After years of contact with so many leaders of volunteers, I have become convinced that many of their concerns stem directly from a lack of substantive support from their agencies' top administrators. This lack of support is not due to malice or unwillingness to be of help but to a lack of understanding about what is really needed from them—and little information actually geared to an executive.

In fact, a series of focus groups held by the University of Texas at Austin in 2009 found that many executives lack a sufficient understanding of what is required for effective volunteer involvement. Other executives confided that they were concerned about possible negative public relations that might be generated by a disgruntled volunteer and feared that they would not be able to resolve disputes should they arise. The findings from this research, highlights of which will be shared throughout this book, are captured in Sarah Jane Rehnborg's *Strategic Volunteer Engagement: A Guide for Nonprofit and Public Sector Leaders*.[1]

Very little has been published about the volunteer-related issues that deserve executive attention. It is probably an accurate assumption that most executives were not taught anything about volunteers in their formal schooling. There may have been some time spent on the interrelationship of executives with their boards of directors, which is one aspect of working successfully with volunteers but—with only a few exceptions, such as the American Humanics curriculum—few management texts or lecturers speak to the specific issues that will be raised in these pages.

That is why this book has been written for *top-level executives* of agencies, organizations, and associations, whether they are already involving volunteers or members or considering starting organized volunteer or member participation.

Target Audiences

This book speaks to top-level organization leaders. Depending on your setting, you might hold one of the following roles:

- Executive director of a nonprofit organization or its board president
- CEO of a large institution, whether profit-making or not
- Director of a government agency
- Leader of a professional society, trade association, faith community, or civic group, in which you must activate members into voluntary participation

If you are not the very top decision maker, you may be part of the management team, a department head, a branch director, or a member of the board of directors (and therefore a volunteer yourself).

While some of the issues presented here may differ for the specifics or size of your particular setting, there are really more similarities than differences between the types of organizations that involve volunteers.

Volunteer management practices are generic whether your work is in social services, the arts, recreation, law enforcement, or environmentalism. And, while there naturally are important practical differences from country to country, the basic premises laid out in these chapters are truly universal and international.

Your organization may have no volunteers at present or may already benefit from a large, well-established volunteer corps. You may have a long list of dues-paying but passive members or donors with potential to become more actively engaged. It is never too soon or too late to examine the concerns outlined in the following pages.

You may be seeking volunteers who are specialists in specific fields or those who are generalists—or both. The types of assignments your organization offers to volunteers may range from long-term, ongoing work to one-time special events; some assignments may need to be done on-site in your facility, while others may involve independent work in the community or online.

This book is not meant to be a distillation of all the resources available on how to develop and manage a volunteer program. Whomever you designate to lead volunteer engagement is encouraged to seek out those resources and learn more about the details of effective, daily volunteer administration. Rather, this book deals with issues that are directly in *your* control as the executive. It is also designed to be thought-provoking and provide you with a basis on which to make necessary decisions.

Research Shows . . .

In 2004, the Urban Institute released a landmark study, *Volunteer Management Capacity in America's Charities and Congregations: A Briefing Report*. The study was commissioned by the UPS Foundation, the Corporation for National and Community Service, and the USA Freedom Corps, and it is probably the strongest argument ever seen in the United States for the value of—in the words of the report—*investment* in volunteer management:

> Funders and organizations that invest in staff volunteer coordinators and training will produce charities and congregations with a greater capacity to their use of volunteers. This report finds that investments in volunteer management and benefits derived from volunteers feed on each other, with investments bringing benefits and these benefits justify greater investments. We conclude that the value that volunteers

provide to organizations they serve should make the effective management of volunteers a key priority.[2]

Further, consider what is revealed in these findings:

- Three out of five charities and only one out of three congregations
  with social service outreach activities reported having a paid
  staff person who worked on volunteer coordination. However,
  among these paid volunteer coordinators, one in three have not
  received any training in volunteer management, and half spend
  less than 30 percent of their time on volunteer coordination ...

- Less than half of charities and congregations that manage
  volunteers have adopted most volunteer management practices advocated by the field ...[3]

- Of charities with a paid staff volunteer manager, only one
  in eight have someone who devotes 100 percent of his/her
  time to volunteer management ...

- The greater the percentage of time a paid staff person spends
  on volunteer administration, the less likely a charity is to
  report problems with recruiting.[4]

The researchers asked comparative questions about resources put into
fundraising; 55 percent of agencies have a paid fundraiser while only
39 percent have a paid coordinator of volunteers. This research was
confirmed in the 2009 *Deloitte Volunteer IMPACT Survey*:

> Nonprofits and corporations are more culturally aligned to solicit
> and manage cash gifts than volunteers. While 61 percent of nonprofit
> employees with primary responsibility for fundraising have at least
> eight years of experience, just 25 percent of nonprofit employees with
> primary responsibility for volunteer management have the same level
> of experience. Further, while only 5 percent of nonprofits have no one
> specifically in charge of fundraising, nearly a quarter (24%) of non-
> profits have no one in charge of managing volunteers.[5]

To those of us committed to the effective engagement of volunteers,
it is an enduring mystery why we must fight so hard to get organizational
leaders to *pay attention* to this resource. The majority of executives

would and do praise volunteers as "vital to our work," "our community connection," or even "the heart of our agency." But in daily practice, this potential pool of limitless talent is largely off the radar screen. Raising money never leaves the agenda—why ignore raising friends? It's easy to get an organization to treat financial donors well—why not value time and skill donors, too? (In fact, these are often the very same people, and we'll be discussing the close connection between volunteer engagement and fundraising later.)

Mainstream or Radical?

Some of the concepts proposed in the following pages may seem radical. Actually, there is a fair mix of suggestions based on time-proven principles and of proposals articulated in print for the first time. In order to stimulate and stretch perspectives, however, I sometimes extend the boundaries of best practices. You are free, of course, to pick and choose among the recommendations here to develop the form of volunteer involvement that will best meet your own organization's needs.

Some readers may be feeling a bit uncomfortable in the suspicion that I am going to suggest lots of structure to bureaucratize volunteerism. Successful volunteering does not come from spontaneous combustion and so does need some structure. Most of our organizations today are already rather complex, and unless we develop clear ways for volunteers to participate in our activities, people in the community really do not know how to become involved. This is true whether the organization is an agency, an institution, or an all-volunteer association.

It is important to avoid wasting the time of volunteers—which is exactly what happens if there has been insufficient planning to define and prepare the work to be done. It is a form of volunteer recognition to evaluate accomplishments and to establish standards for who can become a volunteer and how assignments are made. The best volunteer management serves to *enable* volunteer achievement, not limit it.

All the management principles that work effectively with employees apply equally to volunteers. But surprisingly enough, the theme of this book is not necessarily to treat volunteers in the same way you would treat paid staff. Volunteer administration emphasizes motivators such as choice, a positive working environment, and recognition, to which all workers will respond with increased morale and productivity. This book proposes that it may be better management practice *to treat employees as though they were volunteers*!

Old and New Vocabulary

The volunteer world has expanded to welcome an ever-growing range of new people seeking service opportunities. These folks often do not label themselves as "volunteers," but they are certainly available community resources. At the same time, certain traditional types of volunteering are disappearing or metamorphosing into new forms. Depending on which expert's research you prefer, we are either turning our backs on the old "nation of joiners" or we are "rediscovering community." These observations are not necessarily contradictory, and both may be true. The question is whether your organization can adapt to the valid needs and wants of volunteers today.

The Word *Volunteer*

While still in common use, the word *volunteer* itself can repel as often as it attracts. Many people hear "volunteer" and immediately picture one of many (or a combination of) stereotypes: little old lady in a flowered hat, enthusiastic amateur, do-gooder, helper, sweater set and pearls, candy striper, retired folks with lots of time, and so on. It's odd that these images are usually pejorative, or at least low level, since we all also know that volunteers provide free medical care in developing countries, turn the tide in election campaigns, govern nonprofit agencies, and program open-source software for the Internet. I often get quoted in the press with this sound bite: "Men have always volunteered; they just *call themselves* coaches, trustees, and firemen!"

The point is to recognize your own reaction to the word *volunteer*. If you cannot picture a highly skilled, financially successful, mission-committed person donating time to your organization, it will never happen! Or, rather, you won't create the type of volunteer opportunities most likely to attract high-caliber people.

If the word *volunteering* creates a mental block, try using one of the many others that essentially means the same thing—for example, labels such as the following:

- community service
- citizen participation
- student internships
- pro bono work
- civic engagement

- lay ministry
- donated professional services
- neighborhood action

There are lots of other terms, and you'll learn more about the special issues of some of them later in this book. The important point is to get beyond the words and see volunteer engagement as *tapping the community for skills and talents to direct at meeting your mission or furthering your cause.*

Given this look at all the words that imply volunteering, you might consider another name for this effort altogether rather than "volunteer program." Maybe you want a community resources office or a community engagement team. If this helps everyone to reimagine volunteering, give it a try.

A Working Definition

What's the definition of a *volunteer*? There are many opinions, and frequently the word is applied only when the person doing the service self-identifies with the concept of altruism. But, for the purposes of this book, we're going to take one perspective only: that *of your organization*. In that light,

> *A volunteer is someone who provides time, services, and talents to your organization without going on your payroll.*

It's as simple as that. If they are not employees yet work toward your mission with you, they are volunteers to *you*.

Of course, some types of help bring specific management challenges, which we'll discuss, and there may be good reasons why you welcome only some of the sources of volunteers available. That's OK. Just start with high expectations, openness, and even some creativity, and the rewards to your organization will flow in.

Volunteer "Program" Language

As the definition and use of the word *volunteer* changes, other vocabulary issues have surfaced. For example, it is a valid observation that volunteers are not a "program." The word *program* usually describes a subgroup of specific services within an organization's entire range of activities: the reading program, the gardening program, and so on. We do not speak of the "employee program," do we? That's because employees *provide* program services. So do volunteers.

In this book, you'll occasionally see "volunteer program" language to describe the organized integration of volunteers into an agency's service delivery, but more often I have tried to avoid it.

The reference to "managing" volunteers is also questionable. Some have pointed out that one manages programs, not people. Even more important, however, is that the term *managing* implies that volunteers are always a group of workers to be *directed*. Yet there are many models of partnering with volunteers, including recruiting highly skilled people to consult with paid staff in their area of expertise. To get the most out of volunteer involvement (and probably out of employees, too), the best choice is the vocabulary of *leading*, *involving*, or *engaging* volunteers.

In the same vein, the title given to the person designated to head volunteers has many variations. In my thirty-nine-plus years in the field, I've watched different titles go in and out of vogue. I talk about this in chapter four when we look at staffing. The most sought-after title in the 1980s was "director of volunteers," and health care settings still often use "director of volunteer services." Today, "volunteer program manager," "volunteer resources manager," and "coordinator of volunteers" are popular. Just to show the range, colleagues in the United Kingdom have begun to use "volunteers coordinator."

In this book, I will use the title "director of volunteer involvement" most often because it is reasonably generic, connotes a position of responsibility, and focuses on leading the organization's *strategy of involvement* throughout the organization, not simply the volunteers themselves. Again, there will be more on the subject of titles in chapter four.

One of the newer trends that also affects vocabulary is to see everything formerly called "volunteer management" or "volunteer administration" as old school. The phrase suggested instead is "volunteer *engagement*." The proponents of the volunteer engagement approach see it as placing more responsibility on the executives of an organization to blend their management of employees and volunteers. Some even feel that a volunteer program manager is not needed when paid and unpaid workers are integrated more seamlessly. I agree with most of the goals of the volunteer engagement advocates and have always urged matching vocabulary to vision. But I strongly feel that the basic principles of volunteer management are timeless and universal, no matter what label is applied. Further, while obviously I have been urging substantial executive involvement all along, I remain convinced that designating someone to lead an organization's volunteer effort is key to ultimate success. If "everyone" is in charge, no one really is. The position is complex enough to have dedicated staff tasked with the responsibility of keeping up with the trends, issues, and evolving practices.

Changes in Volunteering

I began my career in volunteer management in 1971 when I was hired to start a volunteer program for the Philadelphia Family Court (in my early twenties and with absolutely no qualifications!). Almost everything in society has undergone change in the years since. And if the whole world is changing, how can volunteering stay the same? It can't, and it hasn't.

The days of people being willing to commit up front to volunteering on a regular, weekly, on-site schedule for many years are long gone— just as employees do not expect to stay at a paying job for twenty-five years anymore. Short-term and even single days of service are what today's volunteers seek (although they may *evolve* longer commitment if they feel good about the first few projects they complete). The Web has launched the completely new concept of virtual volunteering (online service), as well as offering a wealth of free communication tools, ways to deliver training electronically, many sites at which to register volunteer opportunities to attract new applicants, and social networking sites for online community building. The Internet has also brought daily international exchange among volunteerism practitioners and access to professional literature from around the world. And people are more mobile, too, which has led to another new concept: voluntourism.

It is worthwhile to become informed about the many new developments in the field. This book is not intended to cover all the trends but will refer to many along the way. The point is that organizations who identify and understand how volunteering is evolving are most likely to adapt their volunteer management practices to the new norm. Regardless of the scope, diversity, or vocabulary of the volunteer involvement you plan, the basic principles discussed in this book will continue to apply.

Keys to Success

The first step to volunteer engagement success is *vision*. Volunteers can expand the horizons of your organization and your staff. Encourage volunteers to be creative and innovative partners in service delivery, and then expect the best. Self-fulfilling prophecy is a key factor. If your concept of what volunteers can contribute is limited, you will design a volunteering structure that indeed keeps achievement low. But if you are open to the potential of what might develop, you will find ways to encourage volunteers' success.

The second step is *commitment*. You must have the conviction that volunteers are important—that they are the "nonsalaried personnel" of the agency. Volunteers are not "added spice" to your organizational mix; they are one of the main ingredients. As top executive, you can establish and enforce this premise throughout your organization.

As we will examine in the first chapter, it is important to have a clear understanding of why volunteers are valuable in your setting. Articulating the reasons for involving volunteers is an executive level responsibility, and it forms the foundation on which your organization will build its volunteer participation.

Despite the recommendations in this book about best practices, it is useful to realize that *there are no rules* when it comes to the successful involvement of volunteers. This is one area in which inventiveness and creativity still apply. While the techniques of the profession of volunteer management are important, my goal is not to box community participation into a model designed solely as a parallel to staff operations. Barter, walk-in volunteering, collaboration, self-help, shared volunteers, volunteer exchanges—if it works for you, do it! Understand the *principles* of how to welcome volunteers and facilitate effective service and the rest will follow.

As always, we face economic uncertainties, changes in government priorities, and questions about how to pay for the services we want. Whether you are with a not-for-profit agency or a unit of government, you are undoubtedly redesigning your budget and exploring future funding sources. So the question of whether and how volunteers fit into your "resource mix" is as pertinent as it ever was.

It's not just money, of course. Many organizations, perhaps with health care showing the way, are going to be restructuring the basic ways they deliver services to their patients, clients, audience, or consumers. I predict that we will see totally new forms of volunteer support in the years to come. I emphasize this point in the introduction to this book because, more than anything, I hope the reader will come away with the conviction that it is right to be *proactive* in engaging the best, most qualified volunteers in service delivery. As with all other aspects of organization management, the time spent planning for volunteers is paid back richly by the results. Envision a place in which members of the community will gladly give their time to help meet a shared mission of service, and you will take all the right steps to make that the reality of your organization.

Notes

1. Sarah Jane Rehnborg and others, *Strategic Volunteer Engagement: A Guide for Nonprofit and Public Sector Leaders* (Austin, TX: RGK Center for Philanthropy and Community Service, the LBJ School of Public Affairs, the University of Texas at Austin, 2009).
2. Urban Institute, *Volunteer Management Capacity in America's Charities and Congregations: A Briefing Report* (Washington, DC: Urban Institute, 2004), 21. The study can be obtained online at http://www.national service.gov/pdf/vol_capacity_brief.pdf.
3. Ibid., 3.
4. Ibid., 12.
5. Deloitte Development, LLC, "2009 Executive Summary: *Deloitte Volunteer IMPACT Survey*," p. 1, http://www.deloitte.com/assets/Dcom-UnitedStates/ Local%20Assets/Documents/us_2009%20Volunteer%20IMPACT%20 ExecSummary_050409.pdf.

1

Why Volunteers?

In training seminars, I often include a session to examine and articulate the underlying assumptions of volunteer involvement. I present a list of key questions all leaders of volunteers should go home and ask—regardless of how old or new their volunteer effort is. The first—and most critical—question is, *why* do we want volunteers? This question is absolutely basic, yet it catches some people by surprise. Isn't the answer obvious? No. Aren't agencies "supposed" to have volunteers? Not necessarily. Hasn't our organization "always had" volunteers? So what?

As the executive, why *do* you want volunteers? Well, one answer always seems to be "because we do not have sufficient resources (money, staff, or whatever) to do our job without the help of volunteers." Unfortunately, while this response may be accurate, it also is a rather negative statement about volunteers. The implied corollary is that, if there were sufficient money, staff, or whatever, then volunteers would not be necessary. This makes volunteers a *second-choice* resource.

I submit that this reasoning is at the root of a lot of the problems agencies have in activating volunteers and in working successfully with them. Recruitment based on "we don't have enough resources, so we are forced to turn to you" is not positive. Neither is supervision by paid staff based on "I wish I had a paid helper, but I have to settle for you."

Consider how even more important this point becomes during periods of economic recession, when the need for volunteers suddenly seems obvious to agencies feeling the budget pinch. Unfortunately, those organizations that have not welcomed volunteer engagement in good times discover they may be too late to mobilize community support when times are bad. And do they hope to drop their involvement of volunteers if funding once again materializes? You can see how a positive and consistent philosophy about why your organization wants volunteers in the first place provides the foundation for all other decision making about them.

There are indeed some first-choice reasons for wanting to attract volunteers—reasons that have nothing to do with the presence or absence of money. I ask workshop participants to imagine a "utopia" in which organizations such as theirs would have all the money in the world with which to do anything they please: offer one-to-one client service, pay for all types of consultation, take the staff on a retreat to Bermuda, and so on (with the caveat that there is still not enough money to cure cancer, assure world peace, or eradicate the critical needs and issues most organizations have as their missions).

The group exercise question is, *given such a "utopia" in which your organization could pay for anything needed, would you still involve volunteers in some way and, if so, why?*

Maybe Not

It generally takes several minutes for participants to be able to sort out their reactions to this question. And they find it hard to answer, at least at first. Some people honestly admit—with some relief—that they would not involve volunteers anymore. Their reasoning usually revolves around control, accountability, easier working relationships, and other issues that reveal the respondents' attitudes about the perceived limitations of volunteers. And there are always some who just don't like working with volunteers and truly think their agency would be better off with more employees.

Others get sidetracked in observing that some people would still want to offer their services as volunteers—but I quickly point out that just because some people would always want to be volunteers does not mean that every agency would have to create an assignment for them. So the exercise has to take the organization's perspective only.

Despite the yes-or-no wording of the question about involving volunteers, the best answer straddles the fence. In examining the roles volunteers are currently asked to fill, some may well be offered today because they are necessary and whatever money is available needs to be spent on other priorities. In the wealth of my utopia, therefore, those specific volunteer positions might disappear. So the real question is, which volunteer roles would remain necessary and why?

First-Choice Reasons

After some lively discussion, the following are finally identified as being the unique things volunteers offer an organization—so special to volunteers that paying a salary negates or changes them completely:

- Volunteers are perceived to **have credibility** *because* **they are unpaid**. Paid staff are always perceived as "spokespeople" with a degree of vested interest in the outcome of a legislative hearing or funding proposal, since their livelihood depends on the outcome. Volunteers, because their motivation is not profit-oriented, are seen by donors, clients, legislators, and the public as more objective and even as more sincere. This is what makes them such a potential asset in advocacy, public relations, and public education.

  Note that this perception of volunteers as having no vested interest sometimes has nothing to do with the truth. For example, if a volunteer's grandmother founded the organization, then that volunteer has a different form of "vested interest"! Also, if a volunteer has been on the board for twenty years, objectivity may be questionable. But the fact remains that the perception and assumption of the listener or recipient are that the volunteer is more credible.

  It's also worthwhile to caution against assuming that volunteers are necessarily saying only good things about you! Test what volunteers are really thinking, or this perception of credibility can backfire.

- Receiving assistance from a volunteer (rather than from an employee) **makes a difference to the recipient**. Many consumers are distrustful of paid service providers and are therefore more likely to believe and follow a volunteer's suggestions.

  In some circumstances, the important factor is the feeling that the volunteer is doing the task willingly— voluntarily—while the salaried staff are simply "doing a job."

This is why prisoners, for example, are more willing to talk with volunteer visitors than with guards or state social workers. It is why patients in hospitals are more cheered by the visit of a volunteer than a nurse: volunteers demonstrate that neighbors have not forgotten them nor are "turned off" by their illness. Nurses, on the other hand, must provide service, regardless of their personal feelings about the patient.

Finally, some programs such as one-to-one home visitation or Big Brothers Big Sisters would change radically in their purpose without volunteers. If we pay a Big Brother, we give the child another babysitter. The very word *brother* in the volunteer's title indicates that the service is not based on its being a "job." The same idea is at work with the title of "friendly visitor." You don't pay a friend to visit.

For your agency, the service recipient's comfort level with a volunteer may elicit feedback or other information not as easily obtained by an employee.

- Volunteers are **insider-outsiders**. While your paid staff may well live nearby, volunteers are usually considered "community representatives" even if they are neighbors of your employees. This is because most employees approach their jobs from a specific professional perspective and may be too close to the work to see the forest for the trees. Volunteers, on the other hand, bring a wide range of professional and other backgrounds. Because they give you only a few hours at time, volunteers have a broader point of view. They still think like a member of the public but have also made a commitment to your organization, so you can count on their distinct input.

- Volunteers **extend your sphere of influence** and access to additional people, businesses, and organizations in the community. Even the volunteer who helps you once a year becomes another person with knowledge about your work. This ripple effect can spread increased goodwill, in that happy volunteers will speak well of the organization to others. (This is a two-edged sword, of course, because unhappy volunteers can create bad will for you, too.)

- Volunteers are valuable as **objective policy makers**. Even in the wealthy utopia scenario, they are necessary as members of nonprofit boards of directors. Boards are—by law—an intermediary between donors and funders and program participants, acting as "trustees" of funds from which they derive no profit. Since the ultimate power of a board is the decision to close an agency, it is clear that such decision making should be done by people who are not personally affected by such an action nor by less drastic measures such as cutting some programs. Also, the objectivity of volunteers is aided by not being on-site full time. Distance provides perspective.

- Volunteers bring **the luxury of focus**. Paid staff must equitably share their time among all service recipients or a full caseload. Not so for volunteers. They have the option to focus intensively on a particular issue or client, even to the exclusion of extraneous tasks. Volunteers can specialize. This is a luxury of concentration and time not normally justifiable for employees, while volunteers can actually be recruited to provide such individualized attention to one task. (You can even recruit three volunteers to work with one client, if necessary.)

- Because volunteers are always **private citizens**, they are free to contact legislators or the media in a way employees may not be permitted to do because of legal limitations on lobbying or partisan activity (such as regulations in the Hatch Act in the United States). Though this again is a two-edged sword (i.e., the volunteer may use this access to speak *against* you), it means that volunteers can be powerful advocates.

  Similarly, though volunteers act as agents of your organization, they have more flexibility in cutting through some of the red tape of bureaucratic systems, political boundaries, and other artificial barriers. This is increasingly critical in work with an international component. Volunteers—as private citizens with a mission—can make contacts, travel across borders, and promote cooperation in ways that governments and formal organizations find almost impossible.

- If your organization has public education or community development as a part of your mission, then engaging members of the community is actually a **strategy for meeting service goals** as well as a method of service delivery. By volunteering, more members of the public learn what your cause is all about and develop the skills to further it.

- Volunteers are **freer to criticize** than are salaried staff. Again, this is a function of being outside the career-ladder, promotion-seeking concerns that are often legitimate for employees. Volunteers have less to lose when they give you feedback.

- Because volunteers are not dependent on the organization for their livelihood, they can approach assignments with **less pressure and stress**. This is often an asset in accomplishing the tasks to be done.

- Often volunteers contribute **what would not be purchased otherwise**.[1] This includes what is needed rarely, although highly prized if attainable, such as an interpreter for an uncommon language or a high-profile celebrity to speak at a client graduation. It also means a wide range of "extras" that clients and staff value but that are not required for the primary service goal. A good example is the disabilities job placement service that can go beyond simply finding work for someone because volunteers help the client obtain and choose new work clothes. That isn't what the employees are paid to do, but it certainly provides far greater assistance to the recipient.

- Volunteers **can experiment** with new ideas and service approaches that are not yet ready to be funded—or that no one wants to fund for a wide variety of reasons. Historically, in fact, volunteers have always been the pioneers in creating new services, often against the tide of opposition from more traditional institutions.

There is one additional "first-choice" reason for involving volunteers that does, in fact, involve money. But it must be worded correctly. Too often, in an effort to praise the contributions of volunteers, executives (and legislators) say, "Volunteers save us money!" They may even calculate a dollar figure for these supposed "savings." In chapter eleven, we will discuss the cash equivalency measure of volunteers at length. For now, however, understand that volunteers never "save" money. Do you have money available that you did not have to spend because you involved volunteers? Hardly. Much more accurate is the recognition that *volunteers allow you to spend every dollar you have—and then do more*. **Volunteers extend the budget**.

Implications

What does all this imply? First, it shows that there are definitely areas in which volunteers—*because* they are volunteers—can be even more effective than paid staff. Second, it raises the question of whether your agency is maximizing these "first-choice" areas. Specifically, consider the following in your organization:

- Are volunteers being deployed as legislative advocates? as fundraisers? as public educators? in any role that makes use of their perceived credibility?

- Are volunteers providing direct service to consumers, especially in tasks that may benefit from a higher degree of comfort level or personalization?

- Do you have a system for getting feedback from volunteers? Are there channels for making suggestions or stating criticisms?

- Do you keep volunteers informed about what you'd like the community to know about you?

- Do you ask volunteers to establish collaborative arrangements or to cut red tape in some way?

Examine the position descriptions volunteers are presently fulfilling in your setting and determine whether you are benefiting as much as possible from the unique aspects of volunteer service.

So, Why Pay a Salary?

Perhaps you have been thinking about the reverse of the question of why you involve volunteers, namely, "Why should we pay anyone?" It is important (especially for this book) to recognize that the answer is not that a wage gets you people with better qualifications. A volunteer can be just as highly trained and experienced as any employee can be. Instead, offering a salary gives the agency *a predetermined number of work hours per week*, the right to *dictate the employee's work schedule*, a certain amount of *control over the nature and priorities of the work* to be done, and *continuity*.

When you hire an employee, you can require that the person give your organization forty hours a week or whatever number is necessary. Because most people need to earn a living, people can rarely give one agency that much volunteer time per week.

In addition, volunteers are always free to select their individual work schedules. Though you can require volunteers to commit to a schedule and be dependable, people do not usually jeopardize their volunteer positions by telling you up front that they spend a season in a different climate or that their schedules will change every semester to match a course roster. On the other hand, an employee can indeed be told exactly when the agency expects him or her to be present and can be made to submit vacation schedules, for example, for prior approval.

The area of "control" has many levels and will be discussed in more detail in chapter nine. Some of what you may feel you have in the way of control over employees may be more mythical than real. For example, you really have no way of stopping an employee from going to the press with a story—though you can threaten termination of employment and hope the fear of being fired is a deterrent. The more realistic aspect of control is that you can dictate job assignments and expect the employee to fulfill these, even if s/he dislikes the task or even disagrees with it. Further, you can set the priorities within which the employee must emphasize certain tasks over others. A volunteer always retains freedom of choice and can refuse to work on a project for various reasons, without losing the opportunity to volunteer in another assignment.

Finally, a salaried position provides continuity for the organization. Even if the person filling the position changes over time, the function itself remains relatively stable. The public and the rest of staff can expect a certain standard in the way the service is provided by that position.

Recognize that your organization has made choices throughout its development about whether to accomplish work with volunteers, to hire paid staff, or to mesh the two. There are, after all, examples of all-volunteer groups providing a multitude of community services. Your organization's volunteer founders probably raised the first funds to pay salaries. And when you are faced with a budget crisis, the question of who should do what surfaces again.

This whole subject of the reasons for one set of workers versus another, and the need for mutual understanding of abilities and limitations, is so critical to the success of volunteer involvement that we will return to it in several upcoming chapters.

Other Benefits from Volunteer Involvement

As we have seen, there are some clear first-choice reasons for utilizing volunteers, even in an all-the-money-in-the-world utopia, and there are good reasons for paying some employees, too. Since we live in the real, limited-resources world, what are other benefits to an organization for involving volunteers? Volunteers offer the following:

- **Extra hands** and the potential to do more than could be done simply with limited paid staff. This "more" might mean an increased amount of service, expanded hours of operation, or different and new types of services.

- **Diversity**. Volunteers can intentionally be different from the salaried staff in terms of age, race, social background, income, educational level, and so on. For example, they might be recruited specifically to fill gaps in skills not already offered by employees or to be more representative of the client population than paid staff might be. This translates into many more points of view and perhaps even a sort of checks and balances to the danger of the staff becoming myopic or inbred.

- **Skills** that augment the ones employees already possess. Ideally, volunteers are recruited exactly because the salaried staff cannot have every skill or talent necessary to do all aspects of the job. These skills can be very concrete such as being bilingual, knowing how to repair bicycles, or being able to produce a newsletter. Or, they can be less tangible such as being able to relate to teenagers or the homeless.

- **Community ownership** of solutions to mutual problems. Especially if your organization addresses issues affecting the quality of life, when people participate as volunteers, they empower themselves to improve their own neighborhood (which is your mission, after all).

- **Advocacy** for adequate funding. Volunteers can see the value of full-time, paid staff, know what tangible resources are missing, and are often in the best position to understand why your organization needs more money in addition to more volunteers.

- **Loyalty**. Especially in membership organizations, the likelihood of a person staying tied to an organization rises

with even ad hoc involvement in meaningful activity as a
volunteer.

In fact, one way to conceptualize the meaning of a volunteer involvement effort to an organization is to express it as volunteerism author
Rick Lynch does: getting the participation of volunteers gives you "access
to every skill in the community and engages the community as *a partner
in accomplishing your mission*."[2] This is a powerful vision.

In addition to all of the above, studies have shown that satisfied volunteers frequently are so supportive of the organizations with which
they serve that they become **donors of money and goods** as well. They
also **support special events** and fundraisers by attending themselves
and bringing along family and friends. In the case of cultural arts organizations, volunteers thereby help to **expand the audience or public** for
performances and exhibitions.

Ask yourself, is your organization taking full advantage of all these
benefits of volunteer involvement?

The Volunteer-Donor Connection

As an executive, you do have to be concerned with the funding to keep
your doors open. So while I have just stressed the importance of engaging
volunteers for the benefits they bring *as* volunteers, consider this perspective as well: a check never writes itself. All contributions of money
or valuables come from *people* who are *voluntarily* demonstrating their
support of your cause. This implies a strong correlation between those
who give time (to whom we refer as *volunteers*) and those who give
money (to whom we refer as *donors*). Would your consideration of volunteers change if you were to start calling them "time donors" or speak
of "fundraising" as "people raising"?

Do you regularly ask for a report on how many volunteers in your
organization are also financial donors and vice versa? If not, why not?
If yes, have you analyzed what this means? Are the databases for these
two groups integrated or at least accessible to both volunteer administration and development staff?

There is research indicating that starting with a "time-ask" instead
of a "money-ask" ultimately generates more financial giving:

> How to get people to give? The current research tackles this ques-
> tion by highlighting an important distinction between two types of

"asks"—one that involves asking for donation of time and the other that involves asking for money. In both field and lab experiments and across different populations (U.S. consumers and college students), we show that first asking people about their intentions to donate time leads to a significant increase in actual amounts of contribution, compared to either not asking for volunteering donations . . . or first asking people about their intentions to donate money . . . [T]his effect appears to be driven by the differential mind-sets activated by the consideration of spending time versus money. Considering time appears to activate goals of emotional well-being and beliefs involving personal happiness. Such a mind-set leads to greater willingness to make an actual donation.[3]

Asking Volunteers to Give Money, Too

Periodically, the debate surfaces over whether it's appropriate to solicit money from volunteers. Those who are uncomfortable doing so have a sense that this might be "double dipping." Despite research showing that people who volunteer are more likely to also give cash than uninvolved people, the reluctance to ask for money from volunteers keeps the development office and the volunteer resources office operating in distinctly separate spheres.

One stereotype is that volunteers don't have a lot of money. This, of course, is only understood for frontline volunteers, since those engaged in things like planning the gala dinner are conversely assumed to be wealthy enough to pay for anything requested of them. Beware all assumptions! There have simply been too many news items about the little old lady with the sixteen cats who dutifully fulfills her volunteer shift quietly for twenty-seven years, dies, and leaves $4 million to the organization. Even if this fantasy comes true only rarely, the truth is that no one really knows who has money and who does not or who wants to give money to *your cause* and who does not.

But let's get back to the thought that "it just doesn't feel right" to ask faithful volunteers to give money, too. An organization can—and proba-bly should—offer volunteers the opportunity to donate funds, but it has to be done in a way that is clearly different from soliciting people who are not already actively working for you. The key is to start by acknowl-edging that the prospective donor is a volunteer. It's true "recognition" to know this important fact. Nothing is worse than a volunteer receiving the same mailing sent to everyone, as if his or her service is invisible. Try the following sort of appeal:

We are so appreciative of the time and talent you share with us throughout the year as a volunteer. Thank you!

Please know that your volunteer contribution is of great value in many ways. Volunteers ensure that we can spend every dollar we have on needed services and still do more. We also know that giving us your time comes with various costs and expenses to you personally. But because you are so familiar with our work, you know that it takes both participation and money to accomplish our mission.

How can we ask strangers to contribute funds and not give you the chance to decide if you want to add a check to the ways in which you already help us?

Of course, there's no obligation to give money. It's completely your choice.

Done properly, such a solicitation can (and should) feel like a thank you. Possibly, this request for a donation should be sent only once a year, without follow up. The point is to include volunteers in your fundraising efforts but not guilt them into writing a check.

Donors as Volunteers

It may seem reasonable to learn to ask volunteers for money, but what about approaching donors with the invitation to volunteer? People who become known to us through a fundraising campaign are typecast as check writers, not doers. Why?

Recent studies have shown that regular donors can lose interest in an organization over time (it's called "donor fatigue") but, when given the opportunity to volunteer, are recommitted to the cause. Interestingly, it's the recruitment *invitation* that matters, not if they actually volunteer or not.

Asking a donor to get involved in person does several things. It implies that you see this person as more than a hand holding a pen; it offers the person the chance to see for her/himself how wisely you manage the budget, and it gives you access to more skills and talents.

Colleen Kelly says that, at Volunteer Vancouver, "We talk about the three-word phrase 'thank you AND . . .' Our most important AND is an offer to work with us with their talent after they have given their treasure."[4] So it's "thank you for your contribution AND would you like to work with us on developing our (for example) evaluation process?"

There are various times at which you can discuss volunteer opportunities with donors:

- When you thank people for their financial gifts, include a message about volunteering options as information they may want for themselves or to share with family members or friends. If they care about your cause, so might others close to them.

- Keep donors informed throughout the year about volunteer opportunities, particularly ways they might be able to help at a special event, with a short-term project, or as a technical advisor (it helps if you ask donors some basic information about themselves such as their profession).

- Make a personal appeal by letter or phone to longtime donors, acknowledging how much they have contributed over time and therefore ensuring they know you are interested in their skills as well as in their money.

- Avoid lost opportunities. For example, if you sell tickets to corporate donors for something like a table for eight at a special event, keep in mind that the employees who are given the chance to fill those chairs often attend at no personal cost. So why not provide them with information about your organization, including current volunteer needs and an envelope for their own donation?

Wendy Liu and Jennifer Aaker refer to the trend of corporations urging their employees to volunteer, particularly to use their professional skills in hopes of increasing monetary donations as well. Liu and Aaker found that

> such policies may not just affect volunteering behavior; they may have the independent, and perhaps inadvertent, effect of also increasing the levels of monetary donations. From a policy maker's point of view, this research suggests that volunteering for one's community should receive more attention due to its potential dual impact on both greater prosocial behavior and the ensuing happiness for the donor . . . We should think about time, not money.[5]

It's All about Making Friends

If an organization wants to mobilize the greatest amount of community resources—whether time, money, goods, talents, or whatever—it must first make *friends*. Every action taken can cultivate supporters or potential supporters or raise their level of commitment. That's why it's so important to view volunteer involvement in the broadest possible context.

People move in and out of contribution categories depending on changing circumstances. Some can be time or money donors, or both, at different times. For that matter, some may be employees of your organization at some point and clients or consumers of your services at another. Depending on your work, the same individual may have several identities with you at once. And this extends as well to their family members, circle of friends, and professional colleagues—those ever-widening "spheres of influence" I mentioned earlier.

The greatest impact comes when you and your staff recognize the interconnection of *all* your *stakeholders*. No group of supporters is in an independent silo. Volunteering is one of a range of possible relationships to your organization, albeit one that requires direct interaction. Consider not only the immediate outcome of both donated time and skills but also the long-term, boundary-less potential. This changes the question of "Why should we involve volunteers?" to "How could we not?"

To implement ideas in this chapter, see . . .

Leading the Way to Successful Volunteer Involvement: Practical Tools for Busy Executives by Betty B. Stallings with Susan J. Ellis (Philadelphia: Energize, Inc., 2010).

Idea stimulators, worksheets, step-by-step guides, and more in the following section:

- Section 1: "Personal and Organizational Philosophy about Volunteering"

Notes

1. Thanks to Colleen Kelly, executive director of Volunteer Vancouver/ Vantage Point, for making this point when reviewing this manuscript.
2. Rick Lynch, in a workshop presentation, paraphrasing from Steve McCurley and Rick Lynch, *Volunteer Management: Mobilizing All the Resources of the Community*, 2nd ed. (Ottawa: Johnstone Training and Consultation, 2006), 23.
3. Wendy Liu and Jennifer Aaker, "The Happiness of Giving: The Time-Ask Effect," *Journal of Consumer Research* 35 (October 2008): 552.
4. See note 1.
5. Liu and Aaker, "The Happiness of Giving," 554.

2

Considerations in Planning

From chapter one, you know how important it is to consider the question, "Why do we want volunteers?" To articulate the reasons that matter most to your organization, you may need to have many conversations with key stakeholders. Do not assume everyone either knows or agrees why volunteers are wanted. Allow sufficient time for these discussions to proceed organically, reaching all levels of staff, all function areas, and current volunteers, too. Even if—maybe *especially* if—your organization has been involving volunteers forever, articulating the rationale for volunteer engagement becomes a process of recommitment to it.

Statement of Philosophy

Once you have identified exactly why your organization wishes to involve volunteers, it is very helpful to develop a written "Statement of Philosophy" expressing your point of view. This statement can be useful in a number of ways, especially for establishing clear relationships between volunteers and employees, for recruiting new volunteers, and for demonstrating appreciation of community involvement. The Statement of Philosophy then becomes the basis or framework on which you and the board of directors can develop goals, policies, and other decisions affecting volunteers in the organization.

A Statement of Philosophy should affirm the value of *all* the people who work in your organization, whether paid or volunteer, with a delineation of the roles of each. A statement that says only "volunteers will assist in the achievement of agency goals" is insufficient. Similarly, a statement that limits roles, such as "volunteers will supplement, not supplant, paid staff" also does not do the trick. Though this latter sentiment has been gospel in some quarters, it is too limiting. For example, why must volunteers only "supplement"? Why can't they "innovate," or "experiment," or "work parallel to"? None of these roles diminishes the importance of the function of the paid staff.

A better approach to the Statement of Philosophy would be something like this:

> *Our agency encourages the teamwork of employees and volunteers so that we can offer our consumers the best services possible. Volunteers contribute their unique talents, skills, and knowledge of our community to provide personalized attention to clients, enable the paid staff to concentrate on the work for which they were trained, and educate the public about our organization and its cause.*

In a government agency (whether national, state, or local), the role of "citizen participation" deserves clarification in such a Statement of Philosophy. Here is one way to express political, nonpartisan, and practical commitment to teamwork between civil servants and citizen volunteers.

In a residential facility such as a nursing home, the Statement of Philosophy could include something about the interrelationship of the volunteers, paid staff, and the residents themselves. For example, you might state the desire of the facility to encourage residents to participate fully in the activities that create a home environment for all residents.

In a membership association, where it may seem self-evident that membership is voluntary, it is still useful to delineate the difference between joining and being an *active* member. The Statement of Philosophy might say, "As a community of professionals, we promote member participation as necessary to accomplish mutual goals, to assure representation of the field, and as personal career development."

If you are recruiting volunteers for a profit-making enterprise, it is vital to specify that volunteers will be assigned mainly to the personalized, direct client services for which volunteers are uniquely suited.

Where Are You Now?

What do volunteers do right now in your organization? Are you sure you know? Have you captured every variation of unpaid help you receive throughout the year? I recommend that you do a baseline inventory or audit identifying your current volunteer corps. Even if you are just starting to engage volunteers for the first time (beyond the board), analyze your organization to see if "bootlegged" volunteers are already active. For example, consider the following:

- Have you been asking neighboring faith community or school groups to help you once a year with a special event?
- Are students given the chance to do internships?
- Are friends and relatives of service recipients (or the board or the staff) allowed to "help out" if they are interested?
- Do you have advisory councils or special committees helping particular units or projects?
- Do individuals come in periodically to entertain clients, run a holiday party, or deliver things like donated books?

You may discover that you already have quite a list of "volunteers," though you may not have identified them as such in the past. You need to know if you are starting from scratch or indeed have a base of community supporters on which to build. This identification process can be pleasantly revealing. Understanding the full spectrum of who is already contributing unpaid time and many talents is the first step in assessing how well you are managing this resource and planning for what you want and need in the future.

Be sure to involve current volunteers as much as possible in helping to define their situation. Forming an ad hoc planning team of current volunteers may be one way to do some of the work necessary to define a new or improved program structure. Such a team also allows volunteers genuine participation. After all, you are formulating policies and procedures that will affect them (and may change some of the ways they operate now). What better way to show that you, as CEO, value volunteer input than to ask them for advice?

Establishing Outcome Measures

You develop strategic plans with goals and objectives for all organizational programs, projects, and services and should expect volunteers to work toward those just as employees do. But it is helpful to consider exactly what you expect volunteer involvement to accomplish in any period. There is no reason to let abounding gratitude for donated volunteer time restrain an organization from setting standards of achievement. In fact, volunteers usually prefer to have some way to assess their service contribution.

In developing initial and then ongoing goals and objectives, bigger is not always better. Having "more" volunteers this year than last year does not self-evidently mean better service delivery or greater impact. Some organizations would actually be better off cutting their volunteer corps in half and holding those remaining to higher standards! The number of volunteers needed is a *strategy* determined by expectations of productivity. So, if you wish to provide 15 percent more client services next year, somehow you need to add 15 percent more effort. This might be provided by asking each current volunteer to give an extra two hours a month or by recruiting additional, new volunteers.

Recognize, too, that the body count of how many people are in your volunteer corps does not translate into a standard number of hours contributed. Fifty volunteers each giving two hours a month provide the same output as five volunteers who can give twenty hours. The amount of effort necessary to recruit and support the larger number of volunteers is clearly much more intense, without the payback of more service. On the other hand, if your programmatic goal is community education, you may feel that getting fifty people to participate is more beneficial than just five. See? It depends.

Focus instead on the *outcome* and *impact* of volunteer activity. What results do you want volunteers to produce? As with employees, it is possible to monitor and measure the accomplishments of volunteers by stating goals and objectives at the beginning of a period—and then assessing whether these were achieved. See chapter ten for more about evaluation.

In formulating goals and objectives for volunteer involvement, you might consider such questions as listed below:

- What do we expect individual volunteers to accomplish in each position category?

- What ethnic and cultural diversity do we want represented in our volunteer engagement?

- What kinds of skills would we like volunteers to bring to our services?

- What reaction do we want our consumers to have to the service they receive from volunteers?

- What effect do we want volunteers to have in assignments such as public education, public relations, and so on?

- What outreach efforts do we expect our director of volunteer involvement to make this year?

Outcome measures set for the volunteer component should correlate with the overall goals and objectives of the agency. I once conducted a management retreat with the department heads of a large hospital system, in preparation for which the CEO sent me an impressive eighty-page "Five-Year Strategic Plan" for the institution. I dutifully read the entire document, and when I arrived at the retreat, asked why—despite the current participation of almost six hundred volunteers—there was not one word about volunteers in the strategic plan. After much consternation, it became clear that neither the administrators nor their outside consultant had considered it possible to "plan" for volunteers!

As with absolutely every other aspect of organizational life, the amount of time you spend determining what you want volunteer involvement to be will directly affect the quality and creativity of what you get. Ignore this aspect of your organization, and maybe you'll get lucky. But if you incorporate planning for volunteers into overall agency planning, you will naturally take the steps necessary to assure that you reach those goals.

Remember also to include planning for volunteer participation in any preparation for new projects, services, or campaigns. If, for example, you are proposing a new community education effort that will be under the auspices of the public relations department and you expect to train volunteers as speakers in that effort, develop a written objective that sets targets for the public relations staff related to volunteers, just as you would include an objective about creating a video, if that was also part of the plan. As CEO, you have the responsibility for inserting an objective relating to volunteer participation into the plans for any appropriate project and, as we will discuss later, for involving the person in charge of volunteer engagement in such overall agency planning.

The Nonpaid Personnel Department

From the perspective of human resource management, it is clear that the volunteer program is the nonsalaried personnel department of the agency. What does this mean in practice?

If you were given a $600,000 donation today, with the stipulation that it be spent on salaries for new employees, you would know exactly how to proceed effectively. You would probably follow a sequence of tasks very much like this:

1. Assess the organization's needs and pinpoint where new employees would be most useful.

2. Develop job descriptions, including the qualifications you'd look for in applicants.

3. Publicize the openings.

4. Interview and screen applicants, with the expectation that you will have to turn away some candidates in your search for the best people.

5. Select the people you will hire and match them to the available openings.

6. Assign them to a supervisor or manager.

7. Orient these new employees to the policies and practices of the agency.

8. Train these new employees in the specifics of the job to which each has been assigned.

9. Give them a place to do their work and any necessary tools such as a telephone and computer.

10. Start a new record for them in your personnel files.

Once the new employees were on board, you would then be concerned about their supervision, in-service training, and periodic performance evaluation. As top administrator, you'd recognize that if any one of these personnel management steps is omitted or done without high standards, then effective, quality delivery of service is jeopardized.

The premise of this book is that every one of these tasks is equally pertinent to the effective involvement of volunteers, though there are some special twists along the way and a few things that need extra attention.

If you accept this premise, then this chapter will help you plan for the integration of volunteers into your organization.

Defining What Roles Volunteers Will Fill

Chapter one identified the benefits of volunteer involvement for an organization. Are you making use of these in designing work for volunteers—maximizing the special, "first-choice" reasons volunteers can be effective?

The wrong question to ask when trying to define volunteer assignments is, "What could a volunteer do to help us?" The answer is generally tainted by stereotypes about who could be recruited. If you envision a frail octogenarian or a high school freshman completing a required number of service hours, you will give a very limited response to the question of what such a volunteer could do for you. Further, one of the identified "myths" of volunteer engagement that surfaced in Sarah Jane Rehnborg's study of executives is the belief that

> volunteer "work" is best defined as that which staff wants no part of . . . [There is a tendency] to silo away the possibilities inherent in volunteers' efforts. In many instances, the imagined task to be fulfilled has certain predefined characteristics that make agency leaders view it as work for volunteers—separate and, at times, lesser in value than other work of the organization.[1]

The more meaningful question is, "What needs to be done?" This leads to more specific considerations:

- What are we doing now that we would like to do more?
- What unmet needs do our clients have that we presently can do nothing about?
- What unmet needs does the staff have (to support them in their work)?
- What might we do differently if we had more skills or time available to us?

The answers to these and similar questions provide a wide range of possible assignments. Not every idea will be appropriate or possible to implement with a volunteer, but the door will be open to meaningful, creative, and challenging work. In light of this potential, volunteerism consultant and author Rick Lynch often observes wryly in workshop presentations, "There's really no reason for anyone in a nonprofit to be overworked." The point is that too often organizations simply do not consider asking qualified volunteers to help get things done.

You can also be creative in rethinking project management. Perhaps you tried unsuccessfully to find funding for a program. Might you deliver the service by mixing some paid employee time with many people volunteering their time?

It is fundamental that the kinds of volunteers you will attract are directly connected to what you want them to do. If every volunteer position is called an "aide," don't be surprised if less skilled people offer their help. Conversely, if assignments require special talents and leadership abilities, prospective volunteers who have that skill level will gravitate toward working with you.

Many Work Models

While it is true that the principles of human resources development apply to volunteers, it is limiting to conceive of volunteer work simply as unpaid staff roles. Many volunteers will indeed come on-site as individuals, on a regular schedule to complete tasks. But some will come in groups or teams, perhaps for a single day of service or episodically. Others will communicate with you but do almost all their work independently, from home, in the field, or online. In a membership association, member volunteers frequently fill roles on advisory committees or task forces.

Another important work model is that of a *consultancy*, in which an organization identifies a need and then recruits a volunteer with expertise in that area to help define it, explore its dynamics by interviewing those involved, propose an approach or solution—or facilitate the selection of one—and support implementation of the solution. Such a pro bono assignment is not supervised in the way that a volunteer in an unpaid staff role would be. Rather, it's a partnership between the highly skilled volunteer and the staff member (often someone in top management who is responsible for projects in need of key professional skills) most directly involved.

Don't Miss Opportunities

Consider this scenario: A businessman contacts your office and, completely unsolicited, offers you a donation of $25,000. Imagine your reaction. Perhaps it would be some variation of dancing around pro-claiming, "Manna from heaven!"

Now picture a slightly different scenario: The same businessman contacts your office, unsolicited, and explains that he has taken early retirement and hopes to become a volunteer with a worthwhile orga-nization. He has a lifetime of proven business success and wants to contribute a minimum of two days a week of his time. What's your reaction now?

A while back, two retired friends experienced this exact situation. Coincidentally, they each asked for my help in finding meaningful vol-unteer work to do. Neither of them (they don't know each other) found a volunteer placement that suited them. The problem was that they couldn't seem to find an organization willing to create a position to tap their skills. Even worse, they never felt welcomed or appreciated for their offer of contributed time.

These men are fifty-five to sixty-five years old, college educated, with a wealth of management experience. They also have been finan-cial donors to a range of community organizations over the years. To be truthful, neither is particularly well informed about the realities of nonprofit life nor about the issues and problems of the clientele of most human service agencies. They undoubtedly feel that nonprofits are gen-erally poorly managed by well-meaning novices. In other words, to put these men to work effectively as volunteers will require the right bal-ance of respect and training. But it would seem that the rewards would be worth the effort because these men intend to stick with any commit-ment made.

Independently, my two friends experienced frustration, dismissal, and rejection from a combined total of ten organizations. Their first chal-lenge was getting in the door. When they called an agency and explained what they wanted to do, they were often referred to the executive director's office—even when there was a director of volunteer involve-ment. This is because receptionists sense when a contact is at a higher level than "ordinary" volunteer candidates (an indicator of the impres-sion the staff have formed of the present volunteer program). Execu-tives take such calls but are at a loss as to how to respond. Does the gentleman mean that he wants to be considered for the board? No? Well, now, we'll have to think about what we might be able to do with you. Can we call you back? (Several never did.)

Most organizations are unprepared for the unexpected offer of help, particularly if the prospective volunteer is highly skilled. The technical assistance, consultation, or project management that volunteers such as my friends could provide would truly be unaffordable to most nonprofits, yet the effort required to make such a placement work seems insurmountable to many. It may even seem a bit threatening. Think of unexpected volunteer expertise like a "designated gift" that gives you the opportunity to move forward on plans that no one else has the time or perhaps the talent to do right now.

How clear are you on your organization's capability to respond to unusually qualified volunteer applicants? It does take planning and some staff training to be open to a more challenging type of volunteer. But consider another potential consequence of turning such people away: how likely will they be to give money to an agency that is disinterested in anything but their checkbooks? So here's an even more interesting question: when was the last time you actively *sought* people to contribute sophisticated expertise? If you only look for cash, you may well be missing the boat.

As CEO, you have a role to play in making sure that employees brainstorm creatively in finding ways for talented volunteers to become involved. Help employees avoid "dumping" on volunteers all the tasks they find distasteful or low level. While it is wonderful if a volunteer can be recruited who enjoys the things the employee dislikes, thereby pleasing them both, this approach backfires if the employee never intends to share any of the tasks that are more challenging or rewarding.

Starting Small

No matter what your ultimate goals for volunteer involvement are, it is good management practice to start small. Pilot test new volunteer assignment categories, allowing time to work out the procedural details that will only surface once a volunteer is on the job. Give salaried staff the chance to learn how to work successfully with volunteers, and add more people only as the support structure develops.

Perhaps you can select one or two units of the agency in which to begin placing volunteers, expanding to the other units over time.

Policy Setting

Throughout this book, you will recognize issues that can be solved or avoided by setting policies in advance that everyone understands. Since you and the board of directors (volunteers themselves, of course) are responsible for developing and implementing policies, you have the

- What are the pros and cons of adapting our volunteer involvement to the emerging new trends and issues in volunteerism? (Do we know what those trends and issues are? How do we find out?) What criteria should we employ to determine which trends to pursue?

- Have we taken all the risk management steps necessary to protect the client, the volunteer, and the paid staff? (See chapter nine.)

- Do we want to develop collaborative arrangements with existing community groups, and is volunteer action one way to accomplish this?

- What are the ways we might try to support new service initiatives, in addition to funding? As we attempt to raise the needed money, are we attempting to raise the needed volunteers, too?

- Do we make it possible for our paid staff to volunteer in the community themselves?

Schedule time during board meetings to discuss volunteers. Even if this only happens once a year, the status of volunteers increases when they become a formal part of the board's agenda.

In chapter eight, we'll turn the tables and look at how the principles of volunteer management relate to working with the members of your board of directors.

Management Options

Each reader will come to this book under different circumstances. You may be operating in an agency in which there is already a highly structured and well-managed volunteer component, or you may be considering starting a volunteer program for the first time. You may be the head of a large institution or the only salaried staff member among a multitude of volunteers. Whatever your situation, you will have to make some choices as to how you wish to begin or continue involving volunteers.

There are five management approaches, but do not assume that the following are in any sequence of low to high or poor to excellent. The choice truly depends on each organization's needs:

authority to set the rules for volunteer involvement. When people und
stand the rules, they can either follow them or work to change them. I
without rules in place, everyone operates independently—and you h;
no way of enforcing standards.

Each of the chapters in this book suggests an area requiring po
decisions. It is a policy decision to recruit volunteers in the first pl
and to allocate resources to their support. Make the effort to iden
existing policy gaps, especially in terms of the interaction between
unteers and paid staff. Be sure all new (and veteran) employees kr
the standards you have set, and be alert to new situations that req
revision of policies about volunteers.

For example, innovation in technology has created whole new s
ations requiring policies and procedures for Internet access, use of
tops and other personal computing devices, use of cell phones,
players, and so on. As you set your rules for employees, consider v
teers, too—both in giving them access to the organization's techno
and in limiting personal gadgets on-site.

The setting—and then the enforcing—of policies involving v
teers are two of the most visible ways you can demonstrate com
ment to the integration of volunteers into your organization.

The Role of the Board

The subject of volunteers belongs in the boardroom, but it is too r
raised there. Boards of directors should exercise the same lega
fiduciary stewardship with volunteers as with any other organiz
resources. Apart from the things we have already been discussing
unteers are as legitimate a subject of concern to a board of directc
is donated money. Both are valuable resources to the organizatior
both are "development" issues.

Basic data about volunteers should be reported to the board
with other organizational information. The point is not to manage
activities but to observe patterns over time. Volunteers are part
full picture, to be integrated into other organization decision m;
Here are some board-level questions:

- Is it desirable for the volunteer corps to reflect or represe
  the community and consumers we serve? Do we need ;
  affirmative action statement for volunteer recruitment?

Model I: You, as head of the organization, lead volunteer involvement and personally supervise volunteers just as you do paid staff.

Model II: You designate a leader for the volunteer "program," and all volunteers are recruited and supervised by this "director of volunteer involvement" (more on titles in a moment).

Model III: Volunteer engagement is "decentralized," in that all staff recruit and supervise volunteers active in their particular units.

Model IV: This approach is a mixture of models II and III, in which you designate a director of volunteer involvement who recruits and administers volunteers but deploys them to whichever units need assistance; day-to-day supervision is given by the line staff in each unit.

Model V: Volunteers are self-led, generally organized with elected officers, and so on.

Model IV is the most common management option and is exactly like most personnel or human resources department operations for employees. An entire chapter will be devoted to staffing the volunteer program, but you have basically two choices: you can designate an existing member of the paid staff to lead volunteer engagement in addition to his/her other responsibilities or you can create a new part-time or full-time employee position of director of volunteer involvement. (If you're wondering whether a volunteer can run the volunteer program, we'll consider that in chapter four, too.)

For readers in predominantly all-volunteer organizations or membership associations, the principles here hold true although the vocabulary may differ. Who exactly is charged with responsibility for assuring that as many members as possible participate in the organization's work and are happy doing so? Too many groups have a variation of a "membership chair" whose committee focuses solely on finding *new* members or on getting current members to renew their dues. Without having other leaders paying attention to how members are treated all year long, how candidates are selected for committee or project work, what kind of volunteer-to-volunteer relationships are being formed, or who gets thanked and how, worrying about who's paying dues seems a diversion from the essential tasks. Again, if you cannot specifically identify who is monitoring and guiding member engagement, it's probably no one. Is it time to become more intentional in addressing this leadership vacuum?

Organizational Placement

Whatever management option you choose, to whom will you have the person in charge of volunteers report? This decision has an impact on your entire chain of command and sends a message to all employees and volunteers. In a later chapter, we will consider the question of supervision of the leader of volunteers more fully, but for now, recognize that where you place the head of this initiative implies where—even whether—volunteers themselves are integrated into the organization.

There is no "correct" place for the director of volunteer involvement on the organizational chart. Each setting is different, and parameters such as staff size, job functions of other staff members, and so on will affect your decision. However, be aware that whoever supervises the director of volunteer involvement must truly understand what makes that position unique (see chapter four).

For example, if you place the volunteer program under the public relations department, will the director of public relations be able to assist the director of volunteer involvement in his/her responsibilities related to the daily service delivery of the agency? Generally, a public relations department does not have a role in in-house operations or activities. Conversely, if the director of volunteer involvement is placed under, for example, the casework supervisor, will that person be supportive of volunteer-related public outreach efforts? Again, the casework supervisor would normally have none or few responsibilities requiring external work in the community, such as public speaking.

It is useful to consider the connection between the director of volunteer involvement and the agency's director of human resources or personnel (after all, volunteers are both human and a resource!). There are both similarities and differences between these two functions. Structurally, as already noted, both recruit and place workers into your organization. Both require policies and guidelines to clarify expectations of paid and volunteer personnel. But think carefully if you are leaning toward placing the volunteer office within the human resources department. Here are some cautions:

- No matter how good the intentions, volunteers will always be given lower priority than employees—perhaps little attention at all.

- Human resources staff take job descriptions designed by others in the agency and try to fill those slots with the best people who are then completely delegated to each unit. The director of volunteer involvement, on the other hand, ought to be more proactively suggesting ways volunteers can support the work to be done, be much more creative in finding people with expertise or the potential to become an expert, and find placements for people who unexpectedly offer useful talents (the human resources folks can't hire anyone without an allocated salary).

- The director of volunteer involvement may also be much more involved in day-to-day agency activities and supervise some volunteers directly.

Some organizations place the volunteer office under the development or fundraising department. Again, there is overlap (especially if the development office involves special events or donor solicitation volunteers), but development staff have no direct service or program responsibilities, so who can support the director of volunteer involvement in recruiting and placing volunteers for in-house roles? Also, putting volunteer resources into fundraising may imply an agenda to ask for money as well as time, with emphasis on the former.

In reality, the director of volunteer involvement is a *separate, independent department head*, in that s/he has responsibilities substantially different from, though linked to, all other departments and in that s/he is responsible for a large cadre of workers, albeit volunteers. Ideally, the director of volunteer involvement should answer directly to you or another top executive. This also sends a message to the *volunteers*. It says that they have a direct line to the top decision maker. It conveys a similar message to all employees: volunteers are a subject of daily interest to the top executive. When you consider that the volunteer component is the agency's nonsalaried personnel department and that you, as CEO, are responsible for the deployment of all human resources, the decision to place the director of volunteer involvement directly under you is more than justifiable.

If you are the executive of a very large organization, the director of volunteer involvement may have to report to you through a vice president or some other key administrator. Again, recognize the messages you send to everyone through your choice of where to place the volunteer program. Consider the other organizational units answering to the same administrator and assess whether there is an evident rationale for placing the volunteer program alongside these other units—or whether the place-ment implies that volunteers are a "miscellaneous" agency function.

Organizational Chart

Does your present organizational chart include volunteers? Review the chart you show to funding sources or to new employees. Are volunteers mentioned on it at all? First consider, if you are with a nonprofit agency, are the nonpaid members of your board of directors noted? They should be at the top of your hierarchy, shouldn't they? Do you have an advisory council or a fundraising body such as an auxiliary? Are these volunteers visible on the chart? Now what about frontline volunteers?

The main, and therefore priority, work of each employee is generally reflected on an organizational chart. So if you have a "director of vol-unteer involvement," that position is probably shown. But if volunteer management is only a small part of the job of the person responsible for volunteers, how is s/he shown on the chart? Only under the primary title or function? Is his/her responsibility for volunteer management shown on the chart at all? If not, where does this leave volunteers? Are they out of sight, out of mind?

Whether an organization has a designated director of volunteer involvement or someone doing the work part time, it is probable that that individual will appear on the chart as an employee. But too often volunteers themselves are not indicated at all. If they are shown, they frequently are placed under the head of the volunteer program in this misleading way:

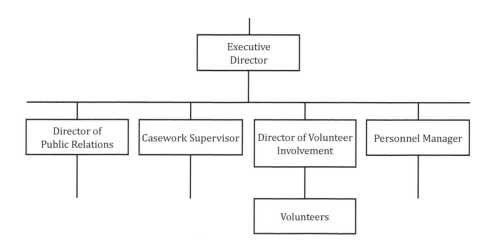

Why is such a chart misleading? It implies that volunteers "belong" to the director of volunteer involvement and effectively lets all other paid staff off the hook in caring about volunteers. Yet, if you have a personnel department, do you place one box saying "all employees" under it? Of course not. Only recruiters, benefits administrators, payroll clerks, and others who are directly supervised by the human resources manager are shown "under" her/him, while all other employees are shown under the departments in which they are placed. The volunteer department works in exactly the same way—channeling volunteers to the appropriate units where daily supervision is provided.

A more accurate organizational chart might look like the illustration on the next page.

Note how this new chart immediately acknowledges how dispersed volunteers are and how many functions they fulfill in your organization. This chart further makes it perfectly clear that each unit is responsible for its volunteer workers. Remember that the human resources department maintains a relationship to each employee, but that relationship is implied, not shown with a solid line connecting everyone back to human resources. The same relationship is true for the volunteer office.

Sometimes CEOs are reluctant to create such an organizational chart in the fear that funding sources will incorrectly conclude that the agency has sufficient resources. It seems somehow dishonest to show so many "staff." One way to handle this to make sure the chart is labeled as a *functional* organizational chart, not as simply a list of employed staff. Then you can indicate employees by circles or squares and volunteers by a differently shaped "box," or solid and dotted lines.

Organizational Image

One more consideration in planning for volunteers is to be sure your "house is in order" before opening the doors to recruit help from members of the public. While no one expects an organization to function perfectly or to have superhuman staff members, volunteers are affected by internal management problems. If the staff squabble or are disorganized, volunteers will be caught in the middle.

The ability to recruit volunteers is strongly and directly connected to your organization's image in the community. If your services are viewed negatively for any reason, it will be hard to attract good volunteers (though people will respond positively to a request to help make things

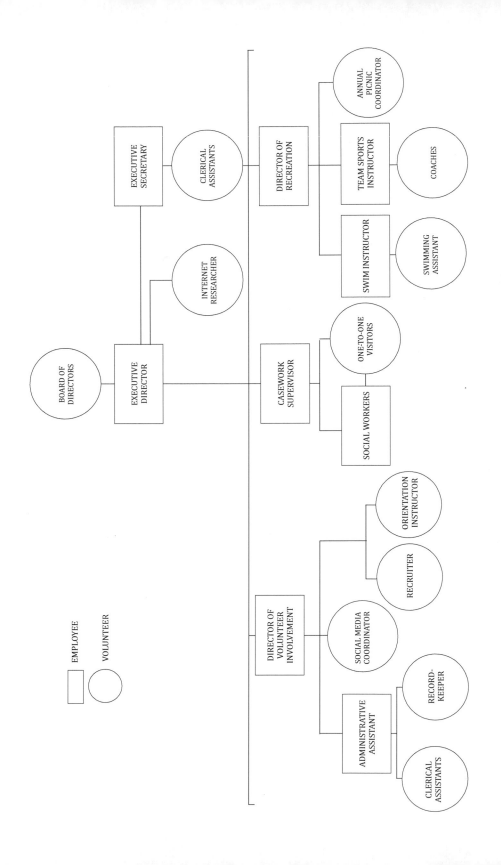

better). On the other hand, if the public sees your agency effectively filling a need, it will be easier to encourage volunteers to join you.

Having *no* image or visibility in the community poses similar recruitment problems. If people are unclear about what it is you do (which might be furthered by a vague or confusing organization name), then you or your leader of volunteers will first have to conduct a generalized public relations effort before you can concentrate on the specifics of volunteer recruitment. After all, how can someone be expected to offer you service if s/he doesn't know what you do?

Mergers

Whether out of concern for more stable funding or to respond to evolving community needs, mergers have become common between similar or compatible organizations—and sometimes between former competitors. Mergers always mean turmoil in the short run, even if ultimately successful. And the more agencies or sites involved, the greater the numbers of people caught in uncertainty, resistance, and fear—even if coupled with hope and gratification.

Volunteers are frequently among the people coping with the effects of a merger, yet they are rarely part of the plan to make it happen. In many cases, volunteers committed themselves to the particular agency now perhaps losing its identity under the merger. Where do their loyalties belong? The reorganization sure to come may include the elimination of staff jobs seen as duplicatory. Will this happen to volunteer assignments, too? Is anyone in a decision-making position thinking about this?

Some mergers have resulted in the attempted consolidation of several preexisting volunteer corps, often with the creation of one central office at one site only. In some situations, this may be quite workable. But in others, it signals the beginning of the end of a thriving volunteer force at the other sites. Unlike employees who want to save their jobs and will hang on during the changes of a transition period, volunteers need to feel that their services are wanted and useful each time they come in. When everything is in flux and then the familiar director of volunteer involvement is laid off with no replacement, it is understandable that some volunteers will leave in frustration.

The key point is that, if you are anticipating or undergoing a merger, put the subject of volunteers on the agenda. Talk with volunteers themselves and learn their hopes and fears. Ask their advice for how to restructure volunteer participation, assuring them continuity within change. If you must consolidate the volunteer office at one site, designate someone at the other sites to be at least the official staff liaison for volunteers, even if this is an interim plan. Demonstrate that you are taking the needs of volunteers into consideration.

If there are two or more independently run associations such as auxiliaries or friends groups, it may be unrealistic to expect them to merge as well, at least not immediately. There may even be advantages to retaining a circle of support for each site. Again, the worst strategy is to ignore the issue or to expect the groups to "work it out" by themselves. You want to send the message that they matter to your organization and that you will work with them to find the best solution for everyone.

Backing Your Involvement Strategy

In this chapter we have examined areas requiring thoughtful planning and preparation. In the next chapter, we'll talk about money. Successful volunteer involvement necessitates not only the allocating of funds but also providing access to other organizational resources.

To implement ideas in this chapter, see . . .

Leading the Way to Successful Volunteer Involvement: Practical Tools for Busy Executives by Betty B. Stallings with Susan J. Ellis (Philadelphia: Energize, Inc., 2010).

Idea stimulators, worksheets, step-by-step guides, and more in the following sections:

- Section 2: "Planning for Volunteer Engagement"
- Section 4: "Hiring and Placing Staff Who Lead Volunteer Engagement"
- Section 5: "Creating a Management Team for Volunteer Involvement"
- Section 7: "Integrating Volunteers throughout the Organization"

Note

1. Sarah Jane Rehnborg and others, *Strategic Volunteer Engagement: A Guide for Nonprofit and Public Sector Leaders* (Austin, TX: RGK Center for Philanthropy and Community Service, the LBJ School of Public Affairs, the University of Texas at Austin, 2009), 8.

3

Budgeting, Allocating, and Finding Resources

Volunteers are not "free" labor. They are a human resource that costs substantially less in hard cash than any other resource, but funds, space, supplies, and other materials must be allocated to support the work of volunteers. The "cost effectiveness" of such allocations is easy to prove: the expenses incurred by a volunteer component are *leveraged* into services valued at many multiples of the original expenditure. Later, we'll look at what the monetary worth of volunteer service really is—and how to compute it.

Avoid the mistake of seeing the volunteer component as "small" simply because there are few paid staff assigned to it. Though personnel costs may be low, other categories in the budget for volunteer involvement can be substantial because of the additional people being put to work.

One of the "Guiding Principles for Volunteer Involvement" highlighted in the *Canadian Code for Volunteer Involvement* reads, "Volunteers have rights. Voluntary organizations recognize that volunteers are a vital human resource and will commit to the appropriate infrastructure to support volunteers."[1] "Appropriate infrastructure" means different things to different people, but without it, volunteer effort is undermined and bound to be less effective than it should be. The annual budget, therefore, supports what is needed and desired.

Choices in Allocating Budget Amounts

There are two ways to budget for volunteer involvement across the organization. One is to gather all the budget items under one volunteer development and support category. The other is to spread the costs over the variety of departments where volunteers are utilized and active, reserving a small budget only for the coordinating role of a central office. There are good reasons for either or both options, depending on your goals.

When all costs associated with volunteer engagement are gathered together, you see what the overall effort really costs the organization. A budget for volunteer involvement demonstrates that this is not a peripheral, easy-to-ignore component of the agency's work. This has significance because some people only value an activity if money is allocated to it. It does, however, make the volunteer office an easy target at a time of budget cuts.[2]

When the costs of involving volunteers are spread to where the work is done, the transparency is of a different sort: volunteers are engaged throughout the operation, and there's at least one line item in each activity area to prove it. Suzanne Lawson notes,

> This is officially called "allocating," but I like the phrase I learned from a senior volunteer leader once: "peanut-buttering"—spreading the costs over several areas where they logically belong. In a local Cancer Society, for instance, that would mean budgeting for recruitment, supplies, recognition, staffing, etc. in the departments of education, service, and fundraising as well as governance, for instance. The budget cut threat is less, but there is a possibility of the volunteer effort seeming to be invisible as an overall priority of the organization.[3]

Let's examine each possible line item in a volunteer involvement budget and discuss the considerations in arriving at reasonable costs. Special needs in the start-up phase of a program will be indicated in each category.

Personnel

As you review the expenditures necessary in the personnel category, consider both direct and indirect costs. As we will be discussing in the next chapter on staffing, the number of full or part-time staff you designate or hire will depend on many factors, including the number and types of volunteers, your hours of operation, and so on.

Salary Range for a Director of Volunteer Involvement

I am often asked about the appropriate salary range for a director of volunteer involvement. This is an unproductive question because of the vast variety of settings in which volunteers work. It is nearly impossible to compare the operating budgets of an institution such as a museum or hospital with a grassroots agency such as a literacy program or food pantry. Clearly, the salary range for any position, including that of the top executive, will differ wildly between such extremely diverse situations.

Determining the salary of your director of volunteer involvement should be based on one criterion only:

What are you presently paying other department heads or key management employees?

The director of volunteer involvement is a *management* position, and the only valid measure of appropriate salary is in comparison with other positions at the same level in your agency. In fact, this is one indicator of how much value you place on the position and, ultimately, on the importance of the contribution of volunteers. The job requires decision making, leadership, and a great deal of public contact on behalf of the organization. If you place the salary on a level with line or clerical staff, you cannot demand management-level credentials or performance from the person you hire to fill the job. You should therefore budget for the position on the basis of its professionalism—and hire accordingly.

Other Staff Positions

The personnel budget category will, of course, include the clerical or administrative assistants and any additional volunteer management staff necessary because of the size or schedule of the volunteer corps. For example, volunteers can and often do work many evening and weekend hours, even if the agency is officially open only on weekdays. Who is available to work with volunteers in *your* off time but *their* on time? Do you need a staff member with hours to match those of the volunteers?

Employee benefits are the next line item, correlating with your current employee benefit package.

Finally, you might want to estimate the cost of the time devoted by other agency staff to the training and supervision of volunteers. While this will not be a direct budget line item, it may help you in identifying the true cost of the resources you are allocating to support volunteers.

Operational Costs and Other Needed Resources

Several of the following items will not be new expenses but will require a reallocation of present organizational resources.

Space and Other Facilities

Volunteer involvement needs supportive office space that affords the following:

- Easy access from the entrance of the building, since prospective volunteers (members of the public) will be coming in for interviews and training. Also, proximity to the entrance will allow the director of volunteer involvement to maintain contact with volunteers arriving and departing on their scheduled workdays and control of the sign-in system.

- Privacy for interviewing prospective volunteers

- Secure storage space for volunteers' coats and other personal belongings (and uniforms, if applicable)

- Group workspace for meetings or other activities

- Workstations for volunteers

Volunteers need adequate space in which to work, in whatever location they are placed. Staff may indeed want assistance with a variety of projects, but has anyone thought through where each volunteer will sit, have a clear work surface, and have access to office equipment? Also, is there anywhere that the volunteer can store his/her work materials in-between visits? Is there any provision for a mail bin or file folder so that messages may be left for the volunteer? Such details make work go smoothly and indicate that volunteers are indeed integrated into the organizational environment.

In addition to the space needed daily, the volunteer office also needs access to the following:

- Space for orientation sessions and in-service training meetings (varying group sizes)
- Adequate restroom facilities (Remember, the numbers of volunteers entering the building daily may be high enough to put a strain on your existing facilities. The school system in Anchorage, Alaska, faced this exact problem during the 1970s when teachers in hurriedly erected Quonset-hut elementary school buildings refused to allow volunteers to utilize the "faculty lounges." It turned out that these lounges contained only a single toilet and that an extra twenty or so adults per day genuinely caused a restroom line for the teachers who then sent the volunteers to the children's facilities. Although this situation occurred a long time ago, the resulting tension between the two groups remains a great example of lack of planning.)
- Space in various locations for sign-in books or other volunteer communication mechanisms, such as bulletin boards
- Possibly, lounge areas for volunteer rest periods (Will volunteers share the same kitchen or coffee and tea area as employees? Is there enough room for everyone?)

Access to space and facilities for volunteer use should be uniform with all other units, on a first-come, first-served basis. If employees can "bump" volunteers from a properly reserved space for no urgent reason, then volunteers learn they have access to the facilities only "when otherwise unoccupied."

Furniture and Equipment

Assess available workspace and furniture in terms of the impact of more people (volunteers) coming into the facility at various hours. Too many organizations have discovered too late that they did not have enough chairs for volunteers who dutifully arrived for work at their scheduled time.

The following are other needs—most of which are one-time, start-up costs rather than annual expenses:

- Coat racks and locked cabinets for volunteers' personal items
- Computers, not only for volunteer leadership staff, but also designated for volunteer use (especially if a number of volunteers have been recruited to do clerical work—it is usually not feasible to expect employees to share their keyboards all the time)
- Slide or LCD projector and screen (for recruitment or volunteer orientation slide shows and videos)
- Bulletin boards
- File cabinets (Keep in mind that the volunteer office is the nonsalaried personnel office and will generate paper files in much the same way as the employee personnel office does, despite computerized records.)
- Possibly, some comfortable furniture for conversation, interviews, or lounging

Telephones

Again, the number of telephone instruments and lines will depend on the size and nature of volunteer activities. But keep in mind that the volunteer office depends heavily on telephone contacts, both for recruitment, public relations, and ongoing communication with volunteers.

If you are creating any project that involves telephoning *by volunteers*—telephone reassurance programs, market surveying, political canvassing, client follow-up—the cost of telephone calls may be a major consideration for you. But with traditional telephone services changing all the time and new advances in cell phones and Internet calling options, this expense category may be one that actually decreases or disappears over time.

Supplies

Supplies is a budget category that is too often treated as minor, while it is really the tip of an iceberg. Budgeting for supplies should be done on the basis of the needs of both the volunteer "office" (a small number of paid staff) and the volunteers themselves (many more people). Consumption of supplies will rise as the number of active volunteers increases: productivity comes at the cost of support materials. A possible list of supplies would include some or all of the items here:

- Paper and stationery
- Pencils and pens
- Printer and copier toner and paper
- Paper clips, staples, and other desktop needs
- Paper towels and other maintenance materials
- Coffee, tea, and paper cups

In a workshop I ran some years ago for school principals, one partic-ipant asked to address his colleagues. He proceeded to tell the true story of his experience in the first year of inviting volunteers into his school. At the March faculty meeting, he admonished his teachers for having wastefully depleted the school's supply of copier toner. His bemused teachers replied, "But now, with all the volunteers, we've been able to give the pupils a chance for individual study exercises, so we've been copying special worksheets in larger numbers than ever before." The principal wanted to advise his colleagues: "If you're going to start hav-ing volunteers, you'd better increase your toner and copy paper requisi-tion." What excellent, practical advice!

One way to estimate your costs for supplies might be to translate the cumulative number of hours served by volunteers (or anticipated being served) annually into "full-time equivalent" (FTE) staff positions. For example, if an employee works 2,080 hours a year (40 hours per week times 52 weeks), then a volunteer program with 150 people log-ging 10,000 hours of volunteer service per year can be said to give the organization the equivalent of 4.8 full-time employee hours of service, or 4.8 FTE. If you normally budget supplies using a formula of $X per employee, to arrive at the supply budget for the volunteer program, sim-ply take $X and multiply it times the total of the number of paid staff and the FTE number of volunteer staff.[4]

Just be careful when you use FTE reasoning. There are some items that must be provided for *every* volunteer, no matter how frequently s/he serves. Sometimes 150 volunteers cannot be reduced to 4.8 FTE; it really will require 150 times $X to meet the need.

Software for Tracking Volunteer Contributions

When I was writing the first edition of this book in the mid-1980s, orga-nizations were just starting to computerize formerly all-paper record-keeping. By the second edition, as desktop computers proliferated and even the smallest of agencies were computerizing, software developed specifically for volunteer management came on the market. Give some consideration to purchasing such dedicated software or, at a minimum, to making sure that the data program you expect the volunteer office to use meets your recordkeeping and reporting needs.

Too often, directors of volunteer involvement are forced to make do with software designed primarily for other purposes. Time and again, colleagues call me in despair at the attitude of management information system or Internet technology staff that volunteer management data are nothing more than glorified address lists that can be added on to some fundraising or accounting software with only a few modifications. The recordkeeping needs of the volunteer office are rather complex, including matching people to assignments and coordinating schedules that change each day, dealing with individuals and groups, and more.

While it is reasonable to want to integrate all the files of your agency into one computer system, the recordkeeping needs of your development office or your casework supervisors are simply not the same as the needs of the volunteer office. On a daily basis, the director of volunteer involvement handles fluid data that changes with the current schedules and activities of volunteers. Available off-the-shelf programs for volunteer recordkeeping are comparatively low cost, especially compared with developing your own software, and generally better. The money spent on the right software will be an investment in improved ability to coordinate volunteers.

For large institutions and as the technology becomes more accessible to smaller agencies, there are online data storage systems, with public- and restricted-access options. This allows volunteers to log in regularly from anywhere, immediately updating service records and entering information about their activities.

The better your ability to record who volunteers are and what they are doing, the more valuable the data you will obtain for monitoring and evaluation purposes.

Internet Access and Web Site Space

Just as all the other departments in your organization, the volunteer office needs to be online. It is no longer just useful to be able to access the Web; it's a necessity. Online recruitment, communication by e-mail with volunteers, virtual volunteering assignments, professional exchange— all this and more has become everyday business as usual. Depending on the size of the volunteer corps, particularly how many paid and volunteer staff are coordinating activities, it may be important to have several Internet-connected computers available at all times.

This raises other related questions, some of which incur costs, including the following:

- Will we allocate pages on our organization's Web site to promote volunteering with us? Will this include such tools as online application forms and updated lists of current vacancies?

- Will we create a password-protected, volunteers-only area of our Web site so that information and resources volunteers need in their work are continuously available to them? Will we establish communication tools to allow volunteers to interact directly with each other, such as discussion boards or listservs?

- Will we give volunteers a password to enter our intranet or other confidential site?

- Will volunteers who do a lot of communicating on our behalf be given an e-mail address with our organization's domain name?

- Will our existing Internet technology staff be able to accommodate designing and maintaining these services or do we need to budget for outside Web design consulting? Or should we be recruiting Web-savvy volunteers?

Printing and Reproduction

Despite today's electronic communication, documents on paper remain an important line item for a volunteer program. The following items all require printing or photocopying:

- Volunteer application forms and other recordkeeping forms
- Recruitment brochures, flyers, posters, mailings, and other tools
- Recognition certificates, invitations, and programs
- Possibly a printed volunteer newsletter
- Possibly a volunteer handbook or manual (in the second year?)
- Training materials

Printing costs have changed enormously because today everyone can generate "just-in-time" materials thanks to word processing and desktop publishing software. Today, we can compose and format our forms, manuals, and other written work and then store each item until we print out only the number of copies required for immediate use. But there is still is a good deal of paperwork needed to support volunteer engagement.

Postage

The amount necessary for postage will depend, of course, on such variables as whether the volunteer program postal mails a volunteer newsletter or intends to use mass mailings of any sort to recruit volunteers. On one hand, postage rates are forever increasing, but, on the other hand, electronic publishing and distribution have decreased dramatically the number of such mailings most organizations need to do. Costs for today's communication may therefore mean purchasing or registering for mass e-mail distribution software and services. However, there are still times when mailing something to hold in your hand matters.

Insurance

The whole issue of insurance will be discussed later in this book. The cost of accident or liability insurance for volunteers may have to be a budget item if your existing agency insurance package does not already cover volunteers. Supplemental automobile insurance may also be a need, if some volunteers are drivers for your organization. Special, one-time event insurance may also be necessary if the volunteers run major fundraising extravaganzas for you.

First talk to your present insurance carrier, but be aware that special programs designed specifically for coverage of volunteer insurance needs are available at reasonable costs (see chapter nine and appendix B).

Recognition

Though it is optional to budget for a major volunteer recognition event such as a party or a dinner, some consideration should be given to how the organization will formally thank volunteers (and perhaps also the staff who supervise them). Certificates of appreciation are not expensive, while gift items can be budgeted at a wide range of costs. Even a minimal amount of money can permit an enjoyable recognition event—punch and cookies can show appreciation just as well as a steak dinner can.

Enabling Funds

Enabling funds are reimbursement given to volunteers for out-of-pocket expenses incurred in the course of volunteer service. This is meant to "enable" people to give their services freely, especially if the cost of volunteering would otherwise prohibit some people from participating. The concept of enabling funds stems from the desire to diversify the corps of volunteers as much as possible. If consideration is not given to out-of-pocket costs, then too many programs will have as volunteers only those people who can afford the "luxury" of volunteering. Older people on fixed incomes, students with little outside income, and low-income people will otherwise be shut out of the opportunity to give their time and energy to causes that they care about.

Some agencies are able to provide in-kind support of volunteers through existing resources, as opposed to having to budget funds to reimburse cash expenditures, including the following:

- Parking lot privileges or van transportation
- Meals on-site
- Free uniforms (or other special items of clothing or uniform cleaning services)
- Refreshments, such as hot or cold drinks
- Access to an agency-run child care service

When an organization can indeed offer these types of items to volunteers, they might be budgeted under the heading of "benefits" and certainly should be described as such in recruitment materials.

One criterion may be what you do or do not reimburse or pay for employees. There is no right or wrong answer, but be aware that if you provide free parking for one part of staff, the other part may want it, too. Or if paid staff pay personally for coffee supplies, will they balk if volunteers are not asked to contribute as well? Suzanne Lawson wisely recommends paying attention to the fine line between what is budgeted or provided for paid staff and what volunteers get:

> If there's a major imbalance either way, morale can be affected . . . For instance, if there is a top-notch leadership development program made available to volunteers but there is no access for staff to participate nor an equivalent leadership development program for staff, staff will soon become resentful. Or, if staff have a comfortable lounge, but volunteers

have no place to make a cup of coffee, volunteers will quickly figure out how valued they are.

... there can be similar volunteer dissatisfaction if one committee gets to meet at a fancy hotel, and all others meet in a run-down conference centre to save money. (It's almost always the finance committee that gets the hotel, have you noticed?!)[5]

She notes *equality* is not necessarily expected or required, but *equity* is expected and shows attention to the needs of both groups who make up the organization.

If you do not have the option of offering such in-kind benefits, consider the types of items that cost volunteers money and therefore might be *reimbursed* by the organization. Some examples are listed below:

- Transportation to and from the assignment
- Child care costs
- Telephone or copying costs for work done at home
- Special clothing needs (uniforms, aprons, work gloves, etc.)
- Money spent directly on clients, such as taking a child to a movie or buying supplies for an art class

Some organizations offer reimbursement to volunteers on the basis of economic need. Clearly, this is a tricky area and requires thoughtful procedures to encourage volunteers to identify their expenses. Philosophically, I believe in making reimbursement available to every volunteer and then allowing those who prefer to consider the money they spend as a donation to say so.

Volunteer expenses should be budgeted visibly to acknowledge their existence. If some (even most) volunteers select to donate these costs to the agency, this can be shown as "revenue" to offset the "expense" category in your financial reports (see chapter eleven). For most volunteers, these out-of-pocket costs are a real financial consideration and good management requires the recognition and reporting of such agency resources.

Travel

Travel costs incurred for public outreach and recruitment fall under the travel line item. The director of volunteer involvement and other program representatives will be making speeches and presentations throughout the community, and such travel or public transportation should be reimbursed.

Travel also should accommodate trips to state and national meetings or conferences by volunteer management staff and volunteers.

Professional Development

Professional development includes funds for the director of volunteer involvement to join various professional societies (see appendix B about volunteerism resources) and registration fees for workshops and conferences, both for the volunteer office staff and for key volunteers. Demonstrating interest in their professional development is one way that an organization can build loyalty among volunteers. It is perfectly all right to ask that a volunteer make a commitment of time for all funds expended on her/his training—just as you would negotiate with a salaried staff member for a work commitment in return for tuition reimbursement. If the time commitment is not honored, then the person (employee or volunteer) would be expected to pay back the money extended.

Volunteerism journal subscriptions and book purchases for an in-house library also fall into the category of professional development.

Volunteer Training

Training expenses may include fees to speakers, video rentals, books, handout materials, and so on to support volunteer training programs.

Expenses to Support the Board

The budget development process is also a good time to remember that board members and members of board committees are also volunteers. Where and how do you reflect the costs associated with board meetings, travel, and out-of-pocket reimbursements? You may show these amounts as "governance" or executive expenses, but be sure everyone recognizes the correlation between these costs and what is budgeted for other volunteer roles.

Other

Every program will have some sort of special need unique to its setting. The point to be made, however, is that volunteer offices often have "odd" requisitions. Who else may ask for three hundred balloons?! The creative aspects of recruitment, motivation, and recognition require supplies that set a tone or atmosphere different from the rest of the facility. So be prepared for the unexpected.

Decentralize Some Expenses

While we have been discussing the allocation of a budget directly to the volunteer program, under the administration of the director of volunteer involvement, it is also legitimate to provide for some of the expenses of volunteers within the budget of each unit that will involve volunteer workers. This allows for categorical accounting and may give you a more realistic understanding of the true costs of volunteer participation.

Finding the Funds

One of the purposes of budgeting is to recognize the total cost of running a volunteer program. However, nothing says that all budget items must be paid for out of current organization monies. Quite a number of the items previously listed can be covered by specific donations (both cash and in-kind) or by special fundraising events.

Funds expended to support volunteers are leveraged into more service than the same amount of money could pay for in salaries. This multiplying factor can be a powerful argument to a corporate donor or a foundation grants officer who might well consider funding support of volunteers in your organization.

Surprisingly, the majority of organizations never ask funders for money designated to support volunteers! Some just don't plan for volunteers before a project starts or underestimate the costs. Some can't believe that anyone would be willing to fund volunteer support. For others, it may be rooted in another myth that Sarah Jane Rehnborg found among the administrators attending her focus groups: you can't *invest* in volunteer efforts. She notes that when the topic of financial investment in volunteers arises, many executives express concern that funders and board members will "see it as 'cheating' to invest in free labor."[6] Nonetheless, she concludes, "Volunteer engagement is a process, no different than fund development or marketing; it connects nonprofits with mission-critical resources. Few question spending money to raise money; spending money to raise people (a prerequisite to raising money) is just as necessary."[7] Whether because of the false reasoning that volunteers are "free," a belief that such money will not be allowed, or the simple omission of the money needed from budget planning, executives send off fundraising proposals without asking to pay for community engagement. The best advice is to state clear goals for the accomplishments of volunteers, explain the anticipated costs, and *request funding.*

An excellent articulation of what it takes to find money to support volunteer involvement was written by Betty Stallings in an article for *e-Volunteerism.* In "Generating Funds for Your Volunteer Program: The Mindset and Methods," Stallings begins by noting,

> Often at the heart of unsuccessful resource generation for volunteer programs is a *lack of true commitment* to generate funds or to allocate existing funds to this effort. In many organizations, volunteer programs are not a priority nor are they valued enough to be allocated needed resources.
>
> It is well known that we fund what we value. So, part of dissecting this issue is to explore the organization's commitment to its volunteer program. Is it a nice thing to have? Is it a nuisance? Or, is it considered essential in reaching the mission of the organization? None of the suggestions for raising funds will land on open ears if this issue of real commitment is not addressed. Having a strong case for incorporating volunteers into your program must be in place before you begin to explore funding options.[8]

She also identifies some of the obstacles to developing effective funding proposals, including

> promoting volunteers as "a program"—possibly viewed in direct competition with other services offered by the organization—rather than *a resource* that empowers the organization to extend *all* of its services. Perhaps we need to consider whether the term "volunteer program" is feeding the internal resistance to funding volunteer engagement adequately.[9]

She notes that too many funders lack knowledge about the necessity of effective engagement of volunteers or its costs:

> But infrequently do funders use an assessment of total volunteer engagement as one of the key measures of a successful program/organization. Thus, it is no wonder that organizations have not taken the steps to initiate and support a strong volunteer program. Funders of the past have rarely understood or rewarded this effort.[10]

Some progress has been made on this front, especially since the publication of the Urban Institute's 2004 study, *Volunteer Management Capacity in America's Charities and Congregations: A Briefing Report*, cited in the introduction to this book.

Develop a Strong Case for Support

Whether you are approaching individual donors, foundations, or corporations, you need to develop a clear and convincing case as to why they should contribute resources to your volunteer program. Stallings offers the following talking points:

1. There is a connection between our mission and effective volunteer engagement.
    . . . request funding based on how volunteers are expanding your capacity to reach your mission, whether that is to end hunger, improve the environment, or empower seniors to live independently. Rather than approaching funders with a budget to support the infrastructure of running a volunteer program, approach them with *the impact* that volunteers will have on the clients you serve . . .

2. Your investment will leverage resources.
    [Funders] want their contributions to be a lead gift that others will match . . . So, my advice is to think of all the ways that supporting your volunteer program will provide leveraging opportunities to gain other resources, expand services, and share successful new ideas with others providing a similar service.

3. We welcome community oversight.
    Any organization that receives private donations or public support is truly "owned" by the community. And thus, engaging the community in the effort makes a great deal of sense, both as watchdogs for the use of the money and as individuals who can expand the services.[11]

She also counsels, as we have already discussed in chapter one, to avoid saying, "volunteers save us money," when what they really do is *extend your budget*. However, it is very effective to talk about return on investment, explaining how each dollar given to support volunteers produces a much greater amount of valuable service. We'll return to this point in both chapters ten and eleven when we discuss evaluation and monetary value of volunteer contributions.

Raise Money to Support Volunteers

Ultimately, whether you will have funds to pay for the budget items required for successful volunteer engagement will depend on your willingness to allocate money from your current revenue or go out and raise money specifically for this purpose.

Ask Volunteers for Money

In chapter one, we noted the interrelationship of volunteers and donors and that it *is* appropriate to ask volunteers to also make a financial gift to your organization—providing that the "ask" acknowledges the value of time donated, as well. Consider extending any solicitation you make to board members to all volunteers:

> Some organizations have even begun to work towards 100% giving by all volunteers, emphasizing that the gift should be comfortable for each person. If you have low- to moderate-income folks volunteering, a gift of $10.00 may be significant to them. The ultimate value of this is that outside funders see how committed the internal supporters are and may be more apt to give a donation when they see that all or most internal volunteers are giving some financial support beyond their gifts of time. This will not change overnight, particularly if you have a culture that indirectly says, "you give time *or* money," but this can gradually change as the fund development and volunteer programs begin to work more closely with one another.[12]

There are other times at which you can give volunteers the opportunity to give money. For example, you can make it optional for volunteers to pay the costs involved in activities to which they are invited guests. Stallings shares this personal experience:

> In one organization [where] I served as a volunteer, many volunteers vocally objected to the costs the organization incurred in their recognition event. To resolve the issue, the organization simply added a space to donate the money back to the organization if they chose to. There was no pressure or any reporting of who did or didn't but nearly 75% of the volunteers in that organization chose to pay for the meal as opposed to having it come from funds that might enhance or expand client services.[13]

Funds Raised at Special Events

The number and diversity of special fundraising events organized and staffed mainly by volunteers are enormous. Yet almost always all the cash raised becomes unrestricted operating funds. Why not allocate at least some of the funds raised by volunteers to support volunteer involvement itself? This seems only fair. After all, some of the funds your development staff solicit ultimately helps pay their salaries. It's also logical to reserve a percentage of the money to assure seed funding for next year and to grow the ability of volunteers to raise even more.

Another approach is to select certain volunteer support costs and run small fundraisers just for those amounts. Let the public know how the money will be leveraged by many multiples by the far greater value of the volunteer work enabled. This sort of approach can easily raise what you need to reimburse volunteer out-of-pocket expenses, special supplies and equipment, or anything clearly supportive of volunteer effort.

Outreach to Corporations

Encourage volunteers to solicit donations to your organization from their employers, especially if they work for any company large enough to have a corporate philanthropy policy. Many employers offer matching gifts both for cash donations their employees make to charitable causes and to add to the value of employees' volunteer services to an organization. These are sometimes called "Dollars for Doers" programs and often apply to the activities of employees' spouses as well. Volunteers may not be aware that they can apply for this type of funding from their employer to multiply what they give to your organization.

Gifts in Honor of Volunteers

Once you begin to see money and time contributions along a continuum and sometimes combined, all sorts of things can materialize. Here's another creative idea from Stallings:

> A way that I frequently make contributions is in honor of a family member or friend who volunteers for an organization. In other words, if your daughter volunteers for the American Red Cross, you can contribute to them in honor of your daughter but—here's a new twist—request that the funds go specifically to support the volunteer program. Gifts in honor or in memory of someone are not new, but I believe that we can proactively establish a designated fund for our needs. Then let volunteers know that if someone asks what they want for a birthday or

holiday, they can say: "Please give a gift to the Volunteer Support Fund at the agency for which I volunteer."

Some organizations are a natural for this type of donation. At a well-known aquarium, their lead volunteers take special guests on back-scene tours of the aquarium. In appreciation for this exceptional treatment, guests were making gifts to the general aquarium fund. It then became obvious (with some encouragement from the volunteer/ fund development department) that the aquarium could create a special "volunteer program fund" to be the recipient of such donations.[14]

Finally, an often unreported financial benefit of volunteers is all that they bring to the organization in the way of in-kind resources and new volunteers. As discussed in chapter one, their spheres of influence are wide and diverse, so they are able to contact many more people and businesses for all kinds of donations.

To implement ideas in this chapter, see . . .

Leading the Way to Successful Volunteer Involvement: Practical Tools for Busy Executives by Betty B. Stallings with Susan J. Ellis (Philadelphia: Energize, Inc., 2010).

Idea stimulators, worksheets, step-by-step guides, and more in the following section:

- Section 3: "Budgeting and Funding Volunteer Involvement"

Also, see the worksheet on budgeting that matches the categories of expense outlined in this chapter of *From the Top Down*.

Notes

1. Volunteer Canada, *Canadian Code for Volunteer Involvement*, revised 2004, http://volunteer.ca/en/can-code.
2. I would like to thank Suzanne Lawson for many of the points she raised in her excellent self-instruction guide, *Budgeting for a Volunteer Program: Money Well Planned and Well Spent*, published by Energize, Inc., in October 2007 as a resource in the *Everyone Ready*® online training program.

3. Ibid., 16.
4. G. Neil Karn, "The No-Apologies Budget," *Voluntary Action Leadership* (Spring 1984): 29–31.
5. Lawson, *Budgeting for a Volunteer Program*, 15.
6. Sarah Jane Rehnborg and others, *Strategic Volunteer Engagement: A Guide for Nonprofit and Public Sector Leaders* (Austin, TX: RGK Center for Philanthropy and Community Service, the LBJ School of Public Affairs, the University of Texas at Austin, 2009), 5–6.
7. Ibid.
8. Betty B. Stallings, "Generating Funds for Your Volunteer Program: The Mindset and Methods," *e-Volunteerism* 7, no. 1 (2006): 1, http://www.e-volunteerism.com/quarterly/06oct/06oct-stallings.php.
9. Ibid., 2.
10. Ibid.
11. Ibid., 3.
12. Ibid., 8.
13. Ibid.
14. Ibid., 10.

4

Staffing Volunteer Involvement

Decisions regarding the staffing of your volunteer initiative deserve careful consideration. A key conclusion of the *Volunteer Management Capacity in America's Charities and Congregations* study was "that the value that volunteers provide to organizations they serve should make the effective management of volunteers a key priority."[1] Yet they also noted how few organizations have created designated staff positions to assure successful volunteer involvement. This is counterintuitive and remains a challenge that each organization must meet.

Betty Stallings surveyed twenty-eight CEOs identified as running organizations with excellent volunteer programs to learn what commonalities exist in what she terms "Volunteer Program Champions." In *12 Key Actions of Volunteer Program Champions: CEOs Who Lead the Way*, she quotes Jay Spradling, assistant chief of police of the Tempe, Arizona, Police Department, who offers this advice:

> Hire the best Volunteer Manager you can find. This single factor has a HUGE impact as to whether your program will succeed or fail. Be prepared to provide a competitive salary and benefits, treat her or him as a manager, and make the investment of your time to keep your

Volunteer Manager position from being a "revolving door" or "training" position.[2]

Similar reports from executives are documented in Sarah Jane Rehnborg's *Strategic Volunteer Engagement* guide, such as when Suki Steinhauser, new CEO of the Communities in Schools (CIS) Program in Austin, Texas, talked about "something she called her 'secret sauce': a new hire in volunteer management whose support made it possible for CIS to involve more than 600 new volunteers in her first year alone, fostering a committed team of community advocates for CIS."[3]

How you go about designating or hiring the leader of volunteer involvement will be influenced by your strategic plan for volunteers. While it should be obvious that your staffing plan must fit the number and functions of volunteers you anticipate, it may not be obvious how to develop a formula to determine the right "fit."

Identifying a Leader

The vast majority of people who lead volunteer engagement do not do so as a full-time job. Rather, they work part-time coordinating volunteers while primarily filling a different function in the organization; they have been asked to assume leadership of the volunteer effort *in addition* to their other responsibilities. In many cases, they were "anointed" into the leadership of volunteers; they did not seek the extra responsibility and felt they had little or no option when their administrator offered it to them. Additionally, they continue to view their original job description as their priority and try to "squeeze in" volunteer-related responsibilities as a secondary set of tasks. In terms of career goals, most of these part-timers have no interest in pursuing the volunteer management field. They see themselves rather as "social workers," "park rangers," "occupational therapists," or "probation officers" and consider the volunteerism "piece" of their jobs as something they will escape someday when they get promoted.

Logically, someone who sees volunteer leadership as secondary (perhaps even as distracting) will rarely give the type of direction that will ensure volunteers achieve their true potential. So why designate a reluctant director of volunteer involvement?

The first step is to decide whether you are able (or willing) to create a new budget line for a designated leader of volunteers. It may be worthwhile to wait in creating or expanding your volunteer component until funds can be found. As noted in the previous chapter on budgeting, a special fundraising event or a special grant request might create the first year's salary, especially if you plan to begin with a part-time staff member. At least this part-timer will devote all of his/her on-site time to the subject of volunteers. And the time will be devoted willingly and enthusiastically because it will be this person's primary job responsibility. The difference in possible achievement of goals because of this factor of primary responsibility cannot be overestimated and outweighs even the time limitations of a shorter work schedule.

If a new budget line is absolutely not possible, then you should begin by discovering who on staff might actually *want* to learn about volunteer management. Even if the interested staff member functions in a work area that seems tangential to what you plan for volunteers, the factors of free choice and enthusiasm should weigh heavily in favor of giving that staff member the responsibility for volunteers.

Defining Expectations

I always ask people who are part-time directors of volunteer involvement in addition to carrying other agency job responsibilities whether they tried to clarify the following important points at the time they accepted their volunteer-related tasks:

- What exactly does "part time" mean? How many hours of the day or week will I be allowed to devote to volunteer management?

- In what ways will my present workload be decreased in order to "make room" for my new volunteer-related responsibilities?

- At what level of program growth will my part-time status be reviewed to determine whether more time is needed for volunteer management or if the agency is ready for a full-time director of volunteer involvement (not necessarily me)?

- What other agency resources will be made available to me in support of our volunteer engagement strategy?

- Does my immediate supervisor understand and completely accept the fact that my previous work patterns will now have to change, especially in terms of decreasing my former output in my primary area of service?

In all too many cases, these questions are not raised by either the new leader of volunteers or the CEO. Because so many of these issues require decision-making authority, it would be helpful for the executive to consider these and other questions *before* selecting an existing staff member to take on the added responsibility of volunteers. Otherwise, volunteer management becomes nothing more than an addendum to an already busy schedule and, in fact, produces stress and tension among the staff as a whole.

It is just as pertinent to consider some of these issues even if a brand-new employee will be hired to focus on volunteer involvement as a sole responsibility but on a part-time schedule. For example, at what point will you start thinking about increasing the number of work hours for the director of volunteer involvement? Or, if you do not want to expand this position, at what level of growth will you consider volunteer participation "capped"?

It Takes a Village . . .

The adage that "It takes a village to raise a child" can be applied to volunteers, as well. It takes the entire organization to provide a supportive environment for volunteer engagement. So whether you delegate primary accountability for volunteer management to an existing staff member or hire a new part-time employee for this role, also assign specific responsibilities for supporting volunteers to other agency staff. This makes it clear that volunteers will be part of *everyone's* job because volunteers are now part of the team delivering the organization's services.

First, as CEO, you are responsible for all the people who work in the organization—paid or unpaid. Just as you support employees in various ways, pay attention to the needs and opinions of volunteers. Again, to quote from Betty Stallings's *Volunteer Program Champions* study,

> Together, the CEO and the staff member designated to manage the volunteer program are the key people in an organization who must provide leadership and support to volunteer involvement. But in the real world, overworked and overwhelmed CEOs are frequently delighted to delegate not only the daily tasks of coordinating volunteers but also all planning and decision-making completely to the director of volunteer involvement. Nothing can be more lethal to a volunteer program.
>
> The director of volunteer involvement can inspire and empower both employees and volunteers to partner effectively to impact the organization's mission. But this staff member cannot accomplish this

alone. It requires significant management team support to integrate volunteer engagement with financial development, public relations, program development and all other key aspects of the organization, all requiring coordination at the highest levels. It is also vital that top leadership express their vision of the potential power of volunteerism, and then take action to assure that the vision can be realized.[4]

Having a designated volunteer management position does not let everyone else off the hook from attention to volunteers. The public relations staff should help with recruitment, the information technology department with recordkeeping and Web placement, and the training staff with skill building. It is up to you to distribute the work where it logically belongs and to specify the chain of command between the new head of volunteer engagement and those other staff members working on behalf of the organization's volunteer-related goals. So even when you are ready and able to designate a full-time director of volunteer involvement, other organizational personnel will continue to have support roles to play in assuring that the volunteers become part of the team.

My organization, Energize, Inc., is so committed to this concept of system-wide responsibility for volunteers that we have produced a number of tools for organizations to use. One is an online volunteer management training program focused on teaching *all* employees, at every level and in all functions, about working with volunteers; we call it *Everyone Ready*® to make the point. We also offer Betty Stallings's *Training Busy Staff to Succeed with Volunteers: The 55-Minute Training Series*, a set of twelve training designs, with PowerPoint slides, ready to present in sessions for staff.[5]

But . . .

Beware of reasoning that, because volunteer management responsibility is shared among work units, you therefore can do without a centralized volunteer office. If everyone is charged with volunteer success, in critical ways it turns out that no one is in charge! Further, because all these other staffers have primary service roles, their work with volunteers naturally becomes secondary, if not tertiary or lower.

What you need is someone designated to be the "point person" on volunteer issues for your organization—someone for whom volunteers are always the main focus and whom you can hold accountable for monitoring and assuring volunteer involvement goals are achieved. This is the person who will keep informed about volunteering trends and issues and who will make sure you integrate the subject of volunteers into whatever planning or discussions are taking place.

I use this simple litmus test. If I want to send an invitation to a workshop about a volunteer management topic, to whom in your organization should I address it? If you can't immediately answer this question, you have no one in charge.

A Word on Titles

Questions may arise about what job title to give the leader of your volunteer component. More than thirty years ago, Harriet Naylor created a "career ladder" for volunteer administration within what was then the U.S. Department of Health, Education and Welfare; it was subsequently picked up in the Department of Labor's *Dictionary of Occupational Titles*, where it still can be found today.[6] This may be useful, but do not feel constrained by anything other than what truly matches your situation. Naylor's ladder proposed three levels:

1. "Director of Volunteers" is top administrator of the volunteer program.
2. "Coordinator of Volunteers" is a manager but not on the top level.
3. "Supervisor of Volunteers" works directly with volunteers but does not handle much decision making about the program as a whole.

In the first two editions of this book, I used the term *director of volunteers* as a sort of generic title—noting, however, that it is more accurate to think of this position as *coordinating* or *mobilizing* rather than as "directing." More recently, favor has shifted to titles such as "director of volunteer services," "manager of volunteer resources," or "volunteer program manager," which properly emphasize that *activities*, not people, are being managed.

Volunteerism author and consultant Steve McCurley offers another perspective, which he proposed during a recent conference presentation. He posits that this position really is not about managing a volunteer program but rather managing the organization's *strategy for utilizing* volunteer involvement. Hence, he suggests the title "chief volunteering officer" (CVO). It's an interesting point of view. McCurley notes that he likes CVO better than his previous tongue-in-cheek suggestion, "director of development for donated human resources."

For this third edition, my title of choice is "director of volunteer involvement." As I explained in the introduction to this book, director of volunteer involvement continues to place the role at the level of an administrator and could be appropriate in any setting but now focuses on guiding the integration of volunteers into the organization.

So, as you read, please substitute whatever title has been selected in your setting, or consider what title you think ought to be used. However, no matter your choice, there is general agreement that any title putting the word *volunteer* first (as in *volunteer coordinator*) is confusing because it can be misinterpreted as an adjective when it is actually being used as a noun. It invariably raises the question, "Oh, you mean *you* are unpaid, too?" Most directors of volunteer involvement prefer to avoid wasting time on explanations and appreciate a more accurate title.

Since the earlier editions of this book, many changes have occurred in the vocabulary of the volunteer world, particularly an increasing withdrawal from the word *volunteer* itself. Today, students speak of doing "community service" or "service-learning," the court system assigns "alternative sentencing," professional societies engage in "pro bono" projects (see chapter seven for a discussion of these and more types of resources). To accommodate and welcome these diverse sources of workers who offer skills and time without going on the payroll, a growing number of organizations are changing the name of their "volunteer office" to something like the office of "community participation," "civic engagement," or "community resources." Then the title of the head of that initiative naturally becomes "director of community resources," and so on. A problem with this is that people seeking volunteer opportunities may not be able to find the right person to talk to and go elsewhere. (Most people don't say, "I'd like to become civically engaged with the local library," or "I want to be a community participant for the Girl Scouts"; most people do say, "I want to volunteer . . .")

If you are going to designate a current staff member to add volunteer management to an existing role, consider adapting that person's job title to include indication of the responsibility for volunteers, as well. First, this clarifies things for members of the public who will otherwise be contacted by a "probation officer" or a "social worker" with seemingly little connection to volunteer involvement. Second, the title expansion tells the rest of the staff that there has indeed been a change in that employee's function.

However, try to avoid sticking the phrase "and volunteers" onto an existing title, such as the real-life example of "coordinator of beautification and volunteers." This only tends to imply that volunteers are an afterthought. If necessary, allow the staff member to use two different job titles, separated as appropriate for different situations.

Defining the Job of Leading Volunteer Engagement

Appendix A provides a "Volunteer Involvement Task Outline" of the role of a director of volunteer involvement. Katherine Campbell and I included the full "Task Analysis" version of it in *The (Help!) I-Don't-Have-Enough-Time Guide to Volunteer Management* (Energize, Inc. 2003). We developed (and have continued to keep current) the complete "Volunteer Management Task Analysis" because we discovered that none of the major books or articles on volunteer administration actually offered a "job description" for a director of volunteer involvement. The job functions were implied, perhaps, but nowhere were all the various elements of the job spelled out. Because you will be writing a job description for your volunteer leadership position, this appendix should be helpful.

In considering the necessary tasks of a director of volunteer involvement, an unusual pattern emerges. The director of volunteer involvement (whether part or full time) operates within a framework of activities that make this position substantially different from any other staff position—except, ironically, your own. It is useful to understand these differences because you will be able to help this leader more effectively if you acknowledge these unique aspects of the work. Also, especially if you are redefining an existing staff member's job to add volunteer management, you must recognize that these differences will affect that person's interrelationships with the rest of the staff.

Here are some of the job elements that make a director of volunteer involvement unique in the organizational structure:

- The director of volunteer involvement is one of the few members of the staff with **responsibility both inside and outside the organization**. S/he must have constant contact with the public, especially in order to recruit new volunteers. This contact is active, not passive—it requires outreach. But s/he is also involved daily with the work of the organization, since volunteers are deployed in so many program areas and require his/her liaison supervision. This is really a very special consideration. The majority of staff have no ongoing "community" job functions; they work solely on client or in-house service provision. Staffers such as a director of public relations, on the other hand, have no actual responsibilities related to the delivery of client services. Usually only you, as executive director, combine both internal and external functions. You and the director of volunteer involvement.

- Because of this public outreach, the director of volunteer involvement's job **requires odd work hours**. Recruitment must accommodate itself to the availability of groups and applicants. This may mean evening screening interviews, weekend special events, breakfast speeches, or Saturday orientation sessions. Conversely, the director of volunteer involvement will sometimes be out of the office during agency working hours, giving presentations or attending meetings. These work habits can be misunderstood by other staff if these special job responsibilities of the volunteer office are not explained. Also, burnout is a danger if the director of volunteer involvement is not given flexibility in adapting her/his schedule to such odd hours.

  Some directors of volunteer involvement are caught in a double bind when they work in settings that do not permit administrators to earn compensatory time. The reasoning is that the demands of top-level management require extra effort occasionally and that this periodic overtime is part of the job already recognized by the higher salary. This rationale is not applicable to the job of the director of volunteer involvement. S/he will continuously have odd-hour commitments and should be able to adjust his/her thirty-five or forty weekly hours (or twenty, etc.) to fit that week's schedule. If a particular period requires an unusual amount of evening or weekend activity, plus daytime responsibilities, the director of volunteer involvement should be able to accrue compensatory time.

- The in-house side of the director of volunteer involvement's job requires that s/he **be aware of the entire organization**. Since volunteers could be assigned to any unit or staff member, the head of the volunteer engagement is not "snooping" when s/he asks about the workload of any area of the agency. From the offices of senior management to the maintenance department, the director of volunteer involvement must be alert to new needs for assistance. Who else but you shares this mandate?

Having to be informed about so many different types of services also forces the director of volunteer involvement to speak many "languages"—requests for volunteers will be submitted in the jargon of each department.

- In keeping with the comprehensive overview just described, the director of volunteer involvement must **deal with staff at all levels** in order to determine volunteer assignments and provide liaison supervision. However, s/he is a *department head*. In day-to-day operations, this can produce confusion or suspicion: why is this department head talking to me about my job? Or, why is this department head talking to one of my people about the work done in this department? Even if all volunteer position descriptions are developed through the channel of the different department heads, once volunteers are assigned, the director of volunteer involvement will be in touch with the actual supervisors, the line staff. This all makes the director of volunteer involvement potentially threatening or, on the other hand, can undermine his/her status as a department head.

- While the volunteer department appears on paper (on the payroll, at least) as the smallest unit in the facility, the director of volunteer involvement may actually **be responsible for more people than any other manager** except the CEO—and perhaps even more than the CEO. This fact cannot be dismissed by such statements as, "Yes, but those people are all part time." Even if the hours given by the volunteers are not equivalent to the hours of service of full-time staff (though they well might be), the director of volunteer involvement still has to interview every applicant, keep records on, orient and place every volunteer, and so on. Here is one area in which "body count" does matter. The director of volunteer involvement must know and relate to *every* volunteer. Remember that each volunteer is a public relations agent for the organization, so the need to have some personal involvement with all volunteers is not unimportant. It is easy to overlook the cumulative effect of the numbers of volunteers who come through the volunteer office in any given period because no one ever sees all the volunteers in the same place at the same time. (Even recognition events usually bring out only a percentage of all volunteers who have been involved in a year.)

- A corollary of being responsible for so many people is that **no one else coordinates a staff with so many different schedules and so many different backgrounds**. The director of volunteer involvement must work with volunteers of all ages (possibly from children to senior citizens), of varying educational levels, and perhaps even with physical disabilities. Now add to this mixture the fact that volunteers select their own working schedules, and you end up with something of a circus—with the director of volunteer involvement as juggler! Some volunteers may work on a very exact, weekly schedule; others work on an as-needed basis. Some come in every Monday and Wednesday morning, some all day Thursday, some every other Friday at lunchtime, and some when the moon is full! The director of volunteer involvement can never "call a staff meeting" yet is expected to organize the work of all these volunteers.

  Another dimension of this factor is that the director of volunteer involvement ends up working in a "fishbowl" environment. Because volunteers arrive and depart at different times of the day, the director of volunteer involvement is continually interrupted—legitimately—by the need to touch bases with the volunteer workers.

- Rarely does anyone else in an organization know how volunteers are recruited and managed. The director of volunteer involvement **is the in-house expert on volunteers** and, in this capacity, acts as their advocate. This includes having to educate other staff about the ways to support volunteers and pointing out inappropriate requests for volunteer services. While other staff may have colleagues in the same profession right there in the agency, a lone director of volunteer involvement may feel isolated.

- The director of volunteer involvement **has a triple constituency** while everyone else in the organization has only two. First, everyone—including the director of volunteer involvement and the volunteers themselves—must be concerned about the needs of the clients, consumers, or patients. All activities must be weighed in terms of whether the best service will be provided to this public. Second, everyone must be supportive of the organization itself. This means that each person must uphold the policies of the agency and must work to achieve its mission. In fact, when an employee (or volunteer) can no longer support the organization's mission or policies, it is time to leave the job.

However, the director of volunteer involvement has a third obligation: to represent the *volunteer perspective*. This point of view may sometimes be in conflict with the first two constituents and may, in practice, cause occasional tension between the director of volunteer involvement and others in the organization. This is appropriate, and the CEO should recognize that the director of volunteer involvement is doing his/her job well when the volunteer perspective is expressed. It might help to recognize that the director of volunteer involvement *facilitates* the involvement of volunteers; s/he does not "control" volunteers.

- The director of volunteer involvement is the only person who **has the mandate to dream** about new projects and creative approaches to existing ones without immediately having to limit such inspiration with the thought, "How will we pay for this?" Though volunteers are not free, they can test new ideas initially without much cash flow. This is a very special role for the volunteer office.

Given these things that make the director of volunteer involvement different from other staff, you might consider how s/he can be of direct support to *you*, the CEO. For example, are you involving the director of volunteer involvement in your strategies for good public relations? Are you sharing long-range planning ideas with him/her so that volunteers can be integrated into planning from the very beginning? Do you ask for advice in working with volunteer board members? Are you utilizing the director of volunteer involvement's contacts across departments, placing volunteers within so many units, to give you insight into the operations of the agency?

The role of director of volunteer involvement has huge potential, but it must be stressed that, to be successful, those charged with this activity must *influence staff over whom they have no authority*. That is why executive support is needed to assure the integration of volunteers throughout the organization.

Qualifications for Being a Director of Volunteer Involvement

All the above assumes that you have an excellent professional leading volunteer engagement, so let's now look at qualifications for this position and how to select the right person to carry out this significant leadership role.

The field of volunteer administration is still developing as a profession. While you should seek someone to be your director of volunteer involvement who has experience in the field, you may have to select someone with *potential* to learn the job. The following are some qualifications you might seek:

- Ability to articulate a positive point of view about volunteers: why they are important, what their potential might be in your setting, and so on. This is a vital area. You don't want to hire someone with negative stereotypes about volunteers. How can s/he then help the rest of staff to work successfully with volunteers? Also, the self-fulfilling prophecy syndrome means that if the person is not positive about volunteers, s/he will never run a creative, energetic program.

- Vision, both for what volunteers can accomplish and of where your agency might go in the future, and the ability to get others in the organization to share that same vision

- Understanding of the expanding scope of the field of volunteerism, including the many types of community resources that have emerged in recent years that may use different terminology for their community service

- Strong management skills

- Strong interpersonal skills, with warmth and a degree of charisma. Potential volunteers are encouraged to join your organization through the image portrayed by the director of volunteer involvement, their first contact with you. S/he must be able to convey friendliness and efficiency and must also be able to get to know each recruit well enough to make appropriate assignment referrals.

- Enthusiasm and energy. The director of volunteer involvement creates an atmosphere for the volunteer program, and it must be upbeat.

- Written and oral communication skills, including comfort with using Internet communication tools

- The ability to apply the principles of adult education in building the competency of paid staff to partner with volunteers and preparing volunteers to join the organization

- Welcoming presentation style and public speaking ability. Remember that the demands of recruitment and training will put this person in the public eye and in front of groups often.

- Familiarity with resources in your local community

- Skill in task analysis. This is important since work requested must be divided into manageable parts that can be assigned to volunteers who give only a few hours at a time.

- Ability to handle and juggle details, especially the demands of scheduling and task delegation

- Willingness to adapt good ideas from other settings to the special needs of your organization

It is imperative that your director of volunteer involvement be a good administrator. But it is *equally* imperative that s/he have the personality needed to be a *leader*—which may call for opposing skill sets! Since volunteers are not rewarded by a paycheck, the director of volunteer involvement must have the ability to motivate people and to maintain high morale among volunteers (and salaried staff).

Interviewing a Prospect

When you interview candidates for the job of director of volunteer involvement, you might ask yourself whether you will feel comfortable working with this applicant personally. As we have been discussing, the director of volunteer involvement is in a position of genuine importance to you as the top executive. S/he should be an assistant to you in planning and implementing new projects. Also, s/he will be a representative of your agency in the community.

It is helpful to ask job applicants what volunteering they themselves have done in the past or are doing now. The way they answer this question—tone and enthusiasm as well as concrete details—should be a clue to their attitude about volunteerism. However, be careful not to fall into the trap of assuming that, just because a person has done volunteering personally, s/he is automatically able to direct an entire volunteer involvement strategy. This line of reasoning is just as faulty as implying that any employee of an agency can also run that agency. Experience as a volunteer is useful background for understanding the value and potential of volunteers, but the skills of recruitment, supervision, or recordkeeping are generally not gained by being a line volunteer handling specific client-related tasks.

On the other hand, if the person has been a staffer (paid or unpaid) in another volunteer management office, an officer of an all-volunteer organization, or a coordinator of a large fundraising event, then you may be correct to assume those experiences would translate well into the management responsibilities of your volunteer component.

How to Find a Director of Volunteer Involvement

Increasingly, it is possible to find people with experience in developing and managing volunteer engagement. It is more important to seek someone who has demonstrated ability to mobilize volunteers in any setting than to insist on finding someone with a complete understanding of your type of facility. The setting can be learned more easily than the techniques of volunteer management. Also, you have lots of in-house resources to train the person about your setting. Who on staff can train the person in volunteerism?

If you accept that volunteer administration is a generic profession, this opens the door to many recruitment possibilities. You might send a job-opening announcement to any of the following resources (described at greater length in appendix B), if they operate in your community:

- Your local volunteer center or HandsOn affiliate
- Your State Office of Volunteerism, Commission on National and Community Service (USA), or any similar "peak body" in a state or province in other countries
- Any local Directors of Volunteers in Agencies (DOVIA) association or similar professional network

- Online job banks that include a category for this sort of position, such as the job banks offered at Energize, Inc. (http://www.energizeinc.com), Idealist (http://www.idealist.org), or NonProfit Times Jobs (http://www.nptimes.com/careers.html).

This is an American list, but many other countries have such resources, too.

Think about which facilities have large volunteer corps. If they are large enough to have several paid staff leaders, there might be someone presently in an assistant position who is ready to move up into a full directorship. This might also be true of some administrative volunteers who have been, in essence, apprenticing as leaders of other volunteers. So it is worth sending a notice to such settings.

The skills of engaging volunteers can be learned in nonagency environments, too. For example, anyone with background in organizing successful political campaigns (either for partisan candidates or for nonpartisan issues) knows a great deal about volunteers, as do special event organizers, alumni association staff, and many fire chiefs. Former presidents of large, all-volunteer organizations also have experience in the nuances of organizing voluntary workers.

As time goes on, you may become aware of a growing number of people who have the credential of Certified in Volunteer Administration (CVA). The CVA designation is awarded by the Council on Certification in Volunteer Administration, an outgrowth of the field's former international professional society. It is given after an applicant has completed a rather extensive certification process, including the development of a portfolio documenting performance-based competencies. The process includes peer review and has a built-in continuing education requirement. Applicants must have at least two year's experience in volunteer administration before they may begin the certification process (see appendix B).

If you interview someone with the CVA designation, you can be assured that s/he has demonstrated a commitment to volunteer management as a profession and a career. You can also be comfortable about the person's basic understanding of the role of a director of volunteer involvement.

Note that CVA certification is not the same as a "certificate" from an academic institution awarded at the completion of a certain number of academic courses or noncredit workshops on volunteer management. Such certificate programs are under way in a number of states (and increasingly online) and represent an important trend in training for volunteer managers.

Beyond that, you must determine for yourself whether the person fits into your facility and can handle the special demands of leading volunteers in your setting.

Many Backgrounds Are Possible

Many people fall into the field of volunteer administration unintentionally. (I did!) Because it is not yet widely possible to prepare for this profession through formal academic schooling, you will find that directors of volunteer involvement come from a wide variety of backgrounds. On-the-job experience is what counts in most cases, though some applicants will also be able to document having attended single courses or continuing education workshops on various topics in volunteer management. In fact, if someone lists previous job experience in volunteerism, you should specifically ask what educational experiences s/he made use of. Has s/he ever attended a volunteerism conference locally, on the state level, or nationally? Has s/he ever taken a volunteer management course? Does s/he subscribe to any of the journals in the field? These types of questions should quickly indicate whether the person has indeed connected her/himself to the wider field of volunteerism, beyond the daily tasks of the job.

Some people will apply for the job because they see it as a stepping-stone into your type of setting. They are not necessarily interested in running a volunteer project, but rather want to do any job that will get them in the door. This motivation is not self-evidently bad, but it should be approached cautiously. Will this person devote her/himself to the needs of the volunteer program while s/he fills this position? Or will s/he look for the quickest way to move into another slot? The applicant must be open to the possibility that s/he will enjoy the position of director of volunteer involvement enough to end up sticking with it and taking it to its maximum potential. You do not need a reluctant director of volunteer involvement.

One reason why some people resist taking a job as director of volunteer involvement is the mistaken impression that it is a field without a career ladder or promotion options. Because it is isolated in most settings from the other staff positions, there seems to be no clear way for a competent director of volunteer involvement to move up. The real career mobility in volunteerism is to seek higher administrative responsibility (your job!). The director of volunteer involvement is already in the perfect spot for learning a great deal about overall agency functioning. S/he will be involved in planning and implementing a wide array of agency projects. If s/he is promoted into a vice presidency or an assistant directorship, overall responsibility for volunteer engagement can remain with that person—only s/he will now supervise the new director of volunteer involvement. Directors of volunteer involvement are actually in training to become CEOs—and when they reach that career point, they should be as supportive of the volunteer office staff as they always wanted their former bosses to be of them!

Clerical Assistance

From the very beginning, the volunteer office needs the help of a secretary or administrative assistant. This is as crucial to a part-time director as to a full-time one. If you have designated an existing employee as leader of volunteers, be sure to designate consistent, available clerical support.

Recruitment campaigns, records on a growing corps of volunteers, and preparation for such things as orientation, training sessions, and recognition events all demand a great deal of clerical activity. The administrative assistant also provides important office coverage while the director of volunteer involvement is out in the community or busy elsewhere in the facility. Such coverage is vital because prospective applicants and active volunteers deserve to be able to make contact with someone who is knowledgeable about the volunteer program. Also, many administrative assistants actually supervise the work of volunteers assigned to tasks under the jurisdiction of the volunteer office.

One frustration often expressed by directors of volunteer involvement is that their requests for clerical staff are met with the rather smug response, "Why don't you get a volunteer to do it?" There is no doubt in the world that it would be possible to recruit volunteers capable of handling the clerical tasks of the volunteer office. The problem is one of *schedule*. One of the main purposes of a salary is to be able to require a predetermined work schedule. If the director of volunteer involvement has to rely on volunteers for necessary clerical work, then s/he may have to recruit as many as eight or ten volunteers to fill all the necessary hours of service. This creates a situation in which the services of volunteers cost the director of volunteer involvement much supervision and coordination time—at the expense of other necessary work. A paid secretary is a vital link in the program's operation. Volunteers can handle a great deal of the program's clerical tasks but not those that need daily, timely attention with consistency and continuity.

Volunteers in Charge?

In somewhat the same vein, executives tend to ask if it is possible to operate a volunteer program with a *volunteer* as the head. There is no uniformly right answer to this question. It really depends on whether you have a willing volunteer with both the capability and the schedule necessary to be the director of volunteer involvement. Finding the *capability* is not the hard part; getting a long-term, multi-hour-per-week commitment is.

If you are lucky enough to have someone available and willing to be a staff member at no salary, by all means accept his/her services. But recognize that you are not necessarily building for the future if you do not budget for an employee. It is better to create a staff position and indicate willingness to pay a salary, and then work with a volunteer for as long as that person can stay with you. In this way, if the volunteer leader has to resign, you are not caught completely unprepared to replace him/her. Volunteers able to give the necessary hours to head a volunteer effort are few and far between. And if you end up recruiting, say, five volunteers to share the job—are you going to supervise and coordinate them?

As this third edition goes to press, there is strong interest in the United States in assigning AmeriCorps or VISTA participants (full-time, stipended placements funded by the federal government) to take on the role of volunteer coordinator for those agencies without one. While this option deserves examination, let me caution you against *relying* on this source of staffing. AmeriCorps members are unlikely to be experienced in what it takes to start a volunteer engagement effort. If there is no one on your staff now who can teach them about volunteer management, how will they be able to do it? Also, they enroll for one year or, at most, two. Do you want a parade of new and inexperienced volunteer involvement leaders year after year? The best approach may be to use an AmeriCorps placement as an opportunity to lay the groundwork for a designated, full-time staff position to follow. Then, by all means, continue to ask new AmeriCorps members to *assist* in the development of your volunteering strategy.

The right volunteers can be excellent midlevel supervisors or team leaders of other volunteers—sort of a team approach to running the office. Such administrative volunteers can be project coordinators for specific activities, orient groups of new volunteers, be shift leaders, or follow up on work being done by other volunteers off-site. This is one way that a director of volunteer involvement is able to handle a growing program. It is a legitimate utilization of volunteers because it can offer flexible scheduling in reasonable chunks of time. However, even a program with several such administrative volunteers will eventually require a paid assistant director of volunteer involvement because the demands of managing a team of administrative volunteers can also grow beyond what one employee can adequately oversee.

Graduate students majoring in some aspect of organizational management may be an excellent source of help in the early stages of volunteer involvement or the piloting of a new volunteer project. They might take on special assignments such as developing a volunteer handbook or assessing how your Web site recruits new volunteers. If it is possible to develop a nine-month internship of two days per week and focus it entirely on volunteer development, your organization may have found a cost-effective and reasonable way to get started.

Also, be certain to designate a staff supervisor who can genuinely help the student or service corps member and who can carry on after the student leaves. In fact, it is important to plan ahead for the transition of leadership when the internship is over, because you do not want a gap in administration over the summer months or longer.

The danger of utilizing a graduate student or service corps member is that volunteer involvement may therefore be viewed as "low level," since the intern will hardly have real authority with which to make decisions or set standards. So your executive involvement in enforcing commitment to volunteers will be imperative. Keep in mind, too, that if you later hire a more experienced director of volunteer involvement, that new person might need to do some course corrections before moving ahead.

If volunteer participation will be or is headed by a volunteer, be alert to the possible ways conflict might develop between these leaders and the paid staff—and do not unwittingly add to it yourself! The biggest problem is that the person may not be treated as a genuine administrator and will constantly be justifying her/his authority. Clearly, you will set the tone for the rest of the staff by the way you model acceptance of this volunteer.

Include the person, by name, on your department head memos. Invite the volunteer to staff meetings, and give him/her time on the agenda as any other department head. Expect the same reports and other accountability from the unsalaried director of volunteer involvement as you would from any other staff member. Supply the volunteer with an office, telephone extension, e-mail address, and business cards paid for by the agency. All these things demonstrate that the volunteer has been accepted by you as the leader of the volunteer program. Another important way to indicate that the volunteer is a part of staff is to show, in agency financial statements, the program budget over which the volunteer department head has jurisdiction.

Designated Liaison Staff in Each Work Area

Even with one or more full-time staff leading volunteer engagement, it's at the front line that the majority of volunteers will need support or, at minimum, someone to provide information. The larger your organization, the more critical it becomes to designate an official liaison from each department, work unit, or physical location to be the "point person" for volunteers assigned there.

This liaison performs key coordinating functions:

- Welcoming new volunteers and assuring they receive whatever orientation, training, workspace, or supplies they need to start being productive
- Maintaining a record of all volunteers currently assigned to the unit, their schedules, their supervisors or contacts, and so on
- Assuring that all communication from the volunteer office is disseminated to paid and unpaid staff in that work area and, conversely, that information is conveyed from the unit to the volunteer office
- Working with the volunteer office to identify additional volunteer assignments
- Representing the unit in planning for organization-wide volunteer events, such as recognition functions

These people are vital to daily management of volunteer involvement for all parties: the staff of each specific work area, the volunteers assigned there, and the volunteer office trying together to make volunteer management consistent and effective throughout the organization.

The work of a liaison is not necessarily demanding or continually time consuming. As with so many other recommendations in this book, however, the responsibility must be handled *intentionally*. So everyone in the unit must know who the point person is, and if something related to volunteers arises, the liaison must be able to prioritize dealing with it.

Other Staffing Needs

As mentioned in the rationale for a program secretary, the volunteer office has some special considerations in terms of coverage. Certainly every unit of the organization wants to be accessible to the public and therefore makes provisions for such things as telephone coverage when all staff are away from their desks. But for the volunteer office, this need is more than just for message taking. The hardest step in applying for a volunteer position is to make the initial telephone call. Therefore, the attitude and tone of the person answering the phone is critical. If the prospective volunteer hears disinterest or even discourtesy, the whole recruitment effort may be aborted. In fact, the agency representative should be saying things such as, "We're so glad you called, and I know that our director of volunteer involvement will be delighted to call you back." This simply is not the way most staff "take messages" for each other!

As CEO, you can make certain that employees are trained to support the volunteer office in its relations with the public. Reception desk personnel and others with frontline public contact responsibilities should project a friendly and appreciative image to all prospective and active volunteers. In a small office, this requirement extends to all staff who routinely answer phones or greet visitors for one another. (This is a great example of behavior change that benefits everyone, not just volunteers.)

Unfortunately, we have all grown accustomed to the ubiquitous presence of automated voice mail systems. Many organizations need to evaluate the cost of replacing a live voice on the telephone with a computer. It certainly projects an impersonal image to clients and the community, especially if people are calling when in distress. For prospective volunteers, voice mail may be an unhelpful hurdle to jump in the process of considering whether to give time. At a minimum, test the system to make sure that contact with the volunteer office is a specific option to select and that it is easy to leave a message. Not to mention assuring that a staff member calls back soon!

Similarly, prospective volunteers are increasingly submitting e-mails and online applications, which carry the expectation of a prompt reply. It is vital to acknowledge that the electronic application was received, pledge to get back in touch within a certain amount of time, and then do so.

One other staffing point is that the director of volunteer involvement is not a substitute for volunteers. If a scheduled volunteer is absent for whatever reason, it is not appropriate to expect the director of volunteer involvement to come to the unit and handle the volunteer's work for that day. This is, of course, no different from expectations we hold for employee supervisors. If an employee is not present, the work is generally held until the person returns; the supervisor does not step in to do it unless some emergency warrants it. Actually, since volunteers are deployed in the facility in various work areas, if a task assigned to an absent volunteer is critical, the most appropriate "substitute" would be a line worker in *that* unit—not the director of volunteer involvement who is not part of that unit.

Volunteer Program Advisory or Steering Committee

Both for purposes of planning and evaluation, it is helpful to develop an advisory committee for the volunteer program or a "steering committee" if the group will actually help make decisions. Such a committee need not be large nor need it meet frequently. But it should be representative of management, line employees, and volunteers. When appropriate, recipients of service should also be included.

Because the director of volunteer involvement must have a comprehensive overview of the whole organization, this committee can work to ensure that all points of view are considered when new projects are begun. The committee therefore supports the director of volunteer involvement by channeling information to the volunteer office and by explaining volunteer activities to others throughout the organization. This is an excellent way to prevent some of the possible tension between volunteers and employees.

Expanding the Volunteer Involvement Staff

Apart from the job description and schedule of the leader of volunteer involvement, at some point you will probably need to make decisions about when you will need a full-time position, when to add one or more assistant directors of volunteer involvement, and when to add one or more clerical support staff.

It is difficult to give absolute guidelines for determining the right staffing pattern. However, the following two criteria should be part of any assessment:

1. *Are volunteers going to be active evenings, weekends, or during hours beyond a regular workweek?* The answer to this question might immediately suggest the need for an evening volunteer supervisor, for example, or might help to determine the regular schedule of the full-time director of volunteer involvement (e.g., 11 AM to 7 PM or Tuesday through Saturday).

2. *What is the maximum number of employees that a supervisor of employees is normally asked to supervise?*

To answer question 2, start by identifying the FTE (full-time equivalent, as we discussed in chapter three in the section on budgeting for supplies) of the volunteers working *directly* under the supervision of the director of volunteer involvement. This might include volunteer positions such as interviewers, clerical assistants, in-service trainers, volunteer office librarians, recordkeepers, and so on. The assessment of how many FTE volunteer staff are being supervised is especially pertinent if the volunteer office directly coordinates certain volunteer projects, such as an annual fundraising event or a daily meal delivery program.

Next, what is the FTE of the volunteers for whom the volunteer office is *indirectly* responsible (but still maintains records, handles recognition, etc.)?

How large would you allow your organization's salaried staff to become without adding to the number of employees in, say, the personnel office? The main point is to apply the same standards to the volunteer office and be sure that adequate staff are available to provide the best management. Keep in mind that one way you demonstrate your organization's commitment to volunteers is how you designate and then support their leadership.

To implement ideas in this chapter, see . . .

Leading the Way to Successful Volunteer Involvement: Practical Tools for Busy Executives by Betty B. Stallings with Susan J. Ellis (Philadelphia: Energize, Inc., 2010).

Idea stimulators, worksheets, step-by-step guides, and more in the following sections:

- Section 4: "Hiring and Placing Staff Who Lead Volunteer Engagement"
- Section 5: "Creating a Management Team for Volunteer Involvement"

Notes

1. Urban Institute, *Volunteer Management Capacity in America's Charities and Congregations: A Briefing Report* (Washington, DC: Urban Institute, 2004), 21. The study can be obtained online at http://www .nationalservice.gov/pdf/vol_capacity_brief.pdf.
2. Betty B. Stallings, *12 Key Actions of Volunteer Program Champions: CEOs Who Lead the Way* (Philadelphia: Energize, Inc., 2005), 7.
3. Sarah Jane Rehnborg and others, *Strategic Volunteer Engagement: A Guide for Nonprofit and Public Sector Leaders* (Austin, TX: RGK Center for Philanthropy and Community Service, the LBJ School of Public Affairs, the University of Texas at Austin, 2009), 24.
4. Stallings, *12 Key Actions*, 2.
5. To learn more about the online training program *Everyone Ready®*, go to http://www.energizeinc.com/everyoneready. For more on the *55-Minute Training Series*, go to http://www.energizeinc.com/store/4-109-E-1.
6. The section of the online *Dictionary of Occupational Titles* with these three volunteer management positions can be found at http://www .occupationalinfo.org/defset3_3479.html. See Service Industry Codes 187.137-014 (supervisor), 187.167-022 (coordinator), and 187.167-038 (director).

5

Understanding the Volunteer-Employee Relationship

It may be surprising to learn that the single most requested training topic in volunteer management is not how to recruit volunteers; rather, it is how to develop good volunteer-employee relationships. Regardless of setting, age, or size of the program, everyone wants to know how to build effective teamwork between volunteers and paid staff. Why is this so hard? Is there something inevitable about tension between these two sets of workers?

One thing is certain. If the subject of volunteer-employee relationships is ignored as a management issue, each employee (and volunteer) will develop his/her own way of interacting. Such diverse approaches will indeed produce confusion if not outright hostility. The main purpose of this chapter, therefore, is to emphasize the need for *the involvement of top administration in setting the tone and policy for effective integration of volunteers* into the organization. This cannot be left in the hands of the director of volunteer involvement. S/he does not have the authority to make rules for the whole organization or to enforce such rules. As the nonsalaried personnel of the organization, volunteers deserve direct attention from the executive level.

Unfortunately, executive directors themselves are often negative about volunteers. Participants in Sarah Jane Rehnborg's focus groups expressed concerns that volunteers are a "recipe for trouble" and

> that they are not in the business of meeting the needs of volunteers, that such a perspective can take away from attention to mission, and that any implication that organizations should expend effort considering the needs of volunteers only makes this community resource less attractive in their eyes. Likewise, [executive directors] report that they fear potential negative exchanges with a volunteer.[1]

It needs to be a stated organizational value that volunteers are team members. It's never "us versus them." To assess whether your agency has laid the foundation for good volunteer-employee relationships, consider the following questions:

- What happens (in terms of actual procedures) when a volunteer makes a mistake or does something wrong? For that matter, what if a volunteer does something great?

- If a dispute develops between a volunteer and an employee, is the employee always presumed to be correct? Is the employee presumed to have more rights? Conversely, are volunteers given more consideration and held to lower standards?

- Are there clearly defined channels for volunteers to make suggestions, voice criticisms, and other feedback?

- How many members of the paid staff have ever had formal training (not just on-the-job experience) in how to supervise volunteers?

- Has any member of staff recently refused to work with volunteers (this means refusing to develop a position description for possible volunteer assistance—not turning down a specific applicant who was not appropriate)? Why? Did anyone question that staff member on his/her refusal?

- Has any employee ever been evaluated on his/her level of competence in supervising volunteers?

- When was the last time an employee was given any tangible recognition for working successfully with volunteers?

- Is it common practice to refer to the "professionals" versus the "volunteers"?

- Do all labor contracts (if you have one or more employee unions) include clarification of the role of volunteers in the agency and, especially, their role in times of a possible strike?

- How many volunteers have left the organization in the past year due to dissatisfaction with their acceptance level?

If you answered these questions honestly (and no one will ever know, so go ahead!), you might find yourself saying, "I'm not really sure." *That's* "benign neglect." If all these questions were reversed and asked about employees, you'd feel responsible as an executive to know the answers. Volunteers tend to be invisible workers.

These questions hint at some of the key volunteer-employee relationship areas requiring policy formation and top executive involvement.

Danger Signs: Refusal to Team with Volunteers

One situation crops up so frequently that it is often not even perceived as a problem: the premise that either an individual employee or a unit supervisor has the *choice* of whether to partner with volunteers in delivering services. In many ways, this is the crux of the entire problem and so deserves scrutiny.

In most organizations, the director of volunteer involvement recruits volunteers and, after initial screening, refers them to the most appropriate placement for which the responsible paid staff will then conduct an interview. If both the prospective volunteer and the employee feel comfortable, the director of volunteer involvement finalizes the acceptance, provides an orientation, and then assigns the volunteer to the day-to-day supervision of paid staff. Some volunteers do work under the direct supervision of the volunteer office, but most are deployed throughout the organization in a decentralized approach to volunteer management. The premise is that line staff are the ones most knowledgeable about the tasks to be done and therefore should work directly with volunteers in accomplishing those tasks.

If you are starting volunteer engagement or strengthening what is already in place, you must deal with the question, do we, as an organization, believe qualified volunteers are vital enough to integrate them everywhere? Please note the word *qualified*. In every instance, this book advocates the appropriate placement of volunteers who either were recruited for special skills or were given training by the agency to fill necessary positions.

Another key decision to make is, will we hold volunteers accountable for doing the work to which they commit and to high standards of performance? If there is any doubt about your answer, paid staff may legitimately resist a double standard of service delivery.

Some of the resistance to working with volunteers comes from negative stereotypes about volunteers. Employees should never be asked to work with uncommitted, unqualified, or unpleasant people—whether paid or not. But if we start with the supposition that volunteer involvement will be managed well and that all volunteers will be recruited to match the requirements of available assignments, then prejudices about volunteers should be dispelled.

As long as employees are given the choice, or act as though they have the choice, of accepting volunteers as co-workers, top administration is sending mixed messages about volunteers, *even* if the organization has volunteer involvement goals and has allocated resources to them. The implication is that working with volunteers is in some way *additional* to the primary work to be done and that partnering with volunteers is *optional*. When no negative reaction follows from an employee's decision not to work with volunteers and, further, when an employee who *does* work with volunteers receives no positive reinforcement, the only logical conclusion is *it does not matter to administration*. Volunteers are "nice" and maybe even "helpful," but they are certainly not *essential*.

Think what would happen if, using a hospital as an example, a nurse unilaterally decided s/he would not work with the physical therapists (PTs). Whenever the PTs come around, s/he politely refuses to work cooperatively. Such behavior sounds so absurd it is even hard to take the example seriously. Yet, in many hospitals around the country, the volunteer services department has had to accept rejection from nurses and other medical staff who simply—with no reasons given or required—opt not to "take" a volunteer. (Feel free to substitute any other kind of setting.)

Currently, in most organizations, the director of volunteer involvement is placed in the position of going around to the salaried staff and asking, "Do you want a volunteer?" The tone is one of, can we do each other a favor? How ridiculous. If the organization has seen fit to establish and fund a volunteer component, then it should not be optional to work with it. All employees must collaborate with that unit in exactly the same way they are expected to work with the physical therapists, the records department, the maintenance staff, or the public relations department.

Again, it is legitimate for any manager to expect to interview individual *candidates* for an assignment, whether in a paid or unpaid capacity. And if the applicant does not measure up, the interviewer has the right to refuse to accept her/him. But this is not the same thing as refusing to consider *any* volunteer simply because someone doesn't want to deal with this special category of worker.

The director of volunteer involvement must be held accountable to find and prepare the best possible volunteers. If s/he cannot do this, it is grounds for dismissal. But if the director of volunteer involvement is indeed fulfilling this responsibility, then no other staff member has the right to judge the volunteer involvement strategy negatively—and therefore must cooperate. If an employee is uncomfortable with volunteers, the proper administrative response should be to offer *training* in how to work successfully with volunteers, not to permit him/her to avoid this aspect of the job.

Ironically, some directors of volunteer involvement have contributed to the perpetuation of this cycle of "acceptance of rejection." They do not confront the resistant employee on the grounds that they prefer not placing volunteers into a negative supervisory situation. So, out of reasonable concern for the morale and motivation of the volunteers, the director of volunteer involvement protectively ignores the staff member who refuses to work with volunteers. While this may be proper management in the case of a particular volunteer ready to work immediately, it is poor long-range planning. The director of volunteer involvement must identify resistant staff members and—with the help of each person's manager and, if necessary, the chief executive—change their behavior.

What Causes Tension

Even if the salaried staff understand the value of volunteer involvement to the organization and its clients, in day-to-day operations the interface between the two sets of workers can be difficult. Both the perspective of the employee and the volunteer must be understood in order to analyze what causes tension between the two. Specifically, it is necessary to identify both the perceived threats posed by volunteers to paid staff and the reasons volunteers may be resistant to supervision by paid staff.

Because this is first and foremost a human relations situation, it is helpful to remember that the dynamics involved do not always relate to real issues but reflect fears, misunderstanding, and prejudice—on both sides. In order to prevent or solve interrelationship problems, it is necessary to consider the possible factors involved.

Threats to the Paid Staff

Some of the real or imagined threats volunteers pose to employees are expressed in the following list. This list is not meant to imply that every staff member harbors these fears but to show that there is a wide range of possible reactions to the offer of volunteer assistance. Recognize that few people will ever actually voice these thoughts aloud, since, in principle, it seems ungrateful to complain about "free help." It is also possible for staff members to acknowledge the importance of volunteers to the organization at large without necessarily being happy about being asked to work directly with a volunteer in their own unit.

Please note that not all the following issues are imaginary. Some, in fact, are quite legitimate. If the staff feel that administration does not recognize some of the possible problems volunteers create, they will be reluctant to tell you their genuine reactions to the idea of volunteers— instead, they will undercut (even sabotage) the effort by refusing to be assigned a volunteer or by providing insufficient supervision to volunteers already on board.

- Volunteers will take paid jobs—maybe my job. *Here is a good example of just because you're paranoid, it does not mean someone is* not *out to get you. Is it really strange that staff are fearful for their jobs, particularly in a down economy? And have you ever discussed volunteers as budget "savers" rather than as budget "extenders"?*

- Volunteers will do a bad job, and I'll be left with the blame or the responsibility to "clean up." (And volunteers can't be fired, right?)

- Volunteers will do a great job, and I'll look less effective. *This relates to the first threat. Will a great volunteer replace me? In fact, what do you think is more threatening: a volunteer who fails or one who succeeds? Because of uncertainty about the true agenda behind the involvement of volunteers, the most successful volunteer programs can also find themselves the ones with the biggest staff-acceptance problems.*

- Volunteers are spies. (To whom are they related? To whom do they talk after work? Are they watching the way I perform?) *The reality is that volunteers do indeed see the work being done—and not being done. If an employee is insecure about his/her performance, the thought of a volunteer uncovering weakness is scary.*

- Volunteers are amateurs. They do not know much, and I'll have to train them from scratch, which takes a lot of time.

- Volunteers are highly trained, and they do not want to be oriented to do it our (my) way. They can't be controlled.

- Volunteers are different from me. They are (*select any that apply*) younger, older, less educated, more educated, a different race or religion, from a different social or economic class, more or less knowledgeable about this community, or some other factor.

- Volunteers gossip. They do not understand confidentiality.

- If these volunteers were really good workers, they'd all have paying jobs. (You mean a lot of them already do? Then how come they're also volunteering?)

- I do not know how to break my work into smaller tasks that can be delegated to a volunteer. I am also not sure that the time it would take me to do this would be won back in any savings by having the volunteer help me. Besides, I'd really rather do it myself so I can be certain it will be done right.

- Volunteers may misuse or corrupt our online systems and should not have access to our electronic data.

- I never learned about volunteer management in my formal education, so I'm not sure how to work with volunteers. But, because I take pride in being a professional, how can I admit that I don't know how to work with volunteers?

- Volunteers want to spend too much time socializing with me.

- We have so little workspace. I don't have the room to work with a volunteer.

- Volunteers are not dependable.

- You can't criticize a volunteer, so how can you make sure the work is done right?

- The client may like the volunteer better than me.

- All the things I can think of for a volunteer to do are the fun parts of my job. I don't want to give those up.

- I am jealous (though I'd never show it) that volunteers get all those thank-yous, special luncheons, balloons, and mugs. They also get to choose their schedules and their work assignments, and they even get to say "no" once in a while.

- My supervisor doesn't understand that working with volunteers takes some of my time.

- When I accepted this job, no one ever told me I was supposed to work with volunteers.

- There are no rewards for working well with volunteers.

- Why should I work with a volunteer? Volunteers "belong" to the director of volunteer involvement, and why should I do him/her the favor of supervising a volunteer?

- I am so new at my job that it is hard for me to explain parts of it to a volunteer.

- Volunteers only see a small part of the picture because they come in irregularly. Therefore, their opinions and suggestions are not worth as much as mine are because I understand the whole situation.

- If we act on all these new ideas volunteers come up with, things will change around here.

- Do I have to say thank you all the time—even if I don't mean it?

- Volunteers interrupt my day or week.

In examining the range of these statements, it is obvious that even the best paid staff members may be concerned about some of these issues. And, again, their concerns may be appropriate, especially if the organization has never clarified its policies about volunteers.

There are indeed practical issues involved in accommodating volunteers that employees should be encouraged to identify and discuss. It's fair to acknowledge that volunteers *do* require staff time; volunteers *do* have more options for saying no; some volunteers *are* on board in order to learn new skills and therefore need extra training; there may, in fact, *be* a shortage of workspace.

Another factor is the diversity of your volunteer corps. Some volunteers will be recruited as highly trained specialists, while others may come to your organization as trainees or to fill generalist roles such as friendly visiting. Unfortunately, this diversity sometimes results in volunteers being judged by the lowest common denominator. For example, because one unit utilizes high school students as volunteers, staff in another unit may be skeptical about the qualifications of volunteers who may be referred to them—they simply have trouble visualizing more skilled or mature voluntary assistance.

Special Cases

Certain employees may have more justification than others for questioning the value to them of working with volunteers. Brand-new staff members, for example, are so busy learning the ropes of their job that they really cannot yet delegate parts of it to someone else.

Some jobs or professions are not "people oriented" in that they involve limited contact with the public and the type of person entering them may prefer it that way. These jobs range from museum curator to zookeeper to medical records manager. At the very least, such staff members may be inexperienced in supervising other people and may resent having this responsibility foisted on them after the fact of accepting a job description without mention of volunteers.

Finally, your setting may have employees in paraprofessional positions. Paraprofessionals are usually low on the "pecking order" of an organization anyway. They are directly threatened by the influx of volunteers because many of the things assigned to volunteers are related to the assistant work performed by paraprofessionals—and so job security is an honest concern. Negative attitudes by paraprofessionals about volunteers are compounded by the fact that often it is the paraprofessional who is inappropriately assigned to supervise the volunteers—and very few paraprofessionals have the training, the time, or even the skill to do this adequately. If you have a paraprofessional level of staff, be alert to the possibility of misunderstanding of roles between them and some volunteers.

Resistance from Volunteers

It takes two to tango. Though the majority of problems between volunteers and employees stem from employee actions, in all fairness, volunteers also contribute to the hostilities. Never assume that volunteers are knowledgeable about volunteering in the context of organization management. They bring the same stereotypes and prejudices to the situation as do employees. Also, volunteers rarely see the big agency picture since they are focused on the specific work they came to do.

Volunteers' real or imagined reasons for resistance to working effectively with paid staff may include the following:

- I am more qualified than the salaried staff, so why should I let them boss me around?

- I am here to help out, and the staff should be grateful. What's all this about requirements and commitment?

- The employees are different from me. They are (*select any that apply*) younger, older, less educated, more educated, a different race or religion, from a different social or economic class, more or less knowledgeable about this community, or some other factor.

- I am not sure what the employees really do. Am I doing their job? What are they doing while I do their job? Why should the salaried staff get paid while I don't (especially if I'm doing their job)?

- I am always told what to do but am never asked to participate in planning the work.

- No one listens to my suggestions. People here seem unwilling to make changes.

- Employees get or take credit for my good ideas.

- No one says thank you.

- Volunteers always seem to get the "idiot work" around here.

- No one ever gives me feedback on my work. I wish I'd learn how useful my efforts are or how I might improve my work.

- I am given tasks to do without being told their context, so I never really understand how my efforts fit into the activities of the organization.

- I always have to search for a place to do my work, and there is nowhere to store my work from week to week.

- My grandmother founded this organization, and these new staff members are not doing what she would have wanted.

- I should be treated as special because I am related to or friends with a (*select one or more*) board member, donor, top executive, or legislator.

- Why do they suspect my motives and ethics? Why can't I get access to data I need?

- Employees are always given the benefit of the doubt in any dispute. They are seen as "right" just because they are on the payroll.

- Whenever I come in, the employees are always at lunch, on a break, or in a meeting. Don't they ever do any work?

- I am given very little training or even good instructions. I am not sure whom to ask if I have a question, especially if my supervisor is at lunch, on a break, or in a meeting.

- The staff are moody and often do not say hello, good-bye, or thank you.

- I do not know who runs this place. A lot of people come and go from the front office, but I've never been told who they are. They rarely greet me in the hall.

- I don't like the label "volunteer." Can't I have a title?

- I'm just a volunteer.

Consider what might be going on in the minds of volunteers in your setting. Are such attitudes a reaction to how they are being treated while volunteering with you or do they stem from other, outside experiences? Understanding how resistance evolves may suggest comparatively easy ways to diminish it.

Of course, you may be heading an organization in which there are many more volunteers than employees. In such circumstances, the salaried staff realize that volunteers are vital, but some volunteers may misinterpret their numerical strength and feel superior to the employees. This manifests itself in volunteers "giving orders" to the staff or resisting when staff delegate work to volunteers.

In a professional society or trade association, an added factor may be that employees were hired for their skills in association management and have no firsthand knowledge or training in the profession or trade the organization exists to represent. So, reasonably, the members feel greater ownership of what's at stake.

Volunteer-to-Volunteer Relations

Interpersonal dynamics affect the way in which volunteers work with each other, too. Apart from simple personality differences, the organization may unwittingly create situations that cause competition or tension among volunteers, or a subtle hierarchy. Here are some examples:

- Inviting only those volunteers who reach a certain high number of hours to attend the recognition event, leaving those who didn't log in the same time but who may in fact have been very productive during shorter hours, feeling undervalued

- Giving higher status to volunteers who do fundraising than to those who provide direct service—such as allowing an auxiliary a seat on the board of directors, without similar representation of other volunteers

- Assigning male/female or young/old volunteers to positions that perpetuate gender and age divisions and keep them apart

- Deferring to longtime volunteers and members in a way that newer ones feel unable or uninvited to contribute new ideas (there's an insider clique with no clear way to get in)

It is often observed that the longer volunteers remain with an organization, the more they take on the characteristics of the paid staff in relation to new volunteers. They can evolve a sense of ownership and entitlement that makes them resist newcomers and their make-waves ideas for change. Go back and look at the list of why employees resist volunteers and consider it from the perspective of a longtime volunteer. It will help you anticipate possible conflict if you are expanding an existing group of volunteers with new recruits.

Be aware, too, that if you are trying to diversify your volunteer corps in new ways, whether by recruiting people of different ages, ethnicities, or backgrounds, you may create discomfort among the original volunteers. How ready are they to work alongside volunteers who do not already fit into the social structures longtime volunteers have evolved?

There are serious consequences to ignoring the chemistry among new and veteran volunteers, especially if the situation is volatile.

Diagnosis

The litany of possible attitudes just presented is intended to demonstrate how wide a range of causes there might be for tension between employees and volunteers, and among volunteers themselves. View both lists as a sort of menu from which to select the specific issues that might be at work in each tense situation. The dynamics of a particular confrontation will be unique to the individuals involved. As CEO, much will depend on your skill in diagnosing what is really going on beneath the surface.

Research what the actual circumstances are and therefore which attitudes stem from facts or myths. If a person has had one negative experience either as a volunteer or with a volunteer, it is unrealistic to expect him/her to be completely open to a second try. For example, if a salaried staff member worked hard to train a new volunteer and then that volunteer left the agency unexpectedly, it is obvious that the staff member will be wary of the commitment of future volunteers.

Sometimes it is helpful to consider why certain employees or volunteers are exceptionally receptive to teamwork with each other. Knowing the reasons for *good* relationships can indicate approaches to take to change negative relationships. Here are some possible factors that would make for favorable support of volunteer involvement:

- Personal history with volunteerism in another setting—if that past experience was positive
- Respect for the work of the director of volunteer involvement
- Direct experience with excellent volunteers or salaried staff (as opposed to direct experience with mediocre volunteers)
- Praise from an executive for innovative work done with or by volunteers

Payoffs to Individual Employees

Naturally, you do not want employees to team with volunteers just because there are consequences for not doing so. Rather, you hope salaried staff see the benefits of volunteers to the organization and themselves.

But it is important to remember that the benefits to the agency for involving volunteers are not at all the same as the "payoffs" to an individual employee who takes the time to supervise or team with volunteers well. For example, just because the *organization* might receive good public relations from informed community volunteers, it does not follow that a particular employee feels rewarded directly for the effort of working well with volunteers.

The payoff to volunteers for teaming with paid staff is that their motivations for giving their time and effort are fulfilled. Consider what the benefits or payoffs might be to an individual employee who is successful in working with volunteers. How do these compare to the list of potential threats and concerns? How can you assure that the benefits really accrue? Here's a starter set of possible rewards:

- When a staff member supervises or organizes volunteers well, s/he demonstrates to administration (you!) that s/he has managerial ability.

- Supervising volunteers is, indeed, on-the-job training for supervising employees.

- Partnering with skilled volunteers is on-the-job training for working with a wide variety of consultants and community representatives.

- Volunteers bring a freshness of approach that can help the employee to see his/her work in a new way.

- Assigned volunteers share the staff member's interests and can therefore reduce isolation and provide support in a way staff in other departments cannot.

- Since volunteers provide the luxury of trying new service approaches without having to seek funding first, volunteers can test a new idea and prove its merit. If the idea to be demonstrated is the employee's, s/he has the chance to show her/his value to the organization.

- Volunteers can lessen the workload by handling a variety of helpful tasks.

- Volunteers can free the employee to do things s/he is specially trained for or likes.

- The previous two points can reduce employee tension and prevent burnout.

- Qualified volunteers can handle aspects of the work for which the employee may actually not be trained or best suited.

- Volunteers can stimulate creativity by adding new ideas and responding to staff innovations.

- Because volunteers may have a range of different life experiences, working together can provide personal enrichment for the staff.

- Volunteers can renew staff's enthusiasm and confirm the importance of the work being done.

These benefits are not insignificant, but employees need to see them as real.

In the next chapter, we'll examine some of the other considerations that make for positive reinforcement of volunteer-employee relations.

To implement ideas in this chapter, see . . .

Leading the Way to Successful Volunteer Involvement: Practical Tools for Busy Executives by Betty B. Stallings with Susan J. Ellis (Philadelphia: Energize, Inc., 2010).

Idea stimulators, worksheets, step-by-step guides, and more in the following section:

- Section 6: "Building Staff Commitment and Competency to Partner with Volunteers"

Note

1. Sarah Jane Rehnborg and others, *Strategic Volunteer Engagement: A Guide for Nonprofit and Public Sector Leaders* (Austin, TX: RGK Center for Philanthropy and Community Service, the LBJ School of Public Affairs, the University of Texas at Austin, 2009), 7.

6

Strategies to Create Teamwork

As chief executive, you have a vital role to play in laying the groundwork for productive teamwork between paid and volunteer staff. Too often, neither employees nor volunteers really know what they are supposed to do with each other. Do not underestimate the need for clear expectations, and do not assume that everyone will "work it out" on their own. Unfortunately, without guidance as to best practice, everyone does indeed develop her/his own approach and you end up with wildly different levels of teamwork operating side by side.

Colleen Kelly says that, at Volunteer Vancouver/Vantage Point, "We believe the most important item in a job description for paid *and* unpaid employees is a link to the mission. Then everyone understands they are in it for the same thing: to deliver the mission of the organization! Common purpose—one workforce."[1] There are several concrete things you can do to establish policies and standards for your organization that will clarify everyone's roles, rights, and options.

Job Descriptions: Employees

A good place to start is to make certain that all job descriptions for employees include a statement about required teamwork with volunteers. In some cases, the job description will indicate that a staff member will have responsibility for supervising volunteers personally. In other cases, job descriptions may simply note that this is an organization in which volunteers are valued participants, and therefore all employees will have to interact positively with them. For department heads and other middle managers, their job descriptions might clarify that volunteers will be active in each component of the organization and that the department heads will be expected to develop appropriate position descriptions, delegate work to volunteers, and help those they supervise to work effectively with volunteers (more on middle managers in a moment).

If all employee job descriptions contain references to interaction with volunteers, then the application process for new hires should also attempt to uncover a candidate's understanding of and experience with volunteering. For example, include questions on application forms and in interviews about whether the candidate has ever supervised volunteers and in what context. It is helpful to learn whether the applicant has ever received formal training in volunteer management, either in a classroom setting (unlikely), on the job in another organization, or perhaps as an officer of an all-volunteer organization.

You can also ask about the candidate's personal volunteer experience, though this alone is not an indicator of ability to *supervise* volunteers on the job. However, you will undoubtedly discover many valuable things about the person's interests and other job-related qualifications from this question, as well as gain a sense of this person's understanding of the concept of volunteerism.

Middle Managers Are Key

Every decision must be implemented across and down the organizational ladder, relying along the way on the buy-in of middle managers: branch or affiliate directors, department heads, unit supervisors, and others for whom volunteers become a factor in their teams' effectiveness. These key people convey overt and subtle messages about expectations and can become an obstacle to effective volunteer involvement by not encouraging their team members' attention to volunteers. In the worst cases, this can amount to sabotage.

Are your middle managers supportive of or resistant to volunteer involvement? Do they understand their "once removed" volunteer support role? Do they have the skills necessary to help their direct reports develop volunteers for the greatest impact?

Middle managers may feel that volunteers drain staff time from priority work. Because these supervisors evaluate employee performance, they have substantial influence over how staff in their units approach all their responsibilities. This extends to whether their staff get the message that success in teaming with volunteers is valued. How well staff design assignments for volunteers, and then train and supervise them, is directly influenced by the middle manager. And it is this person who makes employees feel appreciated—or penalized—for putting effort into volunteer support.

While engaging volunteers holds great potential, integrating paid and unpaid staff is challenging and definitely takes time. The goal is to make sure *the benefits of volunteer involvement outweigh the effort.* Middle managers can best monitor this balance and reinforce the importance of working with the community. They can be great allies or real obstacles to success. Here's why:

- Middle managers set the tone for how things are done in their corner of the organization. Their personal beliefs and attitudes about volunteers will shape the way staff and volunteer teamwork is supported (or undercut).

- Because middle managers train new employees to do their jobs properly and evaluate employee work performance throughout the year, they substantially affect how their staff members approach any area of responsibility, including volunteers. Do they have the vision and expertise to establish expectations and standards for working with community members?

- They have the authority to approve work assignments created for volunteers by the staff. So, if a middle manager's image of volunteers is that they are mainly nice but not very skilled, staff in that unit will design volunteer positions with low expectations (and self-fulfilling prophecy will produce volunteers who don't care to be challenged). Conversely, middle managers who raise the bar on what volunteers are asked to do will help an organization to attract more highly qualified people.

- Middle managers set the agenda for staff meetings and individual supervision sessions. Do they regularly make time to focus on volunteer involvement in their department, unit, or branch? The inclusion or absence of volunteer-related issues on the agenda sends a message—is it that volunteers matter or don't?

Employees can infer from their supervisors that spending time with volunteers is a diversion from their "real" job, to be done (if they wish) only after other, more important work is completed. Or supervisors can visibly recognize and reward staff who help volunteers to do well.

In a large organization, a middle manager may well be supervising a volunteer program manager directly assigned to that department or unit. Are all middle managers consistent in how they coach and support this staffer? Do they understand the tension between doing what's best for their department and also meshing with organization-wide volunteer involvement goals and policies?

In chapter four, we discussed the usefulness of designating a liaison or point person between each unit and the volunteer office. Middle managers will undoubtedly do the appointing of that staff member and then need to permit him/her to do any such work as necessary.

The point, as always, is not to assume that middle managers are on board with what it takes to support those who are expected to supervise volunteers. Take time to discover what this layer of management really thinks and win their enthusiasm for volunteer involvement. Otherwise, frontline staff will be caught in the middle, expected by top executives to put effort into partnering with volunteers, but undercut at the unit or branch level by the person most influential to that employee's job assessment.

Include middle managers in planning sessions, training, and evaluation of the volunteer program so that they feel ownership of volunteer participation in their unit or department. Make sure that they, too, receive personal recognition for their efforts. They need to see that volunteers help their department to "shine" and are contributing to, not diverting from, accomplishing goals.

Be a Role Model

One wonderful way to demonstrate your commitment to volunteer involvement is to develop assignments with which volunteers can help *you*, at the executive level. Expect other management staff to do the same. This shows that volunteers are integrated throughout the organization, not colleagues from which frontline staff will eventually be "promoted out" of having to work alongside.

What are some things that the right volunteer might do for you? I give you a more detailed list in chapter eight, "Executive-Level Volunteers," but to whet your appetite, consider such things as researching local economic and demographic data to alert you to possible trends or writing speeches and creating presentations for you.

If you feel some discomfort at the thought of sharing your own work, you will understand why other staff members react the way they do. Do a reality check and see if following good volunteer management practices leads to a successful relationship. Think about how nice it would be to move some projects off *your* wish list and on to someone else's to-do list on your behalf.

Training

Once you have stated the expectation that paid staff will work with volunteers, make certain that all current employees understand *how* to do so. Keep in mind that almost no one receives training in volunteer management as part of formal professional education and so there should be no shame in admitting uncertainty about successful techniques of volunteer supervision. If the staff are in any profession dealing with human services, be alert to resistance to the notion that their interpersonal skills need some sharpening! Social work begins at home, and many people who provide wonderful service to clients find it challenging to develop teamwork with those whom they label (often incorrectly) as "nonprofessionals." The great thing is that learning how to work with people—paid or unpaid—is a professional development opportunity for anyone's career.

The only way to be certain that staff will approach volunteer teamwork consistently and in accordance with your policies is to provide training. The key is to demonstrate the importance of the subject by allocating time to it. Be sure any new employee learns about your approach to volunteer engagement as one of the topics in orientation to your organization. By mentioning it at the beginning of employment, you are emphasizing your expectation that this worker will treat volunteers well.

If you have never provided volunteer management training to staff, especially to those who have been with you for a long time, you may encounter surprise at this new attention. Staff training must deal with *attitudes* as well as with skill development. A great start toward new understanding is uncovering the stereotypes that employees have about volunteers. Encourage negatives to surface in a constructive way. Employees think they are supposed to value volunteers and need to feel safe in talking about their concerns. Voicing those concerns often diffuses resistance; there is a level of relief in being allowed to urge caution. A side benefit is that the training session can demonstrate that thoughtful suggestions about volunteers will always be welcome.

Directly confronting some of the fears and threats about volunteers is also healthy. This may mean reassuring everyone that no jobs are at risk, for example. It's a chance for the volunteer office to explain to staff how volunteers are recruited and screened and to stress quality assurance about the caliber of volunteers the organization is placing into partnership with paid staff. Discuss the individual "payoffs" for developing teamwork with volunteers as well as the agency's benefits from involving volunteers.

One interesting way to approach the whole subject is to give employees the chance to talk about the volunteering that *they* are doing outside of the job (or something they have done in the past as a volunteer). This sets up the concept of the Golden Rule—comparing how the employee likes to be treated when s/he is a volunteer with how s/he treats volunteers in the agency. It breaks down the barriers of "us" and "them."

Sometimes there is the problem of vocabulary. It is common to refer to salaried staff as the "professionals." One common definition of *professional* is indeed one who earns a salary for one's work. This is the distinction between *professional* and *amateur* athletes, for example. But another definition of the word *professional* is someone who has special training. Staff must be helped to see that not all volunteers are *un*trained; rather, they may be *differently* trained. There are many volunteers who bring educational credentials and relevant work experience equivalent to (though not necessarily the same as) those of the paid staff, even if offering their services voluntarily to the organization. Differentiating between paid and unpaid staff with the word *professional* is insulting and produces tension.

Once you have trained your current staff in volunteer supervision skills, do not overlook the possible training needs of new employees you may bring on board later. Be sure to include some time in the volunteer office in the orientation schedule of new staff members so that the director of volunteer involvement can brief the newcomer about the way in which volunteers are integrated into your organization's services. Assess whether the new person requires more in-depth training, especially since you cannot assume s/he learned about working with volunteers at a previous job.

Put the subject of volunteers onto the agenda of staff meetings periodically, if not regularly. This is another way to send the message that teamwork is expected and that good news and problems concerning volunteers are going to be discussed by everyone. When work in which volunteers are involved is on a staff meeting agenda, invite volunteers to join the meeting, if feasible. This is practical, day-to-day recognition of their contributions.

Because developing the skills of frontline staff in working with volunteers is so critical, Energize, Inc., offers some popular resources, including the year-round, online volunteer management training program *Everyone Ready®* and a ready-to-present training curriculum by Betty Stallings called *Training Busy Staff to Succeed with Volunteers: The 55-Minute Training Series*. Both are described in appendix B.

Position Descriptions: Volunteers

In chapter two, we discussed planning for volunteer participation and some of the considerations in determining what a volunteer might, can, or should do. Employees need to understand any rules limiting what they ask a volunteer to do, or they should be challenged if they raise objections not grounded in fact. The staff may also need support in thinking outside the box to creatively seek the widest range of donated skills to accomplish what is most needed.

It is considered best practice in volunteer management to also provide written position descriptions to volunteers. But it has become common not to use the word *job* so as to avoid any miscommunication that the volunteer work agreement is an employment contract. Whatever you call them, position descriptions clarify roles and differentiate what volunteers do from what employees do.[2]

Writing down an assignment is not an exercise in paperwork. It provides a tool that will be used in recruiting the right volunteer, determining the necessary training for the role, holding staff account-able for supervising the volunteer, and evaluating the work performed. Therefore, it is also the basis for recognizing the achievements of a volunteer or for initiating the process of termination.

The volunteer position description allows the director of volunteer involvement to conduct a meaningful interview with an applicant. It demonstrates that your organization is not simply looking for people to "help out" but expects productive work to be accomplished. On this basis, it is possible to screen out prospective volunteers who do not fulfill the position description's qualifications—without creating any bad will for turning away someone who offers assistance. You set standards from the beginning.

The paid staff member (or leadership volunteer) who will be work-ing with the new volunteer directly must be involved in writing the posi-tion description. This presupposes two requirements:

1. The staff member's own work is efficiently organized so that someone else can assist with it.

2. The person is skilled in task analysis and can divide the work into manageable pieces to be delegated.

The latter is why the director of volunteer involvement has an impor-tant role in helping the supervisor to define a reasonable, appropriate volunteer assignment. Having to write something down is a good way to ensure that there is indeed meaningful work to be done.

As CEO, you should stress the value of written volunteer position descriptions. See to it that time is taken to articulate these correctly and that they are reviewed as often as necessary to remain current. This action alone may alleviate many of the problems between volunteers and salaried staff. When people know what is expected of them, they are happier and more productive.

Think about showing volunteers the job descriptions of the employ-ees, too. This makes the circle of understanding complete and docu-ments that volunteers fulfill roles that are different from, but parallel to, those of the employees.

Volunteer Position Titles

Just as you send a message with the title you give to the person who leads your organization's volunteer involvement, the titles given to vol-unteer roles also set a tone.

First and foremost, the word *volunteer* is never a title; it's a *pay category*. It is the counterpart of the word *employee*, and you obviously further distinguish each paid staff member's position with a work title relevant to his/her job description.

So, if the volunteer work to be done requires a tutor, tour guide, or picnic coordinator, assign the title that reflects the content of the assignment. If the volunteer is going to be in charge of something, let the title show that, too. Not only is this very helpful in recruitment, but it also allows you to delineate, assess, plan for, and recognize specific groups of volunteers rather than speaking of all volunteers as a mass of interchangeable parts.

Second, resist falling into including the words *assistant* or *aide* in volunteer titles. As we have been discussing, volunteers do far more than "help staff." Don't aggrandize a title, but make sure it conveys the level of skill or responsibility necessary. Again, the more attractive the role and its title, the easier it will be to recruit the right volunteer to fill it.

On the other hand, you can appropriately have some fun with titles for volunteers, too. If you are seeking someone who will enter information into a database carefully, why not name the position "records czar," or, as I recommend for volunteers who do Internet research, "cyber deputy"?

The Unexpected Offer of Help

Although developing volunteer position descriptions is a first step in proactive recruitment of the volunteers you most need, there are times when the process works in reverse: a prospective volunteer offers you a skill or interest that you did not expect. How wonderful! It is important to be open to such opportunities, and the director of volunteer involvement should recognize such potential.

Encourage the development of completely new, even experimental, volunteer position descriptions to tap the offered talent. This does not mean that your organization should accept any and every idea, even if it means squeezing a round peg into a square hole. If you can't utilize a skill, there are undoubtedly other community agencies who might really love to have access to it. But if a talent or an entrepreneurial approach (see chapter seven) lands in the organization's lap and *can* be applied to your work, do not be rigid about having a written position description before you can consider it. Reward employees who collaborate with the volunteer to create something new.

Of course, once it's been negotiated what the volunteer will do, then make sure the agreement is written down for everyone to understand and agree.

Written Work Plans

Position descriptions are fine for individual volunteer roles, particularly those that mesh with paid work in the organization, involve regular work shifts, and so on. But this is only the volunteer-as-unpaid-staff model. What about the other ways volunteers might contribute?

When working with pro bono and other highly skilled volunteer consultants, it is appropriate to develop written work plans or agreements. These should outline the scope of the project, goals and objectives, timelines and deadlines, reporting procedures, and measures of results expected. Such agreements are negotiated mutually and should include a statement of how the organization will communicate with the volunteer, such as who on staff will be the liaison, what data will be made available to the volunteer, and so forth. When intellectual property or creative products are involved, include who owns the copyright or usage rights, for example. This sort of work plan clarifies all expectations and therefore paves the way to a successful, mutually accountable working relationship. Once in writing, both parties sign their agreement to this commitment to the other.

Similarly, work plans can be very useful when a community group offers to adopt or participate in a project for your organization, whether as a single event or on an ongoing basis. The work plan is negotiated with the group's leader (club president, class teacher, member of the clergy, etc.) and again includes details of what both parties accept as a working relationship.

Supervising or Partnering with Volunteers

Most paid staff do not have to learn all the techniques of how to develop and run a volunteer program. That is the responsibility of the director of volunteer involvement. But to accomplish specific jobs, the staff should feel comfortable in supervising and collaborating with volunteers as co-workers. All the principles of good supervision of employees operate with volunteers, too. However, there are some special considerations in supervising volunteers. These include the following:

- Volunteers need a positive working atmosphere. Because volunteers come and go during the course of a day or week, they encounter the work environment of a particular period. If the work-site tone is harried and hassled, it will affect volunteers' approach to their work, too. If some volunteers are on duty at lunchtime and therefore always see the staff on break, they will sense a different atmosphere than those who are scheduled at peak client visitation time. Enthusiasm and energy are infectious and really help volunteers to feel motivated. (Creating a good atmosphere for volunteers is one of those elements of volunteer management that rub off beautifully on the paid staff. Everyone benefits from a positive tone in the working environment.)

- To maintain continuity and consistency among volunteers with very different schedules, well-functioning communication mechanisms are essential to keep everyone in the loop.

- Many volunteer assignments involve work to be done outside of the agency's offices. This type of fieldwork includes such independent responsibilities as home visits to clients, solicitation calls on potential donors, leadership of group activities (clubs, sports teams, trips), and, increasingly, online assignments. It is quite possible for a volunteer to serve the organization entirely separated from the work site of the supervisor or staff liaison. This physical separation requires special consideration for defining lines of communication and accountability.

- Volunteers need accessibility to a supervisor or someone designated to answer questions. If an employee has a question and discovers her/his supervisor has gone out to a meeting, the question can wait until the next day. But a volunteer may only be in once a week. In that circumstance, having no one who can move the work forward can amount to a waste of a workday. It is not sufficient to have another staff member hand the volunteer a pile of work to do (though this is light-years ahead of having the volunteer arrive only to discover no one remembered s/he was coming in and no work was left at all!). Concern must be shown for supporting the volunteer's accomplishment of the task.

- Volunteers may get orientation and training but not need the information taught for many weeks or months later. Therefore, the supervisor needs to monitor if the volunteer is feeling competent and has the tools and resources necessary to do the best work. Betty Stallings often shares her favorite suggestion in her workshop presentations, which is the question that one of her daughters was asked midway through a volunteer experience: "Is there anything you have experienced in your volunteer assignment that we have not adequately prepared you for?"

- The volunteer's commitment of time should be respected. If there is no work to be done in the person's assignment area on a particular day, then the volunteer should, in all courtesy, be contacted and told of the problem. S/he can be given the option of revising her/his schedule for the week or of coming in anyway to do some other task. But it should not be assumed that all volunteers will do *anything* just to help out.

  As alluded to previously, nothing is more undercutting of the volunteer's commitment than to arrive on-site and discover that no work has been prepared—in fact, to realize that the paid staff have forgotten the volunteer was even due in. Watching the employee rush around to "pull something together" for the volunteer to do is hardly conducive to feeling really needed.

- There is something in the volunteer world that I have always called "instant accountability." This refers to the reality that, in the supervision of employees, there is a margin for error that does not exist with the supervision of volunteers. If a supervisor is moody, uncommunicative, nasty, or leaves no work to be done in his/her absence, the salaried worker will not like it but will tolerate it—or perhaps will "wait out" the mood until a better day. But the volunteer who is treated discourteously or is left with nothing to do is likely never to return to the organization again. This is not to imply that volunteers are thin-skinned. But if one gives his/her time to a facility and then is treated poorly, why should s/he return? It is a form of masochism or martyrdom to wish to repeat a bad experience under those circumstances.

It might be a measure of a supervisor's skill to realize that every time a volunteer *returns* to an agency, it is a compliment to what occurred on the previous visit.

- Volunteers have freedom of choice beyond what employees are usually given. Employees must complete a wide variety of mandated tasks, even some that are tedious or somewhat unpleasant. A volunteer is free to say no to an assignment, without jeopardizing his/her right to remain a volunteer. This does not mean that a volunteer can randomly select which parts of a task to do and which to ignore. But it does mean that the person can, within reason, select a particular assignment on which to concentrate time and effort.

- There is a degree of "socializing" that is part of volunteering (paid staff do this naturally throughout the workweek without noticing). This can get out of hand, at which point it becomes a reasonable complaint of the employees. But, within bounds, it is fair for a volunteer to want to have some personal interaction during her/his scheduled work time. As long as this does not interfere with productivity, the supervisor might show an interest in the volunteer's activities since last seeing him/her.

- Ongoing recognition, especially in the form of saying thank you, is important to supervising volunteers. In some ways, this amounts to an "exit line" in which a person is acknowledged for his/her efforts that day and is encouraged to return. But the thank-you has to be sincere. Remember that volunteers do not always see the way their work fits into the larger picture. By next week, the project handled this week may seem forgotten—unless the supervisor notes how the volunteer's effort enabled the entire workload to be completed. (Again, it would be nice to say thank you more often to *employees*, too.)

Two important concepts to keep in mind when supervising volunteers are *courtesy* and *self-fulfilling prophecy*. So many interpersonal relationships can be handled smoothly with politeness and friendliness. This is important for any human interaction, but with volunteers the need to be courteous is even more vital. Similarly, when one expects the best, one often gets the best. If one has a low level of expectation about volunteers, volunteers will act accordingly—largely because they will end up being poorly recruited, trained, and supervised.

Volunteers as Trainees

Employees often want to know if they may give critical feedback to a volunteer. The answer is of course. In fact, it is a form of compliment to give a person suggestions for improving work done; it implies that the supervisor has confidence that the volunteer has the capability and will to do a better job. And then the volunteer knows the work is important enough to be reviewed and done to the best of everyone's ability. Empty thank-yous without enthusiasm leave volunteers with the uncomfortable suspicion that their work will be tossed out after they leave. It is better to deal directly with improving a volunteer's work. After all, when people give their time freely, it is in the hope that their effort will produce results—not to waste their time doing something wrong or ineffectively.

One suggestion is to require every new volunteer, regardless of status or background, to be a "trainee" for the first month or so of work. You might even distribute colorful "Hi, I'm new here" buttons to cheerfully set the tone. All newcomers understand that they are in training, if only to become oriented to the organization. For the paid staff, the volunteer trainee period gives permission to correct early mistakes and give instructions. It is also a grace or probation period during which either the volunteer or the supervisor might recognize the placement is not working. Conversely, emerging from the training period successfully is immediate positive feedback.

This is also a bit different for frontline volunteers and those who provide expert consulting. Pro bono volunteers are, by definition, already highly skilled in their professions and so the organization will not have to do any training, per se. But even this group of volunteers needs *orientation* to the organization and some time to be integrated into the work.

Collaboration with Volunteers

Again, not all volunteers work *under the supervision* of salaried staff. There are many assignments that utilize volunteers as independent specialists, consultants, or project leaders. These assignments imply partnership between volunteers and employees, on an equal footing. In fact, in some cases, the volunteer's position (and expertise) may place him/her *above* the salaried staff member in responsibility (see chapter eight for a discussion of board roles as one example).

The principles of good volunteer supervision create effective teamwork, too. Clear and written work agreements, respect for the volunteer's time and contributions, and a willingness to be honest about the value of the work produced encourage successful collaboration.

One special need in these types of assignments is clarification of how the volunteer will keep the organization informed about her/his activities. Specify a *two-way* reporting process and timetable.

Liaison Supervision by the Director of Volunteer Involvement

The director of volunteer involvement maintains an ongoing relationship with volunteers placed throughout the organization and monitors the progress of volunteer assignments. The immediate staff supervisor is responsible for day-to-day supervision on the front line, specific to the work being done. Should any problem arise, that supervisor is the first line of communication and accountability. However, the director of volunteer involvement can be helpful to both the employee and the volunteer by being a third party to differences of opinion.

If the volunteer wishes to change assignments, it would be up to the director of volunteer involvement to weigh the request and act upon it. Similarly, if the staff member wishes the volunteer transferred or terminated, the director of volunteer involvement must be involved. Ideally, the interrelationship is cooperative, open, and not unlike the way in which a personnel or human resources department operates.

Reinforcement and Recognition

Once you have seen to it that all staff receive the necessary training in how to work with volunteers, the next step is to reinforce the process by evaluating paid staff on whether they are carrying out this job function appropriately. Employees should receive feedback on their effectiveness with volunteers as a part of any annual or periodic performance review. This implies further that exceptional effort and achievement with volunteer assistance will receive special recognition (a raise, promotion, or at least a comment)—and that poor teamwork will carry negative sanctions.

Only when good behavior is reinforced and bad behavior carries consequences do an organization's standards carry weight. Unless you are willing to act in this manner, you are only giving lip service to support of volunteers—and the paid staff will each decide unilaterally whether to cooperate with volunteers. Without the risk of administrative disapproval, it is easy to opt for not working with volunteers.

To be fair, enforcement is a two-way street. Volunteers should also be held to high standards, and there should be consequences if productivity is low or if work is not done properly. If some volunteers are undependable or resist instruction, they should be informed of the organization's dissatisfaction. This is as important as providing recognition for volunteers who do well. In fact, it makes annual recognition events more meaningful if everyone knows that mediocre volunteers were weeded out. Employees will be more likely to accept evaluation of their ability to work successfully with volunteers if they know that the same assessment will be made of volunteers. Otherwise, you are sending a mixed message: we want you to accept volunteers as equals, but we won't hold them to equal standards.

Settling Disputes

Just because someone is on the payroll does not necessarily make his/her point of view right or more worthy of consideration if it differs from that of a volunteer. Intellectually, this point might be accepted, but in practice, management actions can imply that employees get the primary benefit of the doubt.

It is true that full-time employees, or even part-time employees with weekly schedules, see a broader picture than a volunteer with limited time on-site can. Also, demonstrating loyalty to a staff member with seniority is understandable. But every situation must be weighed in terms of its particular details, so as to ensure that volunteers are not discriminated against.

How does such discrimination occur? One real example occurred in a large metropolitan hospital in which the director of volunteer involvement received a memorandum from an administrative assistant in another department (on behalf of his/her department head) concerning access to the photocopy machine. The memo asked the director of volunteer involvement to instruct all volunteers whose assignments included photocopying to *stop their work* whenever an employee came to the copying room and step aside. In other words, the administrative assistant felt that employees had "first rights" to the copying machine. What are the underlying assumptions of this memo?

First, the memo implies that the time of the employees is "clearly" more valuable than that of the volunteers (after all, they have the time to volunteer, so they can wait around, right?).

Second, the memo shows misunderstanding of what volunteers are doing in the photocopy room: they are (surprise!) making photocopies. And these copies are being made for departments and employees who need them as part of the hospital workload. So first-come, first-served is a reasonable rule in the photocopy room, no matter what the hourly rate of the person making the copies.

Actually, the full-time employee has more options as to when to return to the copying room. The volunteer, with a limited schedule, needs to complete as much work as possible in the allotted time. So asking the volunteer to wait around while the employee does copying turns out to be more wasteful of productivity than may be realized.

The most notable fact about this memo is that it was sent at all, in the complacent certainty that the paid staff had the right to dictate the use of organizational resources. It expressed the opinion that volunteers should do "whatever it is they do" only when it does not "interfere" with the really important activities of the employees. Assuming the other department head was not intentionally trying to insult anyone, can you imagine such a memo going to any other counterpart manager? And via the sending department's administrative assistant?

The way to begin to deal with such attitudes is to recognize them when they surface. As chief executive, you have the chance daily to reaffirm that volunteers are legitimate workers with equal access to resources. If the volunteers' assignments are appropriately planned, their need for workspace, supervision, and even copying machines can be accommodated with a minimum of stress.

If individual disputes occur between a member of the paid staff and a volunteer, these should be handled in the same manner as any interpersonal problem. The two people should first be encouraged to work out their differences together. It should not be acceptable for the employee to decide unilaterally, "I just can't work with this volunteer; ask him/her to leave." If necessary, the employee's immediate supervisor can mediate the problem, possibly also calling in the director of volunteer involvement for assistance. The volunteer's point of view deserves to be heard and to be evaluated on its own merit. Of course, if there are facts that the volunteer is unaware of because of his/her limited schedule or other considerations, these should be explained. But again, the bottom line is that a salaried staff member cannot rely on being seen as right a priori on the basis of being on the payroll.

If volunteers are indeed in the wrong, the staff should feel that standards will be maintained and that such nonproductive or counterproductive workers will be asked to leave. It is probably necessary to mention that volunteers should also not be protected against criticism or even firing simply out of gratitude for their voluntary service. Reassignment of a volunteer to a new unit or to a new staff supervisor may be an appropriate way of solving a particular interpersonal problem. But reassignment should not be done simply on demand of an employee. This is another version of giving staff all the power with no accountability for their skills in supervision.

Labor Unions

If labor unions are active in your facility, the question of volunteers will come up sooner or later in contract negotiations. There are just as many examples of peaceable relations between union employees and volunteers as there are examples of tension. The way to ensure peace is to *plan in advance*.

Bring up the subject of volunteers well before labor relations become problematic. There are really only two issues about volunteers that concern union leaders: Will volunteers be used to replace employee positions, reduce overtime pay, or prevent new salaried positions from being created? And, what will be the role of volunteers during a possible employee strike?

The latter is simpler to handle than the former. The basic rule about utilization of volunteers in a work stoppage is to treat volunteers as individuals capable of making their own decisions. If volunteers wish to continue with their ongoing assignments during a strike, they should be permitted to do so as a matter of personal choice. However, administration might assure union members that no *new* volunteers will be recruited or mobilized during a strike—nor will volunteers already on board be reassigned to cover work that strikers normally handle.

The bottom line for unions is to receive assurance that volunteers will not be utilized as *strike breakers* to provide the agency with a work force capable of holding off the strikers for a long period of time. Ironically, devoted volunteers may actually *enable* work stoppages by attending to clients' basic needs.

It is legitimate to agree to thoughtful utilization of volunteers during a strike as much for protection of the volunteers as out of fairness to employees. But, on the other hand, do not agree to refuse to allow volunteers admittance to the facility if a strike is on—this violates each volunteer's right as a member of the public as well as a member of the staff to choose his/her own position in the dispute.

The question of "taking jobs" is much more difficult to clarify because almost every organization welcomes volunteers as a way to stretch the budget beyond what available money would otherwise be able to "buy" through employees. While each administrator must honestly deal with the suspicion that volunteers will be used as a way to *cut* a budget, at the same time it is justifiable to firmly assert the position that management has the right to locate and utilize whatever resources will allow the organization to meet its goals and serve its clientele.

Here is an area in which volunteer position descriptions are invaluable. Administration should be able to document that it is the intent of the organization to recruit and assign volunteers to positions that are substantially *different from* the roles filled by employees. This does not mean that all volunteer positions are subservient to employees. It simply means that the slots to be filled by paid staff are the ones shown in the budget and that the position descriptions written for volunteers would not be filled by employees under most circumstances. Employees and volunteers may share specific tasks but have discrete and different roles.

It is probably useful to clarify with union representatives whether volunteers will be assigned as a temporary measure if an employee leaves a job, until a paid replacement is found.

To prevent future tension, it might be helpful to encourage union representation on any advisory committee or evaluation team supporting the volunteer office. But beware of giving the union the power to OK or veto volunteer activities and roles. If your policy of not duplicating staff roles is accepted, the day-to-day implementation of this should not be given to the union for oversight.

One last thought. When negotiating with labor unions, it might be instructive to point out that unions can't operate themselves without the volunteering of their own members!

Budget Cutting

This is a good point to discuss legitimate concerns about budget cutting, since employees are so often wary of new volunteer projects because of questions of job security. Many organizations are faced with an impossible choice: the need to reduce spending while maintaining or even increasing services. Some groups may wish to expand services but rec-ognize that additional funding will be hard to find. This is the type of situation in which it is very appealing to conclude that "we'll do it with volunteers." The fallacy of this simplistic approach has already been dis-cussed. Volunteers may be "free" in the sense of not requiring a great deal of cash outlay, but they are very expensive in terms of recruitment, training, coordination, and supervision time.

As an overall observation, don't wait until a budget crisis to begin to involve volunteers. This reinforces the notion that volunteers are a sec-ond-choice band-aid. Not only will staff resist volunteer help just when they themselves are coping with an increased workload, but it also is hard to sound sincere when recruiting in desperation. The best way to gain expanded volunteer support in lean times is to have incorporated volunteers as a welcome resource much earlier.

If you are faced with staff layoffs, can you turn to volunteers for help? It is next to impossible to fill a gap left by a full-time employee with only one qualified and available volunteer—it would require an intricate schedule of several volunteers, each giving a certain number of hours per week and each bringing the organization a different set of qualifications. Take all the concerns of "job sharing," and multiply them severalfold!

It is also a mistake to assume that somehow it will be easier to find volunteers to handle the low-level, clerical jobs of the agency. Under this assumption, when the budget diminishes, all the professional staff are retained, but the secretaries are let go. The irony is that the organization can survive more reasonably if the public relations staff is cut back or if there are two fewer caseworkers than by losing someone to answer the telephone during all working hours. Equally ironic, it is easier these days to find volunteers willing to handle the more challenging assign-ments of, say, writing the organization's newsletter or helping a family to learn budgeting than to get a full shift of volunteers to do data entry or filing.

The best way to handle the real problem of a reduced budget is to reassess the job descriptions of the *entire staff*, both those who have left and those remaining. This means doing a task analysis of the way things really work in the organization, not just what was put on paper in the distant past. Scrutinize the various tasks that each employee is doing and identify the following sorts of things:

- What is someone doing once a week or periodically rather than daily or on an inflexible schedule?

- What is someone doing that really does not require his/her specialized training? (For example, a lot of time is spent in making follow-up telephone calls, composing letters, etc. that may take someone away from direct service to clients.)
- What is someone doing that might be done more effectively by someone else with special training in that skill?

Once you have identified such tasks, you are ready to realign all the job descriptions. *Rewrite employee positions* so that these contain all the tasks that require daily attention, special training, and so on. Now add the similar critical responsibilities that had been assigned to the laid-off staff members so that the remaining employees are primarily now assigned to the most vital, daily functions. Remove the other periodic or less technical responsibilities—which then become the basis for legitimate *volunteer* position descriptions. You will be asking volunteers to handle work (still important) that can be done once a week or that makes use of special talents for which the volunteers have been recruited.

This approach to the unfortunate need to trim the budget is therefore good management of both paid and volunteer staff. You will be paying for the best utilization of your employees and will attract volunteers in support of your organization. It is also hard for unions to be as negative about this approach, though careful negotiation is probably in order.

In a Financial Crisis

Some readers may be in true crisis mode, whether because funding has been lost or client needs have multiplied. If your choices have come down to eliminating services (or even closing your doors altogether) or turning to volunteer help as a stopgap measure, your mission comes first. Volunteers understand and respect that. It is legitimate to share information about the emergency situation with current and potential volunteers and to ask for their help. You are likely to get it.

There may be some resistance from paid staff, both those facing layoffs and those left to do more work. The key is honest and open communication about your plans to hold things together until new funding can be found. Solicit everyone's ideas for how to operate in the crisis. Set up a timeline for reassessing how things are going and, perhaps, for when to throw in the towel. Volunteers are a vital part of transitioning to a more effective, fully funded organization; they cannot be expected to carry the load indefinitely. Just be conscious not to abandon the volunteers who bailed you out once you have money to rehire paid staff.

In a public agency or unit of government, there is still another factor to consider. Volunteers are the taxpayers who underwrite your budget. In a democracy, particularly one that says it's "of, by, and for the people," citizens can decide for themselves whether your services are important enough to give their time and skills to assure uninterrupted access. While you have the right to accept only qualified volunteers, citizens have the right to offer their help. Labor unions may not see it that way, so your role as executive is to help all to focus on what is essential—that is, the community's needs.

Always remember that volunteers are your most effective advocates for funding your work. Especially in a crisis, make sure you are utilizing volunteers as spokespeople with legislators, donors, and other funders. Raising more money *and* having great volunteers are mutually compatible goals.

Strong Volunteer Leadership in a Crisis

Let's discuss one last observation about retrenchment. Unfortunately, it is not unusual to see organizations lay off their director of volunteer involvement in the first round of staff cuts. The theory is that the director of volunteer involvement is "indirect" staff, and since there are already volunteers in place, there will be few immediate consequences from this vacancy. Then, often without seeing the irony, the same organizations also announce that they are seeking more volunteers!

Clearly, it is my position that the more critical volunteers are to your organization, the more important the position of the person who leads the volunteer program. Not only do you need such a manager to expand the volunteer corps, but also current volunteers can feel unsupported and taken for granted when they lose their staff liaison. On the other hand, if you are laying off employees in large numbers, this probably is not the most diplomatic time to *create* a new position of director of volunteer involvement! So again, plan for volunteers when times are good if you want their help in times of crisis.

Teamwork Prognosis

When analyzed in the way we have just being doing, the factors that affect teamwork between volunteers and employees are not mysterious. In many ways they are the same factors involved in the interrelationships among members of the paid staff. The major difference is that people expect to define paid-work roles but too often ignore the same need to clarify volunteer roles. Assumptions fill the gap when there are no established policies—assumptions that may be wrong.

While some initial tension between volunteers and employees may be understandable, there are equally important benefits to each for establishing a sense of partnership. By paying attention to the issues just described, the outlook is very positive for real integration of paid and volunteer staff.

Finally, it is worth reemphasizing that this chapter and the previous chapter have contained concepts basic to *good management*— regardless of whether the workers to be managed are volunteers or employees. The most effective ways to support volunteers are also the best ways to work with paid staff—not the other way around. The organization that creates a positive working atmosphere for its volunteers usually also benefits from the high morale and productivity of its employees.

To implement ideas in this chapter, see . . .

Leading the Way to Successful Volunteer Involvement: Practical Tools for Busy Executives by Betty B. Stallings with Susan J. Ellis (Philadelphia: Energize, Inc., 2010).

Idea stimulators, worksheets, step-by-step guides, and more in the following sections:

- Section 6: "Building Staff Commitment and Competency to Partner with Volunteers"
- Section 7: "Integrating Volunteers throughout the Organization"

Notes

1. Colleen Kelly, executive director, Volunteer Vancouver/Vantage Point, in a margin note when reviewing this manuscript, November 2009.
2. For more discussion about how to delineate roles for volunteers and employees, see Ivan H. Scheier, *Building Staff/Volunteer Relationships* (Philadelphia: Energize, Inc., 1993).

7

Tapping into the Full Spectrum of Community Resources

One of the most exciting things about involving volunteers is that the potential for tapping the resources of your community is limitless. When you develop a volunteer involvement strategy, you give its leader the mandate to recruit whatever assistance can effectively meet your organization's needs. This opens the door to all sorts of creative engagement of people and cooperation with other organizations. Avoid a narrow definition of volunteering. Seek out the widest range of community resources through your volunteer engagement.

We have already recognized that volunteers come with every possible type of background and characteristic. In this chapter, we'll examine some current trends and issues in who is contributing time and how. Not all these types of volunteers identify with the word *volunteer*, so you may have decided to separate them administratively from other volunteers by creating different points of entry, assignments, and supervisors. In that case, you've created a blurry situation of a special set of service providers, definitely not employees, but not totally volunteers either. I argue against creating such false dichotomies.

Your human resources office is involved in finding, hiring, and maintaining records on all employees—from department heads to maintenance workers. If they are on the payroll, they are employees. The same logic should hold true for anyone who enters your organization to give time and expertise *without* going on the payroll: those people are *volunteers* from a management perspective. Different volunteers may require special processing, liaison with a third party, or specific types of assignments, but they are all legitimately recruited and administered through your volunteer involvement office. Once on board and officially entered into your volunteer coordinating system, they may be deployed in very different ways, as appropriate.

Some of the following sources of expertise and time will be available and suitable to every organization, others for only a few; some will be familiar, others may surprise you. But all are legitimately *community resources* that can be mobilized through the volunteer office. As we discuss each category of volunteer, we'll identify what might be unique to their engagement and note which categories require some top executive involvement in decision making and policy setting.

Generational Possibilities

Every so often I encounter an executive in the early stages of volunteer involvement who says something such as, "We have a lot of retirees around here, so we know we can get volunteers." Setting aside the stereotype that most volunteers are seniors (coupled with the assumption that most seniors—unlike other age groups—have the time to volunteer), the most dangerous element of this sort of thinking is that we tend to create volunteer positions to match the people we can envision doing them. So if you picture seniors, you will begin to design goals and roles for volunteers in a way that will mainly appeal to older people. *First*, you decide what needs to be done, then you go out and find the best people who match your needs. Coincidentally, some of these candidates may be older, but that's different than aiming for older people simply on the assumption they are the only volunteers available.

On the other hand, perhaps the most talked-about social development of the new century is the aging of the Baby Boomer generation, now moving into retirement—although a countertrend is that many Baby Boomers are delaying retirement, either by choice because they haven't slowed down ("sixty is the new forty") or because their retirement savings have decreased in value. Regardless, this population bulge has long dominated everything from clothing sales to television shows as it moves through the life cycle. In the last decade, there have been hundreds of studies of what Baby Boomers will demand and need as they age, including their expectations of volunteering.

This is neither the forum to debate the research findings nor to go into detail about how some organizations are gearing up for retired Baby Boomers as volunteers. But just as this generation questioned authority in their twenties, redefined family and gender stereotypes in their thirties and forties, and so on, it's no surprise that Baby Boomers are taking a different path to aging and retirement, as well.

The really interesting thing, however, is that recent studies of Generation Y, or the Millennials (generally considered as born between the mid-1980s to mid-1990s), are showing a great deal of similarity to the approach of their parent Baby Boomers to volunteering. For example, both groups tend to want the following:

- The chance to apply their talents and education to social concerns (Boomers are the most highly educated generation in history, and the Millennials have a high percentage of college graduates as well.)
- To participate in designing their own volunteer work and projects, not simply to "fill slots" as unpaid staff (See the section on entrepreneurial volunteers later in this chapter.)
- Flexibility in when and how they give their time, with a reluctance to commit to long-term assignments before testing their satisfaction with an organization
- To partner with staff, not necessarily to be "supervised," and sometimes to *lead* the effort, if their expertise is greater

In other words, they reject the old-fashioned concept of volunteers as helpers who will do anything they are asked to do, on a regular schedule, for a long time. And they are probably right! Times have changed, and volunteering needs to evolve—although the most successful organizations have long ago discovered that dealing with volunteers as a treasure trove of community resources is far more productive than narrowly structuring a no-cash temporary labor force.

It's worth noting that, the younger the volunteer, the more likely s/he will expect to communicate with you electronically. Increasingly, this means not only via e-mail but also instant messaging, Twitter, and social networking sites such as Facebook. For most of us over the age of twenty-five, this produces a very steep—and continuous—learning curve! But the results can be amazing, so recruit volunteers to be your cyber deputies and keep on top of online developments.

Families and Intergenerational Volunteers

Since we are discussing age, note that intergenerational volunteering is another permutation. This means younger and older people volunteering together, in which the resulting blending of perspectives creates a synergy useful to the project being done. "Younger" and "older" can be defined differently for each situation, though it most often refers to pairing children or teens with seniors.

A specific subcategory, and one that has gotten a good bit of attention, is family volunteering. This means two or more people, related in some way, of two or more age groups, committing together to do volunteering. It is often a parent(s) and child(ren) but can be grandparent and grandchild, older and younger siblings, and various other extended family members. One interesting variation is when a divorced, noncustodial parent adds a mutual volunteering project to what would otherwise be a "playdate" with his/her son or daughter.

An executive decision may be needed to determine whether your organization can accept volunteers younger than eighteen or younger than, say, twelve. In the case of family volunteering, an adult relative is on-site to supervise, but preteens may want to volunteer with a Scout troop or a faith community group—and some bright youngsters may even wish to sign up on their own. What if a corporation or civic club wants to do a group project and wishes to bring along their children or grandchildren? There are many considerations (and we've dealt with them at length in the book *Children as Volunteers*—see appendix B), but try not to decide based on a knee-jerk reaction of "Gracious, that sounds risky" or "How in the world could a kid help us?" Certainly, there are important management and safety measures that need to be put in place, but there is no inherent reason that young volunteers cannot be valuable assets.

Keep an open mind. I like to say that volunteering allows someone to rise to the level of their capabilities, not just their resume. Bright young people can fill sophisticated volunteer roles that they would never have the chance to do for pay until they get older.

Just to round out this topic, you may even have to determine whether babies and toddlers are welcome in your facility! You may find it strange to consider them volunteers, since they can't choose to do anything without a parent, but it may be an incredibly therapeutic or educational strategy, for example, to recruit parents of infants to come together to visit patients or a classroom. And that goes for pets, too!

It is important to realize that family service opportunities do more than simply expand your reach into possible new communities of service. Research shows that one of the strongest predictors of volunteering in adulthood is the act of having volunteered *with* a family member. In a comprehensive analysis of undergraduate student volunteerism at the University of Texas at Austin, nearly 90 percent of students who had volunteered *with* a family member (not to be confused with simply having family members who also volunteer) continued to volunteer when they left home.[1] These findings are corroborated by other studies as well. Clearly, family volunteering is about developing a new generation of volunteers, an outcome we should all strongly support.

Students

Students of all ages are a source of volunteer help. Many universities, high schools, and a growing number of junior high, middle, and elementary schools have instituted a variety of what are often called "community service" programs. These range from curriculum-based, "service-learning" activities to completely optional, extracurricular volunteer work coordinated through the school. Examples include formal and intensive internships in which students apply their classroom training to the real world and short projects resulting in a paper or academic credit to pass a course. Students seeking volunteer opportunities come from just about any academic major—which means that your organization can benefit from an incredible range of skills and interests, often knowing that a faculty member is there for additional advice if needed.

Debate can surface over whether to call students engaged in service-learning "volunteers." Educators frequently want to distinguish the community service of students from what they falsely perceive as the low-level help that is traditionally labeled as volunteering.

Further, it has become common in many school districts to mandate a set number of service hours as a requirement for graduation from high school, and the same requirement applies both at some colleges and even some graduate schools. "Mandated volunteering" strikes some as an oxymoron and has given rise to the wry term *voluntold*.[2] As with other types of compulsory service explained later in this chapter, people seem much more comfortable with the vocabulary of "community service."

If your agency is a placement site for college or graduate students completing "internships," some will question whether the volunteer office should coordinate these students. Coordination of student interns is an *administrative* issue that is separate from the question of who should supervise such students once they are working in the organization. Do not allow the waters to be muddied by either the academic institution or various "professionals" in your agency. The volunteer office has a clear and supportive role to play in the effectiveness of internships, and here is why:

- From the point of view of your payroll, no matter what vocabulary they use to describe themselves, student interns are volunteers. Interns work in the agency for benefits other than financial reward; academic credit cannot be negotiated at the store for a loaf of bread.

- There are indeed differences between student interns and other volunteers, but these are considerations related mainly to what the interns will be asked to do and who will supervise them. Often, a school will ask for special training experiences to make the internships more valuable. In terms of management, these considerations are not very different from the need to match any volunteer to the best assignment or to accommodate such factors as physical disability. The volunteer office, therefore, can keep the list of all available internship position descriptions and do *initial screening* of all applicants. Then it should be up to the actual staff supervisor to make the final decision on *acceptance* of the intern (just as with any volunteer who would be assigned to a unit).

- By utilizing the volunteer office to centralize all internship applications, you save staff time in contact with the various schools and you make sure that any internship applicant is told of *all* available openings. If individual staff supervisors make the first contact, they will only be aware of what is available in their one particular unit and will not offer the prospective intern the full range of assignment options for the entire organization. Similarly, if a student is not right for one unit, only the volunteer office has the overview necessary to see if there is another possible placement that would be more appropriate.

- If you do not utilize the volunteer office, where will records be kept on student interns? Is anyone keeping such records at all now? As executive, don't you want to know how much staff time is being spent on interns, how many students you have assisted, or what the performance level of interns has been? If for no other reason, it may be necessary to document the work of interns to meet insurance requirements (since, as with all volunteers, there are accident and liability considerations for interns).

- Many student interns contribute far more hours to the organization than the minimum required by the school. Is this extra time not *volunteering* in its purest sense? Also, a percentage of students will want to remain active with the agency after the official end of their internships. Will you then expect them to "transfer" to the volunteer office—or will they remain undocumented (and, actually, unauthorized) in an unclassified state?

  In one workshop I taught, a participant admitted that she knew of at least three students who had simply kept right on doing their internship assignment for over a year after their school ties had ended, but no one reported it until she asked why the young people were still around. Some of their co-workers in the unit were not even aware that the official internship had ended. Parenthetically, is this the best way to help students with their education? Maybe these students were ready to move on to more challenging assignments in another part of the organization, but without the volunteer office in the equation, no one was responsible for making this offer to them.

- Every newcomer to the agency deserves an orientation. If interns bypass the volunteer office and go directly to their line supervisors, they will not get an overview of the entire organization. The volunteer program is already set up to offer orientation, and students should have access to it. Training for the specific task to be done will be given by the supervisor, as is appropriate.

- From a public relations standpoint, if you do not centralize the coordination of internships in the volunteer office, you are expecting the various schools and colleges to track down as many staff supervisors as necessary to place what may be several students. Working through the volunteer office allows the faculty to make one contact a semester, referring all the student internship candidates at one time. Similarly, requests for end-of-placement evaluations can be channeled through the volunteer office (one call for the school) so that the director of volunteer involvement can monitor whether all forms have been submitted as required. Copies of such evaluations can then be kept in the volunteer office with the other records on the students so that future references can be provided easily.

- At one time, the only student internships were those in medicine, nursing, teaching, and social work, and the type of placement and professional expertise of the required supervisor were clearly defined. Today, there are "internships" in a wide variety of subjects ranging from geography to communications. These newer internships are not always so definitive in requiring that a supervisor offer a specific professional background. Whether the internship is of the traditional kind or the more unstructured, experiential learning kind, the volunteer office is your agency's best vehicle for screening applicants and determining suitable assignments.

- Finally, without the involvement of the volunteer office, it is unlikely that students will receive formal recognition of their accomplishments during their internships. Only you and the director of volunteer involvement can represent the entire organization in expressing appreciation.

Apart from internships in which the student is committed to a specific schedule for a duration of time, there is also the question of student "observers." You should have some policy defining your organization's point of view on such observation, largely because it is time consuming for the staff without necessarily contributing anything to service. Once again, the most logical administrative umbrella for student observers is the volunteer office. The director of volunteer involvement can make the arrangements with the school, schedule appropriate visits, keep records of the activity, and perhaps even recruit some of the students as ongoing volunteers.

Finally, take care not to elevate interns above "volunteers." Organizations and individuals may think pejoratively about volunteers, but if you use the label "student interns," the perceptions become more positive:

- Eager learners (though inexperienced or young), generally exploring a possible career

- Someone who is able to give an intensive set of hours for at least a few months

- Someone whose commitment is more serious and supported by a third party, such as a university faculty member

- Aspiring professionals to whom staff have a responsibility to guide and mentor

It is fine to distinguish specific, challenging volunteer assignments that need to be filled by qualified people with more-than-average hours available per week. But why not make these available to *anyone* willing and able to meet the requirements—not just students? Think about the illogic of assuming that a student, often quite inexperienced, can fulfill an intensive role just because s/he is a student, while an adult volunteer who may be truly qualified is relegated to less consequential tasks simply because of being placed into a different category of worker.

The skill necessary to create a meaningful internship is exactly the same task analysis that ought to be brought to any work designed for volunteers. It might even elicit more creativity if staff were asked to develop volunteer roles that allowed the doer to grow and learn—at any age and for any reason.

Both the words *volunteer* and *intern* are *descriptors*, not job titles. Neither really tells us what the person is actually doing, nor necessarily the skills the person brings. But if, to you, one connotes *nice helper* and the other connotes *serious learner*, ask yourself why each can't be both. Then ask yourself whether the distinction has been made in your agency mainly to professionalize internships—and why that wouldn't be positive as an approach to all volunteered assistance.

Groups of Volunteers

While most of the literature and training in volunteer management focuses on working with individual volunteers, many types of volunteer assignments bring together groups of volunteers to accomplish the work. Sometimes the volunteers are individuals who happen to be scheduled for the same shift, but sometimes an already-established community group agrees to provide several of its members to volunteer in your facility together. Whether the source is a faith community, school, corporation, or civic organization, keep in mind that one of the reasons the source is supporting your volunteer project is to develop a sense of identity and unity among its own group members. This may or may not interfere with your desire to generate loyalty to your organization in people who contribute to you as volunteers.

It may not be possible to meet each member of the group individually in advance (or even the day of the project), in which case agreement on the work plan will be reached with the group's leader(s). All the practical issues will be coordinated through the volunteer office, but the point to remember as CEO is that your organization has formed a collaboration with another organization. Be sure that lines of authority and communication are defined and that group volunteers receive the same orientation and training as would any other volunteer. Clarify possible issues such as insurance coverage, especially if organized groups participate in one-time special events, such as large fundraisers.

Discussion of group volunteering often centers on agency-based service. Another permutation applies to associations, in which the membership body is itself already a group. When members actively participate in association work, they often do so in subgroups such as committees or task forces, where the volunteering can either be project oriented or in an advisory capacity. We'll look more at members as volunteers later in this chapter.

Single-Day and Episodic Service

There has been a proliferation of what are called "single days of service," often in commemoration of a person, a holiday, or event. Many are national and even international, but others are sponsored by one company or a local community. In almost every case, the volunteering is structured as a multi-hour group project, although participants may be a collection of individuals or part of a preorganized team (see previous section on groups).

On one hand, stand-alone days of service have always been with us, particularly on the theme of a holiday. Volunteers deliver special meals and gifts on Thanksgiving and Christmas, visit military hospitals on Veterans Day, and plant trees on Arbor Day. The Martin Luther King, Jr., holiday, however, became a formal, planned service event, "A Day *On*, Not Off," and today is one of the most popular days for volunteering. *USA Weekend* sponsors Make a Difference Day each October, an idea that has been replicated in England and elsewhere. April's National Youth Service Day has expanded into Global Youth Service Day. Most recently, in the 2009 Serve America Act, September 11th has officially been designated as the National Day of Service and Remembrance.

As this book goes to press, there are more than a dozen national and international single days of service on the calendar, meaning that someone could be quite busy trying to participate in all of them.[3] Further, at any given time, some business, university, organization, or locality is holding its own day of service, encouraging its employees, students, and citizens to engage in some form of volunteering. It's also popular for local United Ways to organize a "Day of Caring" to allow donors to see their money at work by volunteering for a few hours in a funded agency.

Is there a saturation point? And now the duration of service is getting even shorter than a day or three to four hours. Mandela Day, launched in 2009, challenges people to honor Nelson Mandela's sixty-seven years of human rights struggle by volunteering for sixty-seven *minutes*, while a new organization called The Extraordinaries is attempting to use cell phone text messaging to permit people to respond to requests in only a few minutes on the run.

Regardless of your opinion of single days (or hours or minutes) of service, they are here to stay, since they fit into people's perceived lack of time and generate a certain amount of publicity and energy. Can (should) your organization tap into this type of volunteering?

It takes preparation and organization to make a single day of service successful. Some projects lend themselves very well to short bursts of energy from a group of willing workers, especially when some sort of physical labor is needed. Habitat for Humanity is the master of this concept, building houses year-round with a continuous flow of one-time volunteers rotating in and out under the direction of a skilled crew of volunteers committed for the long term. Similarly, one-day projects build playgrounds, clean up parks, sort donated clothes and food, offer blood pressure screening, and more.

On the other hand, not every organization is able to develop these kinds of projects and the effort to run a day of service may not seem cost-effective. Keep in mind, though, that there is much anecdotal evidence that participating in a service project introduces new people to the host organization, generating goodwill, possible future financial contributions, and even longer-term volunteers. Volunteers, whether consciously or not, use their day on-site to "audition" the agency and form an opinion about what it does and how it does it. Further, it is good visibility for your organization to appear on the list of available service projects publicized in advance of the event.

The key to converting such potential into concrete benefits is to warmly greet service-day participants and provide a brief introduction to your organization before they begin work, including some sort of printed material to take home with them. At the end of their shift, make sure they are sincerely thanked and offered the chance to be put on your e-mail or postal mailing list to keep informed about your work. It's also good to let them know what ongoing volunteer opportunities are available.

Episodic Volunteers

One related category of service is *episodic* volunteering, in which people return periodically to repeat an activity or to work on a new time-limited project when they can. This includes seasonal work that repeats annually, from Christmas caroling to replanting a vegetable garden. Episodic volunteers may be on call for special situations (such as the willingness of people who speak a foreign language to help if and when interpretation is needed), and many organizations maintain an extensive "skills bank" of a wide range of talents or availabilities (such as volunteers willing to work at night or in an emergency).

Episodic service is the focal point of the HandsOn Network, which has affiliates in several hundred cities in the United States and other countries. Started as an option for young businessmen and women to volunteer without committing to a regular schedule, HandsOn (in some cities, affiliates have kept the name "[City]" Cares, as in New York Cares, Philadelphia Cares, etc.) recruits volunteers, screens and orients them, and then puts them on a mailing list to receive a monthly calendar of one-time, small-group service activities—many that can be done in the evenings or on weekends. Volunteers can do one, a few, or none each month. The agencies posting these opportunities benefit from an externally organized group of pre-vetted volunteers, with a volunteer acting as team leader.

Spontaneous Volunteers

Finally, the phrase *spontaneous volunteering* arose in the hours after the terrorist attacks of September 11, 2001, when literally thousands of people contacted hospitals, police precincts, and other emergency responders with offers of help ranging from giving blood to animal rescue. Such an outpouring of volunteers has always occurred in response to natural disasters, both with people coming on-site in a desire to pitch in and in collections of donated items to be shipped to the site.

While such service is what I call "the silver lining in the cloud of disaster," it poses a serious challenge to agencies operating in crisis mode already. The truth is that well-meaning but untrained volunteers can hinder relief efforts more than they can help, unless there is a system in place—and coordinators assigned—to deal with the people who suddenly appear. What is vital is that their good intentions are respected and that someone is there to determine whether any of the spontaneous volunteers do, in fact, have the skills needed that minute. Offering alternate suggestions for where these volunteers might go to be useful, capturing their names and contact information for later communication, and then indeed following up are all good management approaches.

As executive, the question is whether your organization might someday face a spontaneous volunteering situation and if you are properly prepared to deal with it.

Corporate Employee Volunteers

Community-conscious businesses have long participated in charitable efforts, but corporate philanthropy is receiving increased attention and resources. The phrase *corporate volunteerism* refers to the involvement of a company's employees as volunteers in community organizations. Of course, employed people have always been active as volunteers, but *corporate volunteerism* implies that the company itself, as the employer, takes a direct role in encouraging the community involvement of its workers. It has also come to be an umbrella term for some of the in-kind services businesses provide at no cost to nonprofit organizations.

From the purview of this book, what is important about corporate volunteerism is that you, your development office, and your director of volunteer involvement may have to work cooperatively in approaching

corporations for assistance. You may be requesting a financial contribution from a company but may also want to recruit its employees (or
retirees) as volunteers. It is important to present a unified management
team rather than find your organization has contacted a corporation
from several angles at once—looking as though the left hand does not
know what the right hand is doing. Also, it is becoming more and more
usual for a business to respond to a request for money by offering a
"package" of funds, in-kind services, and employee volunteers. As executive, will you be able to utilize such a package effectively without planning together with the director of volunteer involvement?

There is no reason to make corporate volunteers into a special category all by themselves, even if the volunteers are "release-time" employees doing the service during the regular workday and still receiving
their salary from the corporation (for the perspective of your organization, even such paid-leave workers are not going on *your* payroll). If they
are going to fill existing volunteer position descriptions, they should be
integrated into your organization's corps of volunteer workers, just as
would volunteers from any source. In most cases the company employees will actually be volunteering on their own time, so there is even less
reason to differentiate them from other volunteers. The only exception
might be technical assistance and pro bono volunteers, which we will
discuss in a moment.

In recent years, the phrase *workplace volunteering* has become popular to describe any type of employee volunteering, beyond only that
organized by large businesses. Also on this bandwagon are medium-
and small-sized businesses, government agencies, and even nonprofit
organizations. As noted in the discussion of single days of service, some
workplace volunteer campaigns focus on everyone doing service on a
single day, usually in groups or teams. But other models include adopt-
ing a theme or a project for an entire year or more and then organizing employees to do activities focused on that throughout the year, or
simply enabling employees to take time to do individual volunteering
as they wish.

Pro Bono and Consulting Volunteers

There is nothing inherently new about volunteers donating professional expertise, but as this edition goes to press, a variety of summits
and action campaigns are examining the potential of intentionally and
strategically applying business talents to the nonprofit world. Perhaps

the most developed initiative is A Billion + Change,[4] in which the President's Council on Service and Civic Participation and the Corporation for National and Community Service issued the challenge to leverage $1 billion in skilled volunteering and pro bono services from the corporate community. A Billion + Change makes a distinction between skilled volunteering and pro bono services, as explained in their report, "Toward a New Definition of Pro Bono":

> Pro bono is decidedly different from corporate philanthropy, serving on a nonprofit board, volunteering to deliver nonprofit services, and donating in-kind products or services.
>
> Pro bono is the donation of professional services that are included in an employees' job description and for which the recipient nonprofit would otherwise have to pay. It is a subset of skilled volunteering that gives nonprofits access to the business skills and experience they need to develop and implement sound business strategies, increase their capabilities and improve their organizational infrastructure.
>
> By contributing business services and skills to nonprofits, corporate pro bono programs are improving people's lives while adding significant value to their own recruitment, productivity and profitability.[5]

In the FAQs on the A Billion + Change Web site, pro bono volunteering is further defined as "the practice of using work-related knowledge and expertise in a volunteer opportunity. In other words, skills normally used to generate income are provided free of charge to a nonprofit organization."[6]

The 2009 *Deloitte Volunteer IMPACT Survey* concluded,

> Nonprofits and corporations cannot control today's economic crisis, only how they react to it. These challenging times offer a tremendous opportunity to deepen relationships between the nonprofit and business communities. With philanthropic dollars becoming more scarce, the need to hasten the adoption of pro bono as a complementary giving strategy has never been more urgent . . . "Pro bono as currency" is a win-win approach. Those who seize the opportunity to expand their definition of corporate giving could emerge in a stronger position, better able to weather the times ahead.[7]

In a number of communities, special projects are functioning that recruit highly skilled volunteers willing to provide technical assistance and professional consultation on a short-term basis to any agency with need for such help. This also gives the volunteers the chance to donate their expertise to a wide variety of community agencies. In the United States, such programs may be run by a volunteer center as a "skills bank" or by a local chapter of AARP or Executive Service Corps; there are also online registries matching pro bono volunteers with opportunities to contribute their services. Some corporations have established their own skills banks, registering interested employees and then informing local agencies of the types of skills obtainable. Another source of management-level volunteers may be your area's community leadership organization, often sponsored through the Chamber of Commerce.

Some of the skills offered are concrete, such as carpentry, art talent, or computer programming. For such talents, it is not difficult to create suitable volunteer assignments and evaluate success. The bookshelves are built, the brochure designed, the records entered. However, many of the skills available are less tangible and directed at building an organization's management capacity, from expertise in strategic planning to personnel policy development. When an organization accepts this type of professional contribution, it implies that it is willing to open up its management process to consultation from the volunteer—and top administrators need to be directly involved.

Working with a volunteer consultant is no different from working with a paid consultant in terms of the potential benefits from the shared expertise. Many of the techniques for maximizing paid consulting time also apply to getting the most from a volunteer expert: proper identification of the needs to be addressed, a written work plan, homework on your part to offer the consultant useful background materials, good agenda planning, and follow-up of recommendations. When you offer such support, you are demonstrating that you value the pro bono volunteer's time and opinions as though you were indeed paying for these in cash.

Regardless of whether the professional assistance is provided to the vice president or the custodian, the director of volunteer involvement has the same responsibilities in the process as with any other volunteer. The short-term technical assistance role is simply one more type of volunteer assignment. Even the pro bono volunteer who will work directly with you, at the top, should not bypass the volunteer office. We'll discuss this more in the next chapter.

In-Kind Services, Barter, Loans, and Other Donations

When the director of volunteer involvement seeks volunteer assistance for your organization, especially from the business world, s/he often uncovers ways to get needed services at no cost or at significantly reduced cost. Such development of in-kind contributions is a part of the role of the director of volunteer involvement that you should cultivate and support. This sometimes hidden aspect of the job can be misinterpreted as overstepping boundaries (since the director of volunteer involvement is generally not authorized to "fundraise"). Here is another context in which the department of volunteers is really the "department of donated community resources." A creative director of volunteer involvement will turn up all sorts of unexpected opportunities to obtain things that your organization needs or can put to good use if offered unexpectedly.

Because the director of volunteer involvement is out in the community, explaining your mission to all sorts of groups and individuals, be prepared to get offers such as the following:

- Loans of equipment, space for meetings and events, storage space, and even paid staff. These might be indefinite-term loans or simply the chance to borrow something you need occasionally. One agency in downtown Pittsburgh was able to obtain two free parking spaces for volunteers in the garage of the big corporation across the street.

- Gifts in-kind, such as used furniture, office supplies, or items for client needs, crafts projects, and just about anything else you might seek.

- Barter and exchanges, such as a small Web design firm donating services to maintain your online presence, in exchange for public credit and a link to their company's site. This could also mean reciprocal volunteer help: a community group helps staff your fundraising carnival, and a few months later, you ask your volunteers and employees to help with that group's special event.

- Collaboration partners to work on major projects of mutual interest. For example, if you are launching a physical fitness program, it might attract organizations and businesses that otherwise might not see themselves as your team members: restaurants with reduced-calorie meal options, cardiologists, physical therapists, sports teams, weight-loss programs, stores that sell running shoes, and so on.

In fact, proactively seek such offers by keeping the director of volunteer involvement informed of current needs throughout the organization.

Entrepreneurial Volunteers

Best practice in volunteer management is to design meaningful volunteer position descriptions first and then recruit qualified people to fill them. And this process works. But this approach also reinforces the conventional idea that it is the role of the organization *both* to define the needs and to select the ways the needs will be met. This is fine up to a point, but it perpetuates the notion that volunteers are "helpers"— enthusiastic labor bringing the organization's strategies to life. Predeveloped assignments also do not welcome totally new approaches to the problems at hand, may not evoke discovery of unexpected talents offered by a prospective volunteer, and therefore can lead to squeezing square pegs into round holes.

Enter *social entrepreneurship*, which has a number of definitions, including starting a profit-making enterprise and then using all or some of the revenue for charitable purposes. Entrepreneurial volunteering is not necessarily concerned with money, but rather with *innovation*. It attracts the kind of person who likes to experiment and think outside the box.

The idea is to explain the needs you must address and then invite anyone to propose ways to try to solve the problem. This doesn't mean you have to accept every proposal, nor allow volunteers to go off totally independently. But it opens the door to such benefits as these:

- It is possible that someone outside the organization may, in fact, have a great idea no one has yet developed inside the organization. Innovative thinking can come from the most unexpected places. Why not discover and harness it?

- Some people (as discussed about Baby Boomers and Millennials) are more attracted to being innovators than to filling an established assignment, no matter how valid the assignment may be. Offering a chance to be creative or experimental may therefore recruit a totally new population of volunteers.

- People who participate in crafting the goals and strategies of their work are always more vested in the outcomes (which is as true of paid staff as of volunteers). So this may be a counterbalance to the trend toward single-day service, which is the quintessential expression of, "Here's my energy for a few hours, but not my commitment."

So how open are you to input as well as help?

Online Volunteers

The newest category of volunteering was not even imaginable as recently as the 1990s because it has evolved as a direct result of computer technology and online interaction in cyberspace (note that the World Wide Web did not even exist when the first edition of this book was published in 1986!). In fact, a whole new term has been coined to identify "online service" or "virtual volunteering"—the volunteers are indeed real, but they contribute their services via the Internet. And they can do so wherever they are on the globe, at any time that is convenient to them (Jayne Cravens, coauthor of *The Virtual Volunteering Guidebook*, calls it "volunteering in your pajamas"!). It's particularly exciting to recognize that online volunteering levels the playing field to allow people with physical disabilities, limited mobility, or hearing impairments or those living in remote locations to participate in your work.

Online service has developed dramatically in the last decade and continues to grow and expand. Here are just a few of the ways virtual volunteering is offering assistance to organizations and the people they serve:

- *Technical assistance* on any subject imaginable, provided through e-mail and, increasingly, using Voice-over-Internet-Protocol (VoIP) services such as Skype, which today includes the capacity to stream video through webcams. Volunteers with professional expertise offer access to themselves to answer specific questions from organizations, to review documents of various sorts, and to give other support.
- *Online research*, in which knowledgeable volunteers comb the Web for information needed by the organization.
- *Virtual self-help communities* open to anyone sharing the same disease or problem, or having a mutual interest.

Frequently moderated by volunteers, such self-help groups interact by discussion board and chat room, and increasingly as special-interest communities on social networking sites such as Facebook.

- *One-to-one interaction with clients* can be an extension of real-world visiting, mentoring, or tutoring with e-mail interaction supplementing face-to-face meetings between a volunteer and his/her matched client. Such sessions rarely can happen more than once a week, but e-mail permits much more contact. Or volunteers and the people they are matched with online may never meet in person. Keep in mind that, increasingly, e-mail is so commonplace that it no longer seems strange to participate in this sort of interaction. Again, with webcams, instant messaging, texting, and other technology tools, the volunteer and client can stay in touch in fun and satisfying ways.

- *Web site design and maintenance* is a popular type of virtual volunteering, with a number of organizations established specifically to help tech-savvy volunteers and nonprofits find each other.

- *Blogging, podcasting, online video production, and moderating online discussion forums* are all excellent ways to utilize articulate and willing volunteers on your behalf.

- *Fundraising* of all sorts, ranging from placing a "charity badge"[8] onto a social networking site that generates funds through click-throughs to running a sponsored marathon with avatars in Second Life.

- *Developing and implementing your organization's social media strategy*—whether using Facebook, LinkedIn, Twitter, or any of the constantly evolving new tools for social networking online, through mobile phones, or whatever will come along next!

Virtual volunteering can be managed using all the same techniques as real-world volunteer engagement, with position descriptions, interviewing and screening, monitoring, reporting, assessment, recognition, and more. Really.

As the chief executive, your role is to determine such things as policies for who will get password access to restricted areas of your Web site or be given an agency e-mail address and to hold the information technology staff accountable for partnering with qualified volunteers.

Residents or Clients as Volunteers

Another source of volunteers that you may need to clarify and define is your client group itself. As a special form of "self-help," you may want to encourage the people who receive services to, in turn, become givers by participating as volunteers. Some examples of this type of volunteering include the following:

- Retirement center residents taking an active role in visiting, feeding, and helping other residents who are ill enough to be in the nursing care unit

- Patients in a long-term mental health facility helping to tend the gardens and grounds

- Students doing a major clean-up project within their school building

- Residents in a home for those with severe disabilities forming a program committee to plan year-round special events

- Seniors in a nutrition center helping to set the tables before and clean up after their lunch

The common denominator of all these examples is a very fine line between what might be reasonably expected from program participants and what is some type of *extra* service that warrants the label "volunteer." Every organization must come to its own definition of what makes a resident or client a volunteer—and whether and how this group of volunteers differs from "outside" volunteers. In practice, this includes questions such as, will the residents who volunteered be invited to the annual volunteer recognition event?

Some of the types of resident or patient volunteering are really an attempt to foster *participation* in the facility's program so that the experience is more home-like or therapeutic. Other types of client involvement encourage ownership of the activity and reduce the feeling that the person is receiving charity. Self-respect is thereby maintained while getting necessary work done.

The key variable in all this is *choice*. Each person must participate completely voluntarily and should have as wide an array of options for particular assignments as possible. It is choice that places such activity within the realm of volunteering. At the same time, the agency also retains the right to assign (or reassign) a participant-volunteer or even to withdraw permission to be a volunteer if the person is not able to effectively deliver services to others. However, it is imperative that someone who is not eligible to volunteer in no way jeopardizes his/her right to remain a recipient of agency services.

Some organizations have run into difficulty implementing a client-as-volunteer program because of protests from those outside the facility. The major point raised by such protesters is that clients are being utilized as unpaid labor. Several court cases have successfully enjoined agencies from continuing certain types of programs using patients or residents as workers, unless a minimum wage is offered. In most of these cases, the evidence revolved around whether the clients truly had the choice to say no to the work activity.

If you wish to implement a self-help volunteer project, be sure to clarify the issues involved and to utilize the director of volunteer involvement in establishing some structure. It would be highly appropriate to ask the clients themselves for input from the very beginning.

Vested-Interest Volunteers

Another group of potential volunteers with similarities to resident or client volunteers is people with a special or vested interest in your work. This includes family members of residents, patients, students, or other constituents of your facility. Such volunteers are motivated not only by the desire to support your work but also by concern for the welfare of their parent, child, or other relative. The key is to assure that the latter does not overshadow the former.

Apply volunteer management principles. Clarify roles, channels for voicing complaints (or praise), and other working relationships. When is the relative acting as a volunteer and when as a consumer? Are all relatives welcome as volunteers, or must they first apply and be accepted into the program? Will the relative be assigned to his/her relation, or do you prefer that volunteers have some separation from their personal connections? What if the client or student prefers that her/his relative be assigned elsewhere?

Some of these policy decisions should be considered even if relatives volunteer only on a limited basis, such as parents chaperoning a class trip.

Volunteers may have an even more personal interest in your cause, although they may not currently be "clients." For example, health foundations have many volunteers who are themselves diagnosed with the disease being combated. Domestic violence programs involve volunteers with histories of abuse who may still be in litigation against their spouses. Performing arts centers may attract the donated services of performers themselves as volunteers. Again, the more defined the roles of volunteers, the less chance for conflict of interest and the greater the chance for wonderful contributions. "Defining" roles does not mean "limiting" them.

Finally, what are the considerations when major donors wish to be active direct-service volunteers? The donor may be used to personal contact with you, the executive, or the development officer, but the chain of command is probably quite different in the volunteer assignment. Orient the donor about the demands of volunteer work and the requirement to complete the volunteer sign-up process, and help paid staff to feel comfortable in supervising the work done by this volunteer.

Member Participation

If you are an association, professional society, or have any sort of dues-paying "members," you have another volunteer situation. Joining your organization may be voluntary, but just because a person pays dues and affiliates with you does not mean s/he expects or wants to do any work. So active *member participation* is a form of volunteering. It requires internal recruiting and support every bit as much as signing on new members, but who's paying attention to the level of involvement of members once they are on your rolls?

The largest study to date of mutual-benefit associations, *The Decision to Volunteer*, surveyed 26,305 association members affiliated with twenty-three cosponsoring organizations. The authors found that

> when we think about association volunteers, the first people who might come to mind are those who fill board and committee seats. Our study suggests that most association volunteers are performing low-profile services such as mentoring, membership recruitment, technical writing, or activities that might be further off the radar screen for association staff. The risk is in assuming that these ad hoc volunteers require less attention. Rather, we suggest that staff and board members find ways to identify, support, and acknowledge all volunteer contributions.[9]

A previous study, *The Decision to Join*, also noted that ad hoc volunteers are often overlooked yet are a critical member group:

> Whatever is done about ad hoc volunteers, it's certainly worth noting that there is a chasm of difference in the perception of value that is perceived by the majority who are not involved versus the upward slope of enthusiasm that takes off with ad hoc involvement. Those who are not involved lie perilously close to former members in their overarching assessments of the value they derive from associations. If former members are thought of as being dead, the uninvolved are close to comatose. And from that delightful imagery, involvement might be thought of as the life blood of an association, which therefore deserves much more strategic direction than it gets.[10]

What do you want from your members? Attendance, labor, input, advice—or just their dues? Do members vote on anything? How does someone get appointed to a committee or the board? What if they want to offer their help—is it clear to all members how they can do that? Do your membership application and subsequent renewal forms invite participation? Are offers of help followed up or allowed to languish? What if a member wants to bring along a relative or friend to help, too? How do you recognize members who volunteer?

Without question,

> organizational strategies can support or discourage volunteering . . . [M]embers told us that many of the reasons they did not volunteer for their professional association are within the organization's power to address. In fact, the number one reason they did not volunteer was a lack of information about the opportunities . . . an understanding of the essential elements of a volunteer program can increase participation among your members, beginning with a clear understanding among board and staff about the strategic value of volunteers.[11]

Never assume members "know" what they can do or how to offer their services. Be specific in offering volunteer opportunities; recognize that members will be looking for flexibility in the time needed to do the work and will have many competing choices for where to donate their talents (including community volunteer work). However, there is no question that becoming an active member increases a strong sense of affiliation. Further, for a professional society, "We found a strong connection between the number of hours [respondents] volunteered and their satisfaction with professional volunteering. In fact, many regard volunteering as a benefit of membership; they see the association volunteer work they have done as something that has made them better professionals."[12]

Clearly, this is a huge topic, and indeed, association management is a field unto itself (see resources in appendix B). The same issues also apply to running faith communities, neighborhood organizations, civic clubs, and more. For our purposes here, however, the point is that if you have a list of "members," view them as potential volunteers to be mobilized. Then make the executive decisions to define what you want and how such active members will mesh with volunteers who affiliate with you in other ways.

Voluntourists

Although only a small number of organizations will be in a location or situation to be able to tap into this trend, it's worth mentioning the recent increase in opportunities to take a "volunteer vacation" or be a "voluntourist." Voluntourism combines recreational travel with service to the community visited. There are many variations.

The most established programs are actually structured as intensive group service (what was called a "work camp" in the 1940s) that might be focused on constructing homes, excavating archeological digs, cleaning up after natural disasters, monitoring wildlife on land or at sea, and so on. Volunteers pay their own travel costs, which can be substantial. When not working on the assigned project, however, they are free to explore the country or area they are visiting.

Newer and less-intensive forms of voluntourism include the following:

- Hotel chains advertising that overnight guests may participate in a service project for a day at a time, both to do something charitable and as a different way of getting to know the people of the area being visited

- National and international conferences scheduling days of service during their event, again both to return some value to the host community and to offer conferees interaction with local citizens

- Families of employees of multinational organizations who live abroad for periods of time. The employee has a work permit, but in most countries, an accompanying spouse cannot work for pay. Volunteering is a viable option and can

provide organizations with some very skilled people who
may be in residence for as much as a year or more.

- Foreign exchange students who, again, may not earn money
on a student visa but can experience many new situations
outside the classroom through volunteer opportunities.

Finally, although it might be stretching the definition of *vacation* to
include this group, there are many people who own a seasonal home in
a warmer or cooler climate and who relocate each year for a few months
for the preferred climate. These folks not only still feel connected to their
permanent home but also develop a sense of belonging in the community
to which they return annually. They are rarely invited to volunteer and
may feel that no agency wants a temporary worker. Ironically, in today's
single-day-of-service culture, having a volunteer for three months and
knowing they'll be back next year is a welcome resource!

If you are working in an affiliate, chapter, or branch of a national
or international organization, this is a powerful idea worth formalizing.
Work with the other affiliates and your headquarters to make it part of
your culture that your supporters in one area know they are welcome to
transfer their involvement to a new location, whether for a season or, if
they move, permanently.

Court-Ordered Service

It has become customary for court systems to practice "alternative sentencing," in which an offender is given the option of completing a set number of hours of community service work in lieu of a fine or spending time
in prison or as an adjunct to probation or parole. The offenses committed
range from misdemeanors to more serious crimes, and the people range
from drunk drivers to embezzlers. There are many models of alternative
sentencing programs, but all are looking for organizations willing to offer
placements to program participants. (Note that the justice system has
long referred to this as "community service," a fact that confuses and con-
founds educators using that phrase to describe student projects.)

If you agree to accept court-referred volunteers, you will probably
need to set related policy. Here are some of the policy areas to consider:

- Whether you wish to place any limits on the nature of the
offense or on the minimum amount of hours in the sentence.
For example, it may not be cost-effective for you to orient

and place someone who has less than twenty hours of community service work to do, unless you have a number of short-term projects waiting to be tackled.

- How much you need to know of the person's court record before placing him/her. Who in your organization will be told of the person's sentence and for what reasons?

- How you will handle possible infringements of the placement agreement, should they occur. For example, after how many absences will the probation officer or other court contact be notified?

- Whether court-referred workers will be assigned to the same positions as other volunteers. How might this affect attitudes toward all volunteers?

Once again, use the volunteer office as the conduit for these court-referred workers. They are nonsalaried, temporary personnel who require screening, orienting, and so on, just as all other volunteers do. This is also a way to be sure the proper legal records are kept to verify the time served.

Interestingly, data on existing alternative sentencing programs indicate that a significant percentage of people referred by courts to do community service continue to be active as volunteers well after their mandatory time is over. This is a positive side effect for both the person and the organization.

Other Mandates

A number of states integrate community service into their unemployment and public assistance programs. Under such plans, recipients of public monies are expected to demonstrate that they are taking steps to become independent. Their options include attending school or a training program, taking a part-time job, or performing a certain number of "community service" hours as a volunteer. Ironically, other states legislate *against* volunteering by those receiving public funds because of the assumption that the time spent at the volunteer assignment takes away from the person's focus on finding a job.

If your state has a program under which people may do community service—or are mandated to do it—does this provide a pool of possible workers for your organization? Just as with the other government programs already discussed, especially court-ordered service, your agency may have to verify and report on the work done by someone in such a program.

Similarly, some states allow and even encourage people on extended or permanent disability leave to do volunteer work. Perhaps even more interesting, a small number of corporations has been pioneering the concept that, since they pay the bill for temporary disability leave, employees who are reasonably fit but not yet able to return to their regular jobs can be offered the chance or even required to volunteer in nonprofit agencies. The company sees this as a donation to the community, since they are funding the employee's time anyway.

Finally, there are government regulations stating that tenants in public housing projects must demonstrate that they are giving back to the community that is subsidizing their rent. For many years, these regulations were not enforced, but in some areas residents are being required to do some volunteer work each year to comply with the law.

As always, the question for you is, can you see any way to welcome and benefit from these potential resource pools?

Time Bank or Service Dollar Programs

Time banks, also called service dollar or time dollar programs, have been around for a while but are not widespread. They can be instituted in a particular geographic area, within a defined group of people, or under the auspices of one or a network of organizations. The simplest way to explain a time bank is as a form of barter or exchange. People do volunteer work and record the number of hours served with the time bank, which stores those records for a set period of time or indefinitely. Later, those people can "draw on" their banked hours to obtain services on *their* behalf from other volunteers in the system. In some areas, donated hours can be exchanged for local "currency"—paper scrip that is honored by area businesses for discounts and special offers. The international Time Banks Web site reports, "Time Banking is a social change movement in 22 countries and six continents."[13]

There are several theories behind time banks. One is the belief (not shared by all) that people are more likely to volunteer if there is something in it for them later. Another is that some groups, such as proud seniors privately dealing with financial problems, may be ashamed to ask for available assistance to which they are entitled; by giving them a chance to serve others first, they are more willing to let others serve them. The programs that offer buying power are attempting to leverage volunteering into economic development as well.

This is not the place to go into detail about time banks and such issues as the moral obligation to maintain the project over time for volunteers who signed on and gave service with the expectation of an exchange in the future. But you may want to find out if a time bank exists in your area, if you want to participate in some way, or even if you see a benefit to establishing one in your area or even for your own stakeholders.

A time bank can be set up for a limited time, such as one year. If you have many constituents who are likely to be mobilized by an invitation to participate in this type of exchange, try it (being clear that "unredeemed" hours will not be exchangeable after the year ends). Just be sure to have the necessary software and coordination to handle the program successfully.

Stipended Workers

At various times, your organization may have access to volunteers who receive a stipend for their work. The stipend is never more and often less than minimum wage and is intended to enable the person to give a considerable number of hours of service in lieu of a more lucrative job or as a supplement to a low income. Sometimes a living allowance for expenses is included. Most often such money comes from government programs, and usually the agency contributes some percentage of matching funds.

Stipended workers are considered part of the volunteer world because the amount of money they receive is always considerably less than the professional nature of the jobs they do would ordinarily command and because they choose to participate in such service for a set period of time (usually one to two years). The Peace Corps and VISTA pioneered such efforts; United Nations Volunteers (UNV), AmeriCorps, and others continue the tradition. The 2009 Edward M. Kennedy Serve America Act expands full-time, stipended "national service," as well as programs designed as income supplements, such as Foster Grandparents.

From the perspective of this book, the important thing is to consider, first, whether your agency wants to seek such special categories of workers. They do provide a considerable number of hours each week, with some continuity, as well as offer a generally enthusiastic participant. Second, recognize the stipended workers' similarity to volunteers, though in the majority of cases they will work with you full-time for as long as two years. Much as we just discussed regarding student interns, only the volunteer office has the system in place to orient and place people who do not fit into the conventional employment structure.

Funded Jobs Programs

There are a number of federal, state, and local government programs that pay participants a stipend or even a full salary to work in selected community agencies, most often as a form of job training. Such programs often are focused on a particular target population that is difficult to employ, such as teenagers, senior citizens, the disabled, or non-English speakers. As with the stipended forms of national service already mentioned, program models range from ones in which the recipient agency pays a percentage of the worker's salary to ones with no host financial obligation at all.

As CEO, you will need to make a determination as to which workers are to be considered employees and which volunteers. One reasonable approach would be to place any worker receiving financial payment from your organization under your personnel office, while placing non-remunerated workers under the volunteer office.

For bookkeeping purposes, this division on the basis of money works quite well, but there are other considerations to ensure smooth organizational functioning. If the special salaried workers are part time, not clearly skilled, or both, perhaps the director of volunteer involvement needs to be part of the assignment-making process regardless of who maintains chief responsibility for these workers. Once again, who else maintains an ongoing list of the available short-term work in the agency or is prepared to conduct an orientation at any time?

In addition, it is important to make sure that a temporary influx of stipended workers does not displace loyal volunteers. This does not mean that a new source of help should be turned down. It simply suggests that present volunteers should be considered in your planning process and should be approached for suggestions as to what they would most prefer doing, should they be "replaced" by paid newcomers.

Informal Volunteers

In the course of a program year, you may find that your organization benefits from the help of individuals who informally give a few hours of their time in some way (as you will have discovered if you conduct the inventory of current volunteers that I recommended in chapter two). Most often such volunteers are family members or friends of the staff or of current volunteers. And they frequently surface during major fundraising or public events, when your organization needs lots of support work such as carrying boxes, staffing booths, and cleaning up.

Such informal contributions are wonderful. The only caveat is to assess the situation and make sure that, if someone is really serving for many hours annually, you are not simply permitting loose management just because the person is not on the payroll. If someone can be identified as volunteering, perhaps the volunteer program office should enroll her/him more formally. This permits better engagement of the volunteer, inclusion in the thank-yous that follow an event, coverage by your insurance, and the most accurate documentation of community contributions to your organization.

Up to now, I have maintained the party line about defining volunteer work carefully, writing volunteer position descriptions, and maintaining some sort of structure. For most types of organizations, this is the best way to involve volunteers effectively—and not waste the staff's or the volunteer's time.

But there are other ways to be successful, too. Some settings or certain areas of work lend themselves to a much more relaxed, drop-in sort of approach that may attract a wider range of volunteers than anything else. For example, if you are doing a lot of outdoor work requiring many hands, why not send out the word that anyone and everyone who shows up on Saturday afternoons is welcome? Volunteer team captains should be recruited with position descriptions, training, and some longer-term commitment, but each week their labor pool will expand or contract and change. It is true that some weeks will see fewer volunteers than needed and other weeks more. But the goals of generating neighborhood enthusiasm, accomplishing a bit each week, and being welcoming to everyone can be met.

Not every organization will have work conducive to this throw-out-the-rules approach. But you may be surprised at what someone might be able to do to help if you are willing to loosen up. For example, can a volunteer bring a friend along one day even if that person has not applied or interviewed? For some assignments, the best risk management answer has to be no. But for a lot of other work, the answer might be yes. Just be sure you *make the decision to be informal* rather than lapse into it because no one is paying attention.

Vision

If the director of volunteer involvement is consistently seen as heading the organization's community resources office, the interrelationship of all the categories mentioned here becomes apparent. Once you have made the various executive decisions necessary to authorize the director of volunteer involvement to coordinate the full range of volunteers as just described, your organization will benefit from all available community resources on an ongoing basis.

Expect your volunteer involvement leader to do three things: proactively identify agency and client needs, apply volunteer management principles to design ways that people can address those needs, and then mobilize non-cash community resources to meet those needs. Whether you—or the people you recruit—use the label "volunteer" to describe what's happening does not matter at all. The challenge is to expand your organization's vision about sources of help.

This chapter has focused on the wide range of types of volunteers in all communities. An alternative perspective is to consider the differential needs of episodic or short-term volunteers from volunteers in long-term or ongoing opportunities. The Volunteer Involvement Framework™ presented in *Strategic Volunteer Involvement* is a helpful tool for considering the potential of the different volunteer contributions available to your organization.[14] In addition, the Volunteer Involvement Framework considers the unique characteristics of persons volunteering to bring a specific skill to an organization and how these may differ from volunteers open to serving in any needed capacity for which they are qualified.

To implement ideas in this chapter, see . . .

Leading the Way to Successful Volunteer Involvement: Practical Tools for Busy Executives by Betty B. Stallings with Susan J. Ellis (Philadelphia: Energize, Inc., 2010).

Idea stimulators, worksheets, step-by-step guides, and more in the following sections:

- Section 1: "Personal and Organizational Philosophy about Volunteering"
- Section 7: "Integrating Volunteers throughout the Organization"

Notes

1. University's Office of Survey Research for the RGK Center for Philanthropy and Community Service, *Volunteerism and Youth: Survey of Student Volunteerism at The University of Texas*, ServiceLeader.org, http://www .serviceleader.org/new/documents/articles/2003/04/000184.php.

2. I first heard the term *voluntold* used by Canadian colleague Anthea Hoare.

3. Energize, Inc., maintains a list of all volunteerism "days of service" and other events at http://www.energizeinc.com/prof-1.html.

4. To read more on A Billion + Change, see http://www.nationalservice .gov/about/initiatives/probono.asp.

5. A Billion + Change, "Summit on Corporate Volunteerism: Toward a New Definition of Pro Bono," http://www.nationalservice.gov/pdf/08_0211 _probono_case.pdf.

6. A Billion + Change, Web Site FAQs, http://www.nationalserviceresources .org/probonofaq.

7. Deloitte Development, LLC, "2009 Executive Summary: *Deloitte Volunteer IMPACT Survey*," p. 3. http://www.deloitte.com/assets/Dcom -UnitedStates/Local%20Assets/Documents/us_2009%20Volunteer %20IMPACT%20ExecSummary_050409.pdf.

8. For an example of the "charity badge" concept, see SixDegrees.org, http://www.sixdegrees.org.

9. Beth Gazley and Monica Dignam, *The Decision to Volunteer: Why People Give Their Time and How You Can Engage Them* (Washington, DC: ASAE & the Center for Association Leadership, 2008), 3.

10. James Dalton and Monica Dignam, *The Decision to Join: How Individuals Determine Value and Why They Choose to Belong* (Washington, DC: ASAE & the Center for Association Leadership, 2007), 3–4.

11. Gazely and Dignam, *The Decision to Volunteer.*

12. Ibid.

13. Time Banks Web site, http://www.timebanks.org/.

14. Sarah Jane Rehnborg and others, *Strategic Volunteer Engagement: A Guide for Nonprofit and Public Sector Leaders* (Austin, TX: RGK Center for Philanthropy and Community Service, the LBJ School of Public Affairs, the University of Texas at Austin, 2009).

8

Executive-Level Volunteers

Because direct service volunteers are usually on-site, seen, and heard during a routine workday, this group becomes the focus of volunteer management planning. But most organizations also benefit from volunteers engaged in other services: those who make or affect policy, provide expertise to build agency capacity, or raise funds. All nonprofit organizations and professional or trade associations have a board of directors whose members are volunteers. Many organizations also have an auxiliary or other fundraising body, usually organized as a self-led group of volunteers. As introduced in the previous chapter, pro bono volunteers donate their professional expertise through consultancies. Finally, a wide variety of advisory councils involve community members. For some units of government, such advisory councils may even be mandated by law as an opportunity for citizen participation.

As CEO, naturally you must relate to any and all volunteers supporting your mission. What's different with the groups and individuals in this chapter, however, is that, in almost all cases, the top executive is *the connecting link* between such volunteers and the rest of the organization. In this chapter, we'll examine how the principles relating to direct-service volunteers apply equally to these special volunteer roles.

The Board

A whole industry has developed to strengthen the effectiveness of non-profit boards of directors and teach boardsmanship. Most such books, articles, and training events are directed at the chief executive, but many are also designed for board members themselves. Although it is generally acknowledged that nonprofit board members are, in fact, volunteers, in practice the voluntary nature of boards is frequently overlooked. Are the successful practices of volunteer management applicable to boards of directors? Definitely, yes.

In chapter one, we examined the role of the board in developing the agency's philosophy of volunteerism, setting goals for volunteer involvement, and providing oversight of volunteer participation. In this chapter, we are concerned about helping the board itself to be most effective as a group of active volunteers, a goal that clearly involves your leadership, as executive.

Recruitment and Position Descriptions

Recruitment of new board members can be done by following the model of how to recruit direct-service volunteers. Targeting potential sources of board members on the basis of special skills needed or type of representation sought is one way to find the right people. Similarly, having a written position description to show candidates will clarify what your organization expects of *each* individual board member. For board officers, additional pages are needed to describe the requirements of each leadership position. By using such descriptions at the start of a board member's term, you are able to hold people to their commitments—whether this involves attendance at board meetings, follow-up activities during any given month, or an annual financial contribution.

There is a misconception that an organization's bylaws already provide role descriptions for board volunteers. The bylaws define *functions* and division of responsibility but do not specify the practical, operational aspects of being a board member. Also, the bylaws deal with functions that are continuous and timeless. Position descriptions, which should be updated regularly, apportion tasks necessary at any given point in time.

Be honest in writing board member position descriptions. Do not underestimate the time commitment involved in serving on the board. Remember to mention the work expected of board members in between regular board meetings, including preparing in advance for the meetings and serving on subcommittees.

If you hope for—or expect—a financial contribution from every board member, say so. It is reasonable to ask the board to demonstrate their support of the organization with a donation or by some fundraising activity. By openly stating this expectation, you can later solicit money from board volunteers more comfortably.

Developing Effective Working Relationships

Orientation and training are as important for board members as for any other volunteers. Regardless of the expertise for which the board member was recruited, no one is able to walk into a new situation and start being productive without learning the details of that particular situation. It is never insulting to offer board members the opportunity to learn about your organization—and someone who resents such a session is probably an inappropriate recruit.

In your role as chief executive, you will be providing leadership to the board in ways that are very different from supervising in-house volunteers. One major difference is that the board is in charge; they have the final legal responsibility for the way your organization operates. Authority and power rest with them (even if some boards rarely exercise their power), including the right to hire and fire the chief executive. Even more sobering is the realization that the board of directors can legally make the decision to close the entire agency. Some boards make that decision by default, by not raising sufficient funds. But occasionally boards make the active choice to end services, which may reflect the happy fact that those services may no longer be needed.

In order to make the best decisions, board members need your executive direction and advice, particularly in identifying the most pressing issues for the organization at any given time. Your most effective tool is persuasion—explaining and convincing the board of your point of view. You also need to provide resources with which board volunteers can accomplish tasks, explain how their work integrates with the rest of the agency's timetables, and also monitor that board work is getting done. All this requires setting a tone of harmony and energy—"leading from behind" as you motivate board volunteers to give their utmost to the organization.

Periodically, it is nice to provide some recognition to board members for their hard work on behalf of the agency. It is too easy to become wrapped up in the problems of today and overlook the achievements of the past year. Again, because board members are volunteers, doing something to say thank you is always valid.

In some smaller (and even larger) organizations, board members become active in the daily work of providing services. In fact, the traditional way nonprofit organizations grow is that board members do *everything* in the beginning—from making policy to cleaning the office. Later, when funds are raised, a small corps of salaried staff takes over the operational side of the agency and the board redefines its role to goal and policy setting. This transition is not always accomplished without pain. It is hard for board members to relinquish control over activities they handled before the staff came on board. To some board volunteers, the hands-on work is more interesting than the policy decision making and they prefer doing what they see as practical things.

On one level, it is healthy for board members to have some firsthand exposure to the work of the organization. It is questionable how a board can make decisions without some reality testing of the possible effect of certain actions. Also, needs assessment cannot be done objectively if all the data are funneled through the CEO's perspective only.

In a membership association or any organization in which the board is representative of the major stakeholders, it may also be necessary to decide who is the spokesperson in different situations. As the full-time, paid executive, you obviously are deeply engaged in day-to-day management and therefore have detailed knowledge of operational facts. But you may not *represent* the cause or mission the way your board members do. The voice of any professional society must be members of that profession, not someone who is an association manager. This can be muddied if the person filling the role of executive also has experience in the same profession.

Here's a true story. A number of years ago, I presented a workshop for the National Council of Jewish Women (NCJW) in Essex County, New Jersey. When I arrived, their executive director introduced herself to me with a very Irish-sounding name. At lunch, I learned that she was not Jewish, and she asked me if I could figure out why she was hired. It turned out that, during her job interview, she told the committee, "By hiring me, you will know that there will never be a situation in which it will not be crystal clear who should speak for NCJW. I'll be a competent executive; you take whatever positions you feel are right." Quite profound, no?

You and the board must establish the boundary line between yourselves in your own way, based on the needs of the organization at this point in its history and on the personalities and skills of the individuals involved. But it is important for you to recognize that roles must be *defined*. If some board members volunteer on-site on a regular schedule, then they should have a discrete volunteer position description during those periods they wear a different hat, and they are accountable to the responsible paid employee. The dual demands of authority figure and direct worker should be clearly separated.

Subcommittees of the Board

Depending on the type of subcommittees your board has designated, certain employees may be assigned as liaison staff to support the committees' work. This interface requires clarification of roles. For example, will the staff member be a voting member of the committee or serve ex officio? For that matter, is the staff member expected to participate fully in discussions or merely be present to act as a resource when requested?

The matter of who takes the minutes (both for the full board meeting and for subcommittees) deserves examination. Because this task seems clerical, it is common for volunteers to delegate this to paid staff. Unfortunately, this serves to assign the "power of the pen" (or keyboard) to the staff. Minutes present not only facts but also subjective interpretation of what was discussed. The written record of a meeting continues to influence the organization. Volunteers should retain the responsibility for reporting their own deliberations and decisions.

There are no clearly right or wrong ways to develop working relationships between the board and the staff. The variables of each organization must be considered. But the volunteer management principle of *defining* how the team will operate is something that only you, as executive, can employ.

One last point about board subcommittees: they can have members who are not voting members of the board. These volunteers may bring extra skills to the committee or may be in the process of grooming to accept a seat on the board eventually. Either way, both the committee chair and the liaison staff member need to be alert to how this nonboard volunteer is welcomed onto the committee, brought up to speed, and integrated into the committee's work—not to mention, thanked!

How the Director of Volunteer Involvement Can Help

The director of volunteer involvement can be a real asset to you in building the board. Ironically, too few CEOs think of this position in this context—yet who in the organization knows more about the demands of working with volunteers? Specifically, the director of volunteer involvement can help you in the following ways:

- Because the director of volunteer involvement is out in the community, s/he can be of assistance to the board nominating committee in suggesting possible candidates to join the board. Further, the director of volunteer involvement can identify active, committed line volunteers who might be valuable board recruits because of their firsthand understanding of how the organization functions and also because they may have exactly the expertise and experience you need.

- The director of volunteer involvement has lots of experience in writing volunteer position descriptions. Why not put this skill to work for the board?

- When designing an orientation for new board members, why start from scratch? The director of volunteer involvement has already developed a curriculum, handouts, and perhaps even audiovisual aids that s/he uses to orient in-house volunteers. Most of this material will be equally applicable to board members, and you can add whatever other information you need.

- The work contributed by board members should be included in any agency volunteer recognition event. To this end, the volunteer office could assist you in keeping records of board member activities so that each board volunteer can be recognized for his/her special contributions. Any person who volunteers for the organization is a valuable resource— whether that voluntary service is given directly to your consumers or indirectly through policy making.

- Finally, as just discussed, board subcommittees may be composed entirely of board members or of a mixture of board members and nonboard volunteers. The director of volunteer involvement can certainly recruit nonboard volunteers to join such committees and can train salaried staff to provide liaison support to these committees. This is simply another version of good staff-volunteer relationships.

There is no reason to think of board members and other organizational volunteers as completely different. Both groups are community members and, in their own ways, have influence and clout.

How the Board Can Help Volunteer Involvement

Apart from the critical governance issues discussed in chapter one, there are a number of ways that board members can support volunteer involvement. Depending on the stage of development of your strategy and of its present staffing, there may be a need for a board subcommittee called something like the "Volunteer Resources Committee." It can help establish policy for in-house volunteers, assist in recruiting volunteers, and take an active role in evaluating community engagement.

Even without such a committee, individual board members can be called on to make community presentations about the agency, perhaps combining appeals for funds and for volunteer participation. Members can be asked for referrals to sources of volunteers (such as an entree into a professional society) or, particularly if a board member is an executive of a large business, asked to open channels for recruitment (such as publicizing volunteer opportunities in various company communiqués). Finally, board members should be invited to volunteer recognition events for the dual purpose of being thanked and demonstrating the top-level support of agency decision makers for frontline volunteers.

Friends Groups and Auxiliaries

Quite diverse types of nonprofit and public settings utilize auxiliaries, friends groups, and other sorts of self-led associations of supporters, including hospitals, long-term care institutions, libraries, cultural arts groups, parks, law enforcement agencies, and more. Auxiliaries can be independently incorporated or more informally structured; they can be governed by officers elected by their members or report to someone on the staff of the agency. Sometimes members do in-house volunteer work, even coordinating volunteer services before a director of volunteer involvement is hired. But most often, the major purpose of an auxiliary or "Friends of ___ " group is to raise money.

Historically, auxiliaries were responsible for the funding of most of the institutions we hold dear. Also, historically, auxiliaries were female organizations—frequently the wives of the staff or of the board members. In most cases, the auxilians raised the money and turned it over to the decision makers of the sponsoring group. In other cases, the auxilians participated in determining how the money would be spent. These two approaches still exist today. In some organizations, the president of the auxiliary has a seat on the board of directors.

There are many who believe that auxiliaries are a holdover from the past and on their way to extinction. The very term *auxiliary* sounds like a diminutive, and certainly all-female volunteer fundraisers helping all-male paid staff is unacceptable.

Another problem is what is called "aging in place," in which a group was started by supporters decades ago who loved the socializing opportunity and never concerned themselves with growing or diversifying their membership. The result is that, today, the group has advanced in age, no longer has a core of active participants, makes less and less money, and can't find anyone to be an officer.

If this scenario sounds familiar, please face an uncomfortable fact: you (or your predecessors) have *allowed* the situation to deteriorate by being unwilling to become engaged in dealing with the problems as they evolved. Whether out of appreciation for the group's past contributions, not wanting to offend anyone and cause a public relations nightmare, or simple dislike of what may seem like petty internal squabbling, far too many executives look the other way. Yet this group is operating in your organization's name and represents you to the community.

It is possible to have a successful friends group, if you know what its purpose is and are willing to set up mutually determined guidelines, clear chains of authority, and open lines of communication. As executive, you can lead the process by posing and answering these key questions:

1. Is the interrelationship of this auxiliary (or whatever you name this self-governing group) and your agency clearly defined? Is the auxiliary independently incorporated and therefore autonomous, or do you, as sponsor, have some formal decision-making role to play in its governance?

2. If the auxiliary is not self-incorporated, what is the parent organization's responsibility or liability in terms of tax reporting, auditing, and so on? Whose tax identification number is being used for the auxiliary's bank account? To whom do the bank accounts really belong?

3. Who are the members of the auxiliary? What are the criteria for joining, and are new members recruited with these criteria in mind? Does the auxiliary perpetuate exclusionary practices such as limiting membership only to women, to people able to pay membership dues, or other rules? If so, are these discriminatory practices justifiable?

4. Is the auxiliary still strong, or is it a remnant of its old self from years ago, with members aging fast and no longer able to give or generate financial contributions comparable to those in the past?

5. Is there an actual or implied hierarchy in which the auxiliary has more status than the in-house volunteers?

6. What is the relationship between the auxiliary officers and the director of volunteer involvement? Is there a direct line of authority (in what direction)? Why or why not? (Similarly, is there a clear relationship between the auxiliary and the development office?)

7. Does the auxiliary president expect and receive direct communication with you as CEO? Why or why not?

8. If your friends group organizes major revenue-producing events on behalf of your agency, how do these activities mesh with the projected plans of your development staff or special event staff? Are plans determined mutually in advance? Who has the final say over theme, ticket prices, and other elements of the event that might affect your organization's public image? Who keeps the records and submits reports (and to whom)? Who thinks about insurance and other legal issues? Who sends thank-you notes when an event is over?

9. Do you receive regular reports from the auxiliary on all aspects of its operation, including membership statistics and financial statements?

Unless you clarify these types of questions in advance, you may someday discover that this year's auxiliary leaders have a very different point of view about what to do (in your organization's name) than you ever anticipated.

As mentioned earlier, if your organization is partnering or merging with another agency or facility, does this affect two or more friends groups? The politics of mergers are delicate in the best of cases, so it is important to consider all the affected constituents. There are no standard ways to assure the success of combined or separate-but-equal auxiliaries, but it is always a mistake to assume unquestioned loyalty, especially to a restructured institution. Invite supporter group leaders to develop the best strategies with you, and they will develop ownership of the process.

Interrelationships

How you communicate together is a matter of situational management. If you are working with a strong, viable auxiliary that raises lots of money for your organization, certain ways of interacting will derive from the situation. Also, if the auxiliary is clearly focused solely on fundraising, it is easy to draw the line between auxilian volunteers and in-house, direct service volunteers. In fact, in that type of separation, any auxilian who *also* wants to become involved in direct service should be interviewed and placed into a volunteer assignment through the volunteer office, as would any other nonauxilian volunteer. When working on-site, that person would be a docent, patient escort, teen group leader, or whatever volunteer title applies. Her/his additional role as an auxilian would not affect the in-house volunteer function.

As mentioned before, in some facilities, the auxiliary runs the direct-service volunteer program. This may be quite workable, but avoid the requirement that anyone who wants to volunteer has to *join the auxiliary*. This is one way to perpetuate discrimination and outmoded tradition, especially if there are special criteria for becoming an auxiliary member. The very word *join* connotes dues, annual renewals, and other features of an association that have nothing to do with tackling a specific work assignment with an observable outcome.

Perhaps more importantly, few auxiliaries are able to accommodate the type of volunteer who wants to come in for one month to recatalogue your library or who is on call to help with press releases when needed. These types of assignments are rarely filled by people seeking to join the auxiliary or wanting the additional social aspects of group activities or even membership meetings. As CEO, you can establish guidelines to assure that any qualified person wanting to offer volunteer help is encouraged to apply rather than being turned down at the first contact because s/he does not qualify as an auxilian.

At the extreme end of the spectrum, there are even scenarios in which the auxiliary actually pays the salary of the director of volunteer involvement. This almost always creates a multiheaded monster. Is the salary a designated donation to the facility over which you have complete control? Or does the auxiliary, as donor, have any say in who should be hired, at what salary, or other managerial decisions? Even more complicated are questions of whether this new staff member is now permanently on your payroll or theirs, to whom the manager answers, which one of you sets goals for the year and then evaluates performance, and so on.

Revitalizing a Weak Auxiliary

The real challenge to you as executive is the situation in which you have a weakening auxiliary and a growing, vital in-service volunteer program. You will have to examine the possible risks involved in placing the auxiliary under the jurisdiction of the volunteer office or the development office in an effort either to retire the group or to build it up again.

Facilities in inner-city areas have in recent years seen a trend in auxiliaries whose members never set foot in the actual agency—who prefer, in fact, to keep several miles between themselves and the concrete reality of the problems the facility is trying to address. Again, some of these volunteer groups are successful in raising a great deal of money through suburban thrift shops, elegant dinners, and other events and receive publicity and status for their efforts. This fundraising is vital and should not be denigrated because the volunteers disassociate themselves from the recipients of service. However, it is only fair to give comparable credit to those volunteers who, though not wealthy contributors, are willing to come on-site, roll up their sleeves, and work directly with daily service delivery. This type of personal involvement deserves some status, too.

Given today's volunteering climate, the concept of an auxiliary only makes sense if you feel that you want to maintain a fundraising group with a sense of unity. The social aspects of auxiliaries are indeed important to accomplishing the work, for many fundraising events require long hours of service and it is much more pleasant to volunteer in the company of friends. But you should expect the auxiliary to set goals, submit reports, and make a visible contribution.

It is legitimate to question low performance. After all, the auxiliary only exists to support your organization, even if the members have evolved an "us and them" mentality. Unfortunately, because some auxilians are wealthy or influential, executives may be reluctant to "make waves" by challenging the status quo. Further complicating this may be discomfort at seeming to criticize older women. The real problem in too many cases is that auxilians were left to their own devices years ago, and it is difficult to recapture a good working relationship after so much neglect.

As the top administrator, you establish the standards. Auxilian volunteers deserve to know how they can be of most help, just as other types of volunteers should be recognized for their equally vital contributions to the organization. Ultimately, it is the agency's image in the community that is most affected if an auxiliary or friends group is allowed to atrophy.

Face facts. If a once-vital auxiliary has atrophied beyond repair, it may be time to celebrate past accomplishments, elevate remaining members to emeritus status, and disband the group to make room for something new. Or, allow the existing group to do less and less while forming a parallel but up-to-date association alongside it. Then put most of your time and energy into supporting the new volunteers and avoiding the mistakes of the past.

Volunteers Directly Reporting to You

In chapter six, I noted that one way to promote teamwork between employees and volunteers was to be a role model yourself in working directly with volunteers. Then, in chapter seven, I described the wide spectrum of ways that people of all types might contribute their services to your organization. Any of them might report to you and other top executives directly, depending on the assignment or project. Here are a few examples:

- *Pro bono consultants.* The more sophisticated the project or the more integrated with strengthening your organization's infrastructure or management capacity, the more likely that a highly skilled volunteer will need a liaison at a high-enough level to make decisions, provide resources, and implement necessary changes. This is what happens when you pay outside experts. Auditors, evaluators, software designers, and the like are rarely asked to work solely with frontline staff. Because you will be recruiting volunteers with the skills needed for the goals of pro bono consultancies, focus on what the work requires, not the pay scale of the person doing it.

- *Senior fundraisers.* Whether a member of the board or not, any individual who is capable of reaching out to major donors, convincing foundations to give you grant money, or organizing high-return events is a volunteer you want to nurture—and that means periodic attention from the highest level of the organization.

- *Volunteers with skills you need to do* your *work.* Depending on what's happening at any moment—and on your own skill set—the sky's the limit in terms of the strategic assistance the right volunteer can offer. Consider such tasks as the following:

  - *Speechwriting* or other ghostwriting—at a minimum, interviewing you for what you want to say and producing a draft for you to refine; also, someone who can create professional-looking presentations

  - *Being a cyber deputy*—trolling the Internet to keep you current on whatever topics or issues you identify

  - *Industrial spying*—visiting community agencies or attending civic meetings as a "member of the public" and then reporting back to you. This isn't meant as an underhanded activity. It's a test of how someone who is not an official representative might be treated by others. Think of it like a food critic who orders a meal incognito.

  - *Surveying*—asking questions of any stakeholders, formally or informally, on your behalf and then reporting on the findings

  - *Participating in focus groups and think tanks.* You already know that volunteers represent a real cross-section of the community, so periodically convene some of them as your eyes and ears. Cluster invitations to these discussion sessions by characteristics such as age, gender, length of residency in the area, profession, or any other perspective you want to examine.

  - *Researching almost anything*, such as identifying local economic and demographic data to alert you to possible trends or doing prospect hunting for potential donors

  - *Reading* through the growing stack of professional journals in your office and annotating articles of direct interest to your setting

  - *Creating budgets* and other proposals with three scenarios: worst-case, reasonably expected, and blue-sky, offering pros and cons of each

    ○ *Advising* on anything: strategic planning, pricing models for community services, investments and financial sustainability, and more

    ○ *Training* for paid and unpaid staff on any topic, from customer service to data management

    ○ *Coaching* you to advance in your executive skills

Note that the more creative you are in seeing volunteers as true resources, the better a role model you become for everyone else in the organization. Colleen Kelly, executive director of Volunteer Vancouver/ Vantage Point, ironically notes "how much easier the CEO's job is if she is smart enough to really engage volunteers, and not just endure the ones she *has* to work with: her board!"[1]

Advisory Councils

As with boards of directors and auxiliaries, advisory councils are special categories of volunteers with direct relationship to you as the CEO. If you are heading a unit of government, you may be working with a legally mandated advisory council or commission including some or all members designated by virtue of their public positions or appointed by political leaders. Or you may have a council voluntarily established by your agency to gain more community input. Either way, members of your advisory council will respond most productively to motivating behavior on your part.

    Clear expectations are imperative. Just because you have an "advisory" council does not mean that anyone has promised to use the advice given! Take the time to define exactly what the role of the advisory group is—and what it is not. Do not imply power when there is none. Most advisory groups have an impact through influence and persuasion rather than through decision-making authority.

    For this reason, it is good to avoid the use of the word *board* in relation to *advisors*. When someone joins a group called the "Advisory Board," there may be an implication of authority well beyond anything intended. Designations such as "Advisory Council" or "Community Representative Task Force" are more accurate.

    If what you really want is a group of people to actively manage a project or do hands-on work, don't mislabel them as an advisory council. Call them a steering committee, leadership team, or anything else that acknowledges them as a working body.

Conversely, if your main reason for creating this body is to honor past presidents and big donors or to get influential people to permit you to use their names on letterhead, also do not call this an advisory council. Dream up an honorific such as "Emeritus Council" or "Vital Supporters Circle," and be clear with the members and with the public what the group does and doesn't do.

Using the Principles of Volunteer Management

Recruitment of members onto an advisory council should be done with the same consideration as the recruitment of any other volunteers. Criteria for membership should be determined and a process instituted for interviewing, screening, and orienting candidates and new members. Clarify whether a person serves as an advisor because of her/his personal credentials or by virtue of a position s/he holds. If the latter, does the individual automatically resign if s/he changes jobs? A written role description for each member, with additional tasks for council officers, is also a critical tool. Be sure to indicate terms of office or else you may imply that advisors serve forever. The director of volunteer involvement can be of assistance to you in this process, just as described in working effectively with the board of directors.

Getting the Best Advice

If you have formed an advisory council, utilize it! People who have volunteered prefer to be active than to see their names used on letterhead for political clout without having had any input into what the organization is doing.

One of the obstacles to genuine involvement of advisory councils is the feeling that the only way to activate them is to call a group meeting. Ironically, full council meetings tend to work contrary to the goal of getting advice. Most advisors have been recruited because they represent a specific constituency: an ethnic group, neighborhood, profession, funding source, or other stakeholders. In a group meeting, these very different people attempt to reach consensus on issues. In the process of reaching consensus, special interest and minority opinions are overlooked or played down. But, as executive, it is often those very minority opinions that you most wanted advice about!

There are two ways to counteract this tendency to make the advisory council function as a group. One is to ask advisor volunteers to provide service in two distinct ways: participate in one or two group meetings of the full advisory council per year and also spend a few hours consulting with you one-to-one. Sometimes what you need is the perspective of someone with a very specific point of view. You can best gain this information individually—group meetings will dilute the opinions of any one particular advisor.

The other way to assure the benefit of many diverse points of view is to make sure advisory council meetings *never take a vote*. Taking a vote implies that the council can make policy, which it cannot, so allowing the majority to express only one opinion is misleading anyway. Instead of trying to distill all members' perspectives into one, try the following:

- Get the council to list all the *pros and cons* of any idea under discussion.

- Have the group generate a list of all the *questions* they can think of in reaction to a particular issue (sometimes a good question is more valuable than a lengthy statement of opinion).

- Ask for the minutes to reflect the "minority opinion," just as the Supreme Court will publish the perspective of those justices who disagree with the ruling of the Court.

- Ask council members to suggest community *resources* that might assist with a particular project.

You will get a great deal of useful advice while making advisor volunteers feel recognized for their input. Another approach is to hash out ideas through an online discussion forum, which also has the benefit of permitting contributions from experts anywhere in the world, at a time convenient to them.

If your advisory council has been selected for its high degree of professional expertise, you may occasionally want the group to give you the benefit of their specific knowledge and instruct you on what course of action to take. In such special cases, taking a vote may be desirable. But differentiate between those situations in which you want general advice and those in which you are, in essence, delegating decision making. Otherwise, the advisors will assume that all their input carries the weight of giving instructions, which is probably not the case.

You do not have to establish an advisory body as a standing committee. In fact, it is sometimes most useful to recruit advisors for an ad hoc, time-limited task force focused on one particular need for expertise. Tasks could range from advising on site selection for a new building to the design of an evaluation study.

Finally, be sure everyone understands the difference between the roles of any advisory council and the organization's board of directors. For example, does the advisory council advise you, as administrator, or the board, as governors? Lines of authority can quickly become blurred, especially if you routinely encourage volunteers such as past board presidents to continue their service to your agency by joining the advisory council. Because you are the one person with a leadership role in both groups, you can demonstrate the differences between them by the way you plan each set of agendas, deliver reports to each group, and so on.

To implement ideas in this chapter, see . . .

Leading the Way to Successful Volunteer Involvement: Practical Tools for Busy Executives by Betty B. Stallings with Susan J. Ellis (Philadelphia: Energize, Inc., 2010).

Idea stimulators, worksheets, step-by-step guides, and more in the following section:

- Section 8: "The Board's Role in Volunteer Engagement"

Note

1. Colleen Kelly, executive director of Volunteer Vancouver/Vantage Point, in a margin note while reviewing the manuscript of this book, November 2009.

9

Risk, Liability, and Other Legal Issues

Some of the issues that arise from the involvement of volunteers relate to risk management practices and questions of law. There are real legal concerns regarding the liability of and for volunteers, while other issues are quasi-legal in nature. Because of the seriousness of such questions, they require executive involvement.

The *principles* discussed in this chapter are universal and worth considering no matter where you are located. But the *legal* perspective here is American, though laws can differ state to state (we try to note when local regulations need to be checked). Readers outside the United States are urged to learn about the laws in their own countries for what is and is not permitted for them.

I urge you not to let this chapter scare you off from involving volunteers. Volunteers are *not* inherently riskier than employees, nor more accident-prone. It is always good management practice to consider risk prevention and minimization, but please do not slip into risk *avoidance*. There are consequences both for doing something and for *not* doing something. If fear of risk stops you from turning to volunteers as a resource completely, you will lose all the potential benefits of their contributions.

Keep in mind that discussions of potential legal problems always center on worst-case scenarios. As you weigh your options for the utilization of volunteers, objectively analyze the range of difficult situations that could occur and the likelihood of their occurrence. Consider each volunteer assignment category separately. Are the possible problems (and their potential cost) so great that they begin to offset the benefits your organization derives from various volunteer activities? In most cases, you will probably conclude that the net effect of volunteer involvement is positive enough to justify working with volunteers, though you might take precautions to prevent the occurrence of any worst-case situation.

Most legal questions pertaining to volunteers apply equally to employees. Just as you do not allow complex potential legal difficulties to inhibit you from hiring salaried personnel, the existence of similar legal questions should not become a roadblock to the utilization of volunteers.

Risks in Volunteer Activities

There are risk exposures in virtually every endeavor, including volunteer activities. Such exposures must be addressed so that volunteers can support the organization's mission. They *can* be addressed successfully by any volunteer-involving organization that commits to doing it systematically and continually. The ideal approach involves a combination of identifying risks, evaluating their severity, reducing or eliminating the most serious ones, and transferring certain risks to one or more insurance companies. Addressing risks in volunteer involvement should be undertaken as part of a comprehensive risk management program for the organization.

William R. Henry, Jr., longtime director of the Volunteers Insurance Service (VIS), wrote a Self-Instruction Guide for the *Everyone Ready*® online training program titled *Insurance and Risk Management Issues for Volunteer Programs: What Every Decision Maker Should Know*. He introduces the topic by speaking plainly:

> *Volunteers Don't Come with Safety Features Preinstalled.*
> It is likely that your volunteers are motivated primarily by their support of the organization's mission and not by the fact that they possess particular skills. They might or might not have those skills or the judgment required to make good decisions while on duty. In order for them to perform effectively, you need to make certain that they are prepared

to work safely and make the right call when judgment is required. It is the organization's responsibility to create an environment where volunteers are carefully selected and trained, where they can work without unnecessary risk to themselves or others, and where they understand their responsibilities in the event problems arise that threaten their own safety or the safety of others.

Volunteers Know They Have Risks.
Volunteers know that, with some jobs they are called upon to perform, there is a risk that they will be injured, or might be sued by someone claiming that the volunteer injured them, damaged their property or caused them some other harm. State and federal volunteer "immunity" statutes offer very limited protection. The nonprofit organization hoping to attract and retain volunteers can help its cause by assuring current and potential volunteers that it is addressing these concerns in an appropriate way—both in operations and in the insurance protection it provides.[1]

Henry advises writing a risk management policy statement to underscore that the effort to limit risk is important and supported by senior staff and the board. He offers this sample policy from The CIMA Companies, Inc., which administers VIS, advising each organization to customize it for its own situation:

(Name of organization) is subject to certain risks that affect our ability to operate, serve customers and protect assets. These include risks to employees and volunteers, liability to others, and risks to property.

Controlling these risks through a formal program is necessary for the well-being of the organization and everyone in it. The jobs and services the organization provides, the safety of the workplace and other benefits all depend to an extent on our ability to control risks.

Management has the ultimate responsibility to control risks. Control includes making decisions regarding which risks are acceptable and how to address those that are not. Those decisions can be made only with the participation of the entire workforce, because each of us understands the risks of his or her own tasks better than anyone else in the organization. Each is responsible for reporting any unsafe conditions he or she sees. Also, each is encouraged to suggest ways in which we can operate more safely. We are committed to the careful consideration of everyone's suggestions, and to taking appropriate action to address risks.

Accidents and other situations involving loss or near-loss will be investigated as part of the effort to manage risks.

Every employee's and volunteer's performance will be evaluated, in part, according to how he or she complies with this policy.[2]

Fear of being sued is a great motivator for implementing risk management practices. But litigation ought not to be the driving factor. It is right and proper for an organization to want to keep its clientele, employees, and volunteers safe and to protect its assets. Chances are that you have already worked on reducing risks in other areas. If you haven't done so already, now is the time to add consideration of volunteers to your ongoing risk management.

A Systematic Review of Risks

Organizations do risk management all the time, whenever they screen, train, manage performance, check in with a client, fix a loose handrail, and so on. But

they just do it rather haphazardly. And when a hazard comes to light, responses are more often rushed and ill-conceived knee jerks rather than well-reasoned and measured strategies. Looking closely at roles, functions, and responsibilities, identifying, evaluating (both likelihood of occurrence and magnitude of harm), and—in a deliberate, conscious and orderly fashion—planning to reduce and otherwise manage risks is strongly advisable wherever volunteers undertake responsible/ risky work or are placed in positions of trust.

This is the assessment of Linda Graff, shared in an e-mail after reviewing this manuscript. Her important book, *Better Safe . . . Risk Management in Volunteer Programs & Community Service*,[3] recommends that organizations take the systematic route—*before* an accident, loss, or tragedy materializes. The book provides a practical, step-by-step guide to undertaking such a process. There are even off-the-shelf risk management systems available that are very helpful guides.

Control

Whether stated directly or not, many of the questions asked about volunteers center on the concern for control, as in, "But I won't be able to control volunteers!" To which I often reply, "And are you under the delusion that you can control employees?" Round two goes as follows:

"But I can fire an employee." My retort: "If you have to fire someone, you obviously lost control first."

Legitimately, administrators want to be confident that their staff members provide services in accordance with the policies of the organization. Such confidence is bolstered by the belief that there is a clearly understood system of rewards for doing the job right and consequences for doing it wrong.

When managing employees, rewards available include a pay raise, a promotion, more vacation time, or some other tangible demonstration of positive recognition. Consequences are also tangible and range from withholding a pay raise to the ultimate threat of termination of employment. In the last analysis, both top executives and line workers feel that it is the threat of being fired—the mere possibility of it—that keeps employees "in line."

This is the crux of the debate about volunteers and control. What threat can an organization hold over the head of a volunteer that is as controlling as losing one's income?

This question reflects a number of interesting attitudes. First, it indicates the managerial perspective that the threat of punishment is the best motivator for generating good work. Second, it confuses the available punishment with a guarantee of *prevention* of some unwanted behavior. And third, it neglects the important fact that the initial reasons why the volunteer chose to come to the agency had nothing to do with a salary.

Managerially, it is more effective to govern through rewards than through negative consequences. Recognizing and visibly showing appreciation for work done right is far more motivating to everyone on staff than responding only to negative acts. Clearly, it is possible to reward volunteers in a variety of tangible ways similar to recognition of employees, including promotion to more responsible assignments.

For some paid workers, the fear of being fired or even of a lesser consequence will indeed stop them from doing something wrong. But the person who no longer cares about the organization, is too weak to resist temptation, or believes him/herself clever enough to avoid detection will act despite any threat to his/her job. Also, many acts you as an administrator may consider "wrong" may be done in innocence, out of ignorance, or through strong personal convictions that happen to differ from the agency position. It is therefore a delusion to think that it is possible to prevent wrongdoing through the threat of punishment.

The best way to feel confident about control of the organization's service providers is to start with careful screening of employees—and volunteers—at the time they apply to the organization. This includes clarifying expectations on both sides, particularly about any areas of service that might involve philosophic points of view. It is perfectly acceptable to write and cosign a letter of agreement spelling out such things as purpose of the volunteer work, anticipated outcomes or products, length of commitment, and other key mutual decisions reached in the application and interview process. Just be sure that this document includes a description of what the organization, in turn, is promising to give the volunteer.

Another tool to assure compliance with the organization's rules is training. Both employees and volunteers deserve full instruction on how to do their work in the best way. This whole process is then reinforced by supervision and evaluation, including positive recognition for doing the job well. Even with this approach, prevention of problems cannot be guaranteed, but the likelihood of wrongdoing is not determined by who receives a salary and who does not.

For employees, the threat of being fired carries the fear of loss of income. While money is not a factor for volunteers, the idea of no longer being allowed to participate in the work they care so much about is equally threatening. Losing the chance to be involved matters a great deal.

Yes, this means it is possible to "fire" a volunteer.

Some administrators harbor the nightmare that if they tried to fire a volunteer, that person would simply say, "You can't tell me to leave; I'm a volunteer." First, the chances of this happening are so remote that it should never stop you from terminating a volunteer. The person who tries to argue with you probably has some other problem, be it an ax to grind or mental illness. Most healthy people would never stay in a place where they were no longer wanted. Second, from a legal standpoint, you do indeed have the right to designate who will be an agent of your organization—whether paid or not. Under any circumstance, document the reasons for firing the volunteer, just as you would do with an employee.

In short, control is really not dependent on paying a wage. Your best management approach for paid staff and volunteers alike is to motivate through approval.

Confidentiality

This subject is closely linked to control and, in fact, is often raised as a smokescreen to hide the underlying fear that volunteers are uncontrollable. Confidentiality is an important and serious issue, but it is a *training* issue, not one tied to paid versus voluntary employment.

Volunteers should be screened and trained to understand the meaning of client confidentiality and the necessity of maintaining it. In fact, violation of confidentiality should be stated as cause for immediate dismissal. However, whether or not a person gossips has nothing to do with level of pay. Volunteers are no more prone to speak about a case outside of the agency than are employees. In fact, the probability may even be less. Volunteers rarely discuss their volunteer work with their friends (one of the reasons why so many members of the public harbor the mistaken belief that no one volunteers anymore!), while salaried staff, especially those in various professions, are more likely to describe the happenings of their week in a social context. Further, volunteers come in contact with clients for a few hours a week, while employees spend forty hours a week with the agency's consumers. So who has more to talk about?

Any agent of the organization deserves to have access to whatever records or information are necessary in order to accomplish her/his assigned tasks. Conversely, this means that no one should be allowed to peruse records not relevant to an assigned case or to eavesdrop on other workers' activities. Both of these principles should apply equally to employees and volunteers. You do not give any and all employees access to client records. For example, the maintenance department would hardly have a good reason to read counseling case records. Just as you are able to differentiate which employees may be given confidential information, you can select which volunteers require such data to complete their assignments.

If a volunteer is given work to do that involves a particular client, it undercuts all chance for success to deny that volunteer access to the necessary background information. Much of this stems from suspicion that somehow the volunteer is dabbling in providing service and only the serious (i.e., paid) worker should know the full story. Remember that this book makes the assumption that you have made sure all volunteers are appropriately selected and matched only to assignments that they are capable of fulfilling.

If you still have some doubts, go directly to the client and ask for permission to reveal records to the volunteer. After all, ultimately the client's decision is what matters most.

However you choose to handle this issue, the end result must be that you stand behind the volunteer as a legitimate representative of your organization.

Screening Applicants and Doing Background Checks

While no organization would hire someone as an employee without first interviewing them and doing some level of screening, it is all too common for those same organizations to be lax in how they consider applicants for volunteer positions. It may no longer be a matter of choice. In the United States and a number of other countries, if you are serving any population that could be considered vulnerable, you may be required by law to do background checks, including criminal histories and child abuse reports. Learn what rules apply to you.

In *The Staff Screening Tool Kit*, John Patterson defines the purpose of screening as "identify[ing] individuals who have identifiable characteristics that increase the risk of placing them in particular positions."[4] He further identifies four types of screening assessments:

1. To identify individuals who would pose an unacceptable risk if placed in certain situations.

2. To prevent the inappropriate placement of individuals in your organization.

3. To properly exclude dangerous individuals.

4. To properly exclude individuals considered too risky for a particular position.[5]

Screening is connected to but not synonymous with "hiring," "recruitment," or "placement." In her extremely valuable book, *Beyond Police Checks: The Definitive Volunteer & Employee Screening Guidebook*, Linda L. Graff explains, "While screening might well be considered part of each of these other processes, it has become a function of such import that it now warrants separate attention in the overall human resources/volunteer program management process. Screening has become as much a process of exclusion as inclusion."[6] Further,

> whether the candidate is applying for a paid job or a volunteer position is immaterial. Particularly where candidates work with vulnerable populations or are to be placed in positions of trust, screening has become as much a matter of doing everything reasonable to "keep the bad apples" out (John Patterson, 1994) as about achieving a proper fit between the candidate's skills/interests and the demands of the position. No organization should consider itself exempt from these transformations in screening.[7]

There are costs associated with formal screening, which Graff acknowledges:

> More intensive screening is typically more costly, and in times of fiscal restraint, organizations try to realize cost-savings wherever possible. This may be particularly germane to volunteer involvement. Boards and administrators, seeking to enhance services while cutting costs through increased deployment of volunteers, are reluctant to expend precious resources on extensive volunteer screening. The "they're just volunteers" rationale sometimes prevails. Unfortunately, however, in the face of tragedy or loss, the courts may be of the opinion that if an agency did not have the resources to fulfill its mission to a reasonable standard, it perhaps should not have been engaged in the activity at all.
>
> No employer is exempt from the ever-higher legal and ethical standards now being applied in courts of law and in the court of public opinion.[8]

In addition to fees, there is also the issue of time. Because the United States has no uniform or national background check system, it can sometimes take weeks to learn the results. This wait is hard on everyone involved.

You may wonder whether asking volunteers to be fingerprinted or submit to reference checking will make some people shy away from following through on their wish to volunteer. In practice, the opposite is often true. First, applicants with something to hide will most often self-screen out of the process rather than be discovered—which is a plus. Applicants likely to pass all the tests understand why these are important, want to know that you are protecting everyone, and see it as a badge of honor to be approved.

Graff offers sound advice on what she calls "The Ethic of No Surprises":

> It is recommended that organizations adopt a "full disclosure policy" regarding screening. Such a policy specifies that candidates have the right to know (and will be informed) at the outset of the application process, about minimum qualifications, automatic disqualifiers, and all screening procedures that will be deployed with respect to any position for which they apply. It simply is not fair for candidates to invest time, effort, and sometimes resources, in an application process only to find out part way through that a minimum qualification for the position eliminates them from further consideration, or a screening

mechanism to be used will reveal information that will automatically disqualify them.[9]

She also recommends assuring applicants of confidentiality and the right to know the results of all inquiries on their own backgrounds.

These days there are many places to turn for information on the legalities of screening and the best ways to do it. See appendix B for a starter set of resources.

Finally, one common mistake is to consider screening a task done only when someone first joins your organization. Rather, it is a continuing process that needs to be kept updated over time, particularly when a volunteer or employee moves into a new position. Background checks are a snapshot in time, a look backward, and can only reflect behavior that came to official attention; they are not necessarily predictors of future behavior. But once you've accepted someone onto your team, you have a variety of methods to keep assessing suitability:

> Mechanisms such as buddy systems, on-site performance, close supervision, performance reviews, program evaluations (particularly those which elicit client input), unannounced spot checks, and discipline and dismissal policies and procedures are, in effect, on-going screening mechanisms that allow the organization to be certain that the candidate was, and continues to be, the right person for the position.[10]

Opportunities, Not Obstacles

Implement effective screening procedures, but avoid being so inflexible that they become an obstruction. Sarah Jane Rehnborg, the author of *Strategic Volunteer Engagement*, teaches graduate courses in a school of public affairs. She requires some student community service, generally expected to be forty hours of work over the course of a semester. In an e-mail to me when reviewing the manuscript of this book, she shared her frustrations as a faculty member with screening hurdles:

> After countless disappointments I have found it necessary to pre-select service sites because of the barriers established by organizations for volunteering. Students have shared countless examples of not having their telephone calls or emails returned, and of the slow and haphazard pace with which criminal background checks are performed. In one situation, a student was subjected to three separate thumb-prints, all of which were flawed by the organization and never resulted in a police report. Making this matter worse was the fact that the work

she had planned to do was in the volunteer manager's office assisting with research and developing orientation materials, tasks that never involved client contact or interaction with classified or otherwise protected information. Although nonprofits frequently call requesting students, the barriers encountered often prevent highly skilled, eager young workers from ever accessing the service opportunity desired.

It is as important to have *reasonable, justifiable* exceptions to the rules as to have the rules in the first place! If the volunteer will not directly interact with clients, must he wait for fingerprinting results before starting to serve? If a pro bono volunteer will do the work of the promised consultation in her place of business after a single meeting in your facility, does she need a tuberculosis test? Must you require individual references for the members of the choral group volunteering to provide holiday entertainment? Your answers may still be yes, but at least consider the effect of rigidity on your ability to welcome contributions from the entire community. Keep in mind that clients, visitors, vendors, paid consultants, and others spend time in your setting with little or no screening at all.

Questions of Law

The management of volunteers presents many of the same legal issues as the management of employees: What laws regulate the conduct of the organization in setting the parameters of the work to be done and the terms on which the people to do the work are selected and supervised? How should your program operate so that these laws are followed? Volunteers, like employees, also can be accidentally injured or accidentally cause some injury to others while they are carrying out their duties. The leaders of an organization need to understand these potential liabilities and take steps to minimize the organization's exposure, such as practicing good risk management and maintaining insurance, just as is done with respect to employees.

The following pages will articulate some of the questions you might raise with your organization's lawyers and that you might consider as your organization examines the management of volunteer participation. The purpose here is not to provide any professional legal advice. Only a full discussion with your attorney will give you specific information about the federal, state, and local laws that apply to your program or to your country. An attorney who knows your organization can help you consider, in advance, steps to minimize your legal exposure.

Keep in mind, however, that few lawyers are fully knowledgeable about legal issues directly related to volunteers. They may assume that the principles and guidelines of dealing with employees and subcontractors always apply exactly the same way to volunteers—and they may be wrong. Ask to see case law or discuss their rationale for the advice they give you. Most important, make sure they understand fully who volunteers with you, what you want volunteers to do, and how you are managing volunteer engagement. They cannot bring personal prejudice to the table, such as considering all volunteers as unskilled, over age sixty-five, or other stereotypes that do not represent how your organization views volunteer involvement.

I often present a rather maverick perspective on the role of lawyers, accountants, risk managers, and insurance agents. I believe that their role is *not* to tell us what we *cannot* do; instead, they should listen to what we want to do and then advise on the legal and proper ways to do it. Attorneys want to avoid lawsuits, but sometimes it's necessary to do something risky (not illegal) to achieve your mission. Always ask what the costs are of stopping a great service idea because someone may someday sue.

There is a growing body of literature about the legal and insurance issues relating to the management of volunteers. Some of these materials are included in appendix B. While this chapter notes some of the general legal issues, the excellent materials that now exist provide the best sources for executives to explore these issues in more depth.[11]

The Employer-Employee Relationship

Earlier in this book, I suggested that you consider volunteers as your nonsalaried personnel department. That characterization is useful in thinking about legal issues as well as managerial ones, not because all the same laws apply to volunteers as employees, but because one should consider many of the same issues—and whether many of the same laws apply—with regard to volunteers.

Any discussion of legal issues involving volunteers would be much simpler if there were a single, neat legal definition of a *volunteer* that works across the board. Unfortunately, most of the legal issues involving volunteers involve the question of whether laws designed to apply to *employees* also apply to volunteers. However, there is not even a single definition of *employee* that can be used to simplify the discussion. For each issue, one must examine the definitions of *employee* and *employer* used in the legal sources and decide whether they apply to volunteers. For example, an individual might be considered an employee for purposes of a state antidiscrimination statute, even though no salary is paid, because the person receives significant in-kind compensation. The same individual might not be covered by workers' compensation law because no salary is paid.

Employment Law Issues

Issues of whether a volunteer fits within the legal definitions of employee arise most prominently in thinking about the application of labor and employment laws to volunteers. Even some laws that would seem to have no application to volunteers, such as the Fair Labor Standards Act (FLSA) in the United States, might in fact have some relevance.

Laws prohibiting discrimination against members of protected classes generally do not apply to volunteers. Courts that have analyzed these laws have concluded that volunteers normally are not included in the definition of *employee*. However, as noted previously, the scope of these laws may vary, especially at the state and local level. Some such laws may indeed protect volunteers, which means that a volunteer might bring an action alleging discrimination. It is probably safest— and good policy—to use the same type of standards you have for avoiding discrimination in hiring and firing employees in the management of volunteers. The questions that are irrelevant and improper to ask in interviewing a prospective employee do not become acceptable when the person applying for the position is a prospective volunteer. Similarly, questions of access for volunteers may arise under the Americans with Disabilities Act, just as such issues arise with employees, clients, visitors, and other persons.

You should also use care in delineating categories of work to be performed by volunteers and employees. Having the same position filled by some people who are volunteers and others who are paid employees may raise real legal concerns. First, if the employees in question are members of a labor union, you could be in violation of a union contract if volunteers are used to "replace" union members. Second, the FLSA, which sets minimum-wage standards and is designed to prevent exploitation of certain categories of workers by certain types of employers, may prohibit an arrangement in which employees and volunteers do similar tasks in the same organization.

The FLSA may also raise questions about employees who wish to volunteer for the organization on their own time. You should be careful to ensure that such dedicated employees are doing volunteer work that is wholly unrelated to their normal paid work and that such volunteering is clearly *voluntary*. While the law is not entirely clear, at this point, the best advice would be to use the following guidelines:

1. Be sure that no pressure—overt or implied—is given to make an employee feel that extra time is *expected*. It should be a free choice to volunteer.

2. Insist that the employee *apply* for a volunteer position, filling out a volunteer application form and going through the volunteer office for placement. The employee should sign in and out on the volunteer attendance form, separate from any employee time logs.

3. The assignment the volunteer carries should be demonstrably different from the job description of the person's salaried position.

Liability for Acts of Volunteers

In the past, most nonprofit organizations were not liable for harm caused by anyone working for the organization, whether salaried or not, but were protected by a legal doctrine called "charitable immunity." Most states have now abolished this shield from liability, and nonprofit organizations are now liable for damage caused by any of the organization's workers, just as any business would be liable.

There is a general legal principle that a company or organization is liable for injuries caused by its workers doing things on their behalf and at their direction. A number of states have also applied this doctrine to instances in which a volunteer caused the damage.

In order for your organization to be liable for damage caused by a volunteer, three conditions generally must be met:

1. The volunteer must have negligently or intentionally caused the damage; or

2. The volunteer must have been performing his/her assigned work at the time of the accident; and

3. The volunteer must have been within the control of the organization.

All three of these requirements involve complex legal concepts that vary from state to state and that your lawyer can define more fully. The bottom line, however, is that in most states your organization would be fully liable for any harm caused by a volunteer participating in a structured volunteer program, regardless of how careful your management or supervision.

An organization may also have direct liability for failing to take proper steps to supervise or support volunteers, if the organization itself is "negligent" in these activities and some harm ensues. There are also circumstances in which a volunteer will be considered the "agent" of an organization with the power to bind the organization to legal obligations.

Anticipating Potential Liability

While the above summary of the law may surprise some readers, this is no different from the law for paid employees. Rather than risk having to pay the full cost of damage accidentally caused by a volunteer (such damages awarded by a court can be considerable), most employers of salaried and nonsalaried servants take two types of precautions. First, they engage in risk management to help reduce the chance of accidents ever occurring. Second, they purchase insurance that will pay for the damage in the event an accident does occur.

As discussed earlier in this chapter, your organization probably practices some degree of risk management already. For example, you may require employees or volunteers to have certain experience or training before performing specific tasks. Requiring that a volunteer have a lifesaving certificate before being assigned to conduct a swimming program is a form of risk management, since certified lifeguards are more apt to take the necessary safety measures than those without such formal training. Risk management involves anticipating the most likely ways a volunteer could accidentally cause damage and then devising reasonable and cost-effective ways to reduce the likelihood of these accidents. Preventive techniques include requiring special training or education of volunteers, ensuring proper supervision of volunteers, and screening volunteers for certain personality traits (responsibility, maturity, ability to handle stress, etc.).

While the requirement that a volunteer lifeguard have a lifesaving certificate is an easy form of pre-employment screening, other screening issues may raise more complex concerns. Again, if the volunteer will be working with a vulnerable population, such as children, a child abuse screening may be in order (or even legally required) to prevent the organization from placing clients at risk (see the excellent publications and Web sites listed in appendix B for a full discussion of these issues). Other organizations may feel the need to screen certain categories of volunteers to be sure that they do not carry infections such as HIV or tuberculosis. Again, use the guidelines developed for screening employees to decide how—and whether—to screen volunteers.

One important risk management tool is the clear communication of expectations and responsibilities of both the volunteer and the organization. Written position descriptions are therefore useful in describing the duties and qualifications of the volunteer and the support the volunteer will receive. Some organizations go further and ask volunteers to sign formal contracts. A contract for the provision of volunteer services, if it is to be enforceable, must still meet the usual requirement that each side must receive some benefit. Contracts are often used to provide remedies in case of a breach, but that may be inappropriate in situations involving volunteers. A written position description may accomplish the same purpose of verifying each side's obligations and the necessary qualifications of the volunteer.

Another tool in the risk management arsenal is orientation—and it is never too late to orient volunteers, even if they have been with your organization for a long time. William Henry asks, "Do you consciously include information related to risk management and safety?"[12]

What follows is a short list of the orientation basics related to safety. You might consider incorporating these items into a packet to give to all volunteers, so everyone understands what you expect and require:

- Chain of command: To whom does the volunteer report? Whom do they see in the organization when they need something, or have a complaint or problem?

- General safety rules and emergency procedures.

- Time sheets and why it is important to complete them consistently to have a record of when everyone was on site or representing the organization.

- Photo/video release forms, for your newsletter or other publicity.

- Information about insurance coverage, if applicable.[13]

It is, of course, essential that you have some liability insurance to cover damage caused by volunteers, and you should check to see what your current policy covers. It is important that your insurance *explicitly* covers damage caused by volunteers. Since insurance brokers and carriers may be unfamiliar with volunteer programs (and may even harbor the prejudice that volunteers are especially risky), you should be ready to explain the steps your organization takes to adequately train and supervise volunteers. With volunteers, as with employees, you will need to weigh the cost of insuring certain activities against the benefits you derive from these activities.

Volunteers' Personal Liability

In addition to the liability of the organization for harm caused by volunteers, the volunteers themselves may have personal liability. The basis of the volunteer's liability would be the same as that of an employee: negligence or some other breach of a prevailing standard of care or rule of law.

In some situations, federal and/or state laws protect volunteers from potential liability; these are sometimes referred to as "Good Samaritan" acts. The federal Volunteer Protection Act (VPA) of 1997 "immunizes," or protects, volunteers who are working for certain nonprofit organizations and governmental entities, as long as certain conditions are met. These include that the volunteer was acting within the scope of his/her responsibilities; was licensed or certified to the extent required; was not engaging in willful or criminal misconduct, gross negligence, reckless misconduct, or intentionally being indifferent to the rights or safety of whoever was hurt; and was not operating a vehicle. Many states also have similar laws that protect volunteers personally from liability, so long as the volunteer was not acting maliciously or in bad faith. The terms of these laws vary considerably.

Legislators worried that fear of liability was hindering volunteer recruitment and reasoned that immunity would encourage volunteering. Also, the scarcity and cost of insurance has become prohibitive for many nonprofits. However, it must be noted that concern for volunteer liability is more a matter of *perception* than reality. There are very few lawsuits on the books regarding volunteers, as Horwitz and Mead note in a 2008 law journal:

In a search of all cases with written decisions over the past forty years (therefore, covering the period both before and after the immunity acts), we found sixty cases against these volunteers, almost all of which would fall outside the scope of the volunteer protection acts. Of the sixty cases, twenty-three were against volunteer firefighters (usually based on negligent driving and, therefore, exempt from state statutes); three were for negligent driving by other volunteers; eight were sex related (usually against youth leaders for child molestation and, therefore, intentional torts exempted from immunity); and nineteen involved non-tort claims, such as antitrust, Fair Labor Standards Act, discrimination, interference with contract, and other claims brought in the employment context. From 1978 through 2006, only seven cases alleged a straightforward negligence claim; of these, five invoked state volunteer protection acts and two invoked the VPA, with one invoking both.[14]

In addition to the small number of cases on record, there is little evidence that immunity from liability is a major factor in someone's ultimate decision whether to volunteer, although the question does arise regularly, particularly in relation to joining a board of directors.

It is possible for an organization to purchase insurance at a relatively modest cost that protects volunteers in cases of alleged personal liability, and you may wish to investigate such insurance on behalf of volunteers.

The reality in most cases is that, regardless of the volunteer's possible personal exposure, an injured party will look to the organization as the "deep pocket" from which payment will be demanded. Your organization will usually want to defend a lawsuit on behalf of both the organization and the volunteer, just as you would do if an employee were sued along with the organization.

Liability for Injuries to Volunteers

A volunteer who gets injured may attempt to recover medical or other costs from the organization. Whether the volunteer is entitled to such compensation depends on the circumstances surrounding the accident and whether the organization or any of the people acting on its behalf acted in a negligent manner. This situation is, for legal purposes, just like that in which a client or other third party is injured by the volunteer. Once again, you should check to see if your insurance covers this situation. In some states, certain categories of volunteers are covered under workers' compensation laws. Again, check with your lawyer to find out about the specific requirements of your state's law.

One way to reduce the chances of your organization being sued for injury suffered by a volunteer is to have the volunteer sign a waiver of liability. In consulting with your lawyer about the usefulness of a liability waiver, you should realize that such waivers are often not as effective as they might seem. A waiver only operates as a bar to legal action if it can be shown that the signer fully understood the risk involved and the meaning of the waiver and signed it voluntarily. Even so, a waiver may be useful because it provides an opportunity to discuss possible risks with the volunteers and because some volunteers will honor the waiver agreement and not sue in the event of injury. If you involve minors as volunteers, you should also consider whether you need to ask for a parental permission slip.

The volunteer who gets injured may have other sources of compensation, such as personal insurance, which would make it unnecessary to proceed against your organization. However, you may want to provide insurance coverage to volunteers. Most often, such insurance provides for payment only in "excess" of other coverage available.

Car and Drivers Insurance

If volunteer assignments involve driving a motor vehicle, be sure to check appropriate insurance coverage. Though the specific concerns may be affected by whether the volunteers are authorized to drive an agency car or van or utilize their private vehicles, liability is an issue in both cases. This may be especially important if the volunteers who drive for you are older and may, over time, become less able to keep your clients and themselves as safe as you wish.

Board Member Indemnification

Members of your board of directors can be liable for various "errors" or "omissions" committed in the line of decision making for the organization. In recognition of this, many organizations have purchased insurance to protect their board in case the individual members are named in a suit. Under such insurance, the insurer will usually cover the costs of any lawsuit and will pay any damages awarded, within agreed-upon limits. The recent laws protecting volunteers from personal liability also apply to board members. These laws vary from state to state. You should check on when board members can be sued in your state and should investigate insurance options.

Antitrust Laws

Trade and professional associations have been subject to both federal and state antitrust laws for a long time. The Sherman Antitrust Act, the principal American antitrust statute, became law in 1890 (Canada's Competition Act preceded it by a year). Section 1 of the Sherman Antitrust Act prohibits "contracts, combinations, or conspiracies . . . in restraint of trade." Since the purpose of professional societies and business associations is to gather their members together for exchange on issues affecting their common cause, they are tiptoeing on the edges of antitrust law:

> By their very nature, associations are a "combination" of competitors, so one element of a possible antitrust violation is generally present, and only some action by the association that unreasonably restrains trade needs to occur for there to be an antitrust violation. Consequently, associations are common targets of antitrust plaintiffs and prosecutors.[15]

According to the Electronic Transactions Association, there are "five principal antitrust problem areas. These are: price-fixing, division of customers, membership, standardization and certification, and industry self-regulation."[16] In lay terms, an association must avoid anything that could be interpreted as restricting anyone's ability to conduct business (such as strict rules of membership that might keep some individuals from benefiting from information or contacts available to others) or providing the chance for businesses or professionals to make agreements that adversely affect consumers. To remain within the law and avoid antitrust liability, associations should

> adopt a formal antitrust compliance program, and this policy should be distributed regularly to all association officers, directors, committee members, and employees. The policy should require, among other conditions, that all association meetings be regularly scheduled—with agendas prepared in advance and reviewed by legal counsel—and that members be prohibited from holding "rump" meetings. Above all else, members should be free to make business decisions based on the

dictates of the market—not the dictates of the association. Any deviation from this general principle, such as the adoption of a Code of Ethics that infringes on members' ability to make fully independent business decisions, should be approved by legal counsel.[17]

The key is to conduct business openly and avoid even the appearance of engaging in activity that might be seen to have an effect on prices or competition. This applies to all members, but the point is that those who volunteer as officers, as committee members, and in other leadership roles need to be aware of and enforce these rules.

Copyright and Ownership of Work

If you engage volunteers in the production of intellectual property, you should clarify who owns the final product and its components, what rights (limited or unlimited) each of you has to use the material, desired credit lines, and expectations of remuneration.

For example, if a professional photographer donates pro bono services to capture a special event for you, what is included in this volunteer contribution? Will every single photograph become the property of your organization to use (or not) as you please? Does this include digital and on-paper rights? Is there a limit to the number of copies you can make or on how long you may use the material? What credit line will be required, if any? Are there any expenses to reimburse or royalties or fees to be paid? Does the photographer have the right to use your photos again in any way without your prior approval? These sorts of questions are exactly the same whether you hire the photographer or the service is volunteered. But take the time to answer such questions and put your agreement in writing. Don't assume that a volunteer automatically intends to give you everything for free.

Questions of copyright, ownership, and future use relate to a number of potential volunteer roles, including writers, artists, Web designers, and trainers. Clarify, clarify, clarify.

Resolve Concerns

All these legal issues raise complex questions that an attorney can help you fully understand and resolve. Such consultation should help you to anticipate possible legal problems before they arise and to strengthen the way your organization involves volunteers. The resources in appendix B may help you define your questions and clarify your thinking on particular legal and insurance issues.

To implement ideas in this chapter, see . . .

Leading the Way to Successful Volunteer Involvement: Practical Tools for Busy Executives by Betty B. Stallings with Susan J. Ellis (Philadelphia: Energize, Inc., 2010).

Idea stimulators, worksheets, step-by-step guides, and more in the following sections:

- Section 6: "Building Staff Commitment and Competency to Partner with Volunteers"
- Section 9: "Assuring Legal Compliance and Managing Risk"

Notes

1. William R. Henry, Jr., *Insurance and Risk Management Issues for Volunteer Programs: What Every Decision Maker Should Know*, Self-Instruction Guide for the *Everyone Ready*® online training program (Philadelphia: Energize, Inc., 2007), 3.
2. Ibid., 17, quoting The CIMA Companies, Inc. (http://www.cimaworld .com).
3. Linda L. Graff, *Better Safe . . . Risk Management in Volunteer Programs & Community Service* (Dundas, Ontario, Canada: Linda Graff and Associates, 2003).
4. John Patterson with Charles Tremper and Pam Rypkema, *Staff Screening Tool Kit* (Washington, DC: Nonprofit Risk Management Center, 1994), 2.
5. Ibid.
6. Linda L. Graff, *Beyond Police Checks: The Definitive Volunteer & Employee Screening Guidebook* (Dundas, Ontario, Canada: Linda Graff and Associates, 1999), 6.
7. Ibid.
8. Ibid., 2.
9. Ibid., 14.
10. Ibid., 9.

11. Much of the material in this chapter on American law was written, reviewed, and revised by Jeffrey D. Kahn, Esq., who is now senior vice president of Audit, Compliance and Privacy for Children's Hospital of Philadelphia and legal consultant to Energize, Inc. Kahn has long been interested in legal issues related to volunteers and wrote the original version of this chapter early in his law career. In fact, his article on "Organizations' Liability for Torts of Volunteers," *The University of Pennsylvania Law Review* 133 (July 1985): 1433, was the first law review article in the country on this subject and continues to be referenced by other researchers. In 1992, Kahn coauthored the guidebook *Managing Legal Liability and Insurance for Corporate Volunteer Programs* (Washington, DC: Nonprofit Risk Management Center).

12. Henry, *Insurance and Risk Management Issues*, 13.

13. Ibid.

14. Jill R. Horwitz and Joseph Mead, "Letting Good Deeds Go Unpunished: Volunteer Immunity Laws and Tort Deterrence," John M. Olin Center for Law and Economics Working Paper No. 08-009, University of Michigan Law School, 2008, http://papers.ssrn.com/sol3/papers.cfm?abstract _id=1150835.

15. Jeffrey S. Tenenbaum, Esq., "Antitrust Primer for Association Board Members," ASAE & the Center for Association Leadership Online Knowledge Center, January 2007, http://www.asaecenter.org/Publications Resources/whitepaperdetail.cfm?ItemNumber=24301.

16. Electronic Transactions Association, "Antitrust Laws & Trade Associations," http://www.electran.org/content/view/82/108.

17. Tenenbaum, "Antitrust Primer for Association Board Members."

10

Evaluating the Impact of Volunteers

You expend time, money, and other resources on the involvement of volunteers, so it is clearly good management practice to evaluate whether the effort and expense have been worth it. Beyond return on investment, it is important to assess what volunteers accomplish and how well they do it. In fact, such assessment is of equal interest to the volunteers themselves, since no one wants to give time to do something that has no impact.

Some agencies routinely overlook the volunteer component when they do an internal evaluation study. As CEO, you can see to it that services provided by volunteers are evaluated with the same concern as those delivered by employees.

Evaluation has two components: assessment of the cumulative accomplishments of the entire volunteer engagement effort and individual performance assessment of each volunteer and of the director of volunteer involvement. Let's start with program evaluation.

What to Assess

One of the most uncreative—and unhelpful—questions posed to leaders of volunteer involvement is, "How many volunteers do we have, and how many hours did they give us this year?" Unfortunately, this is too often the extent of "evaluation" for the volunteer component. A tally of hours served without analysis of what was accomplished and how well it was done is not worth compiling. It is a left-handed compliment to assume that somehow the importance of volunteer involvement is self-evident. It is up to the top executive to require some demonstration of the value of volunteers.

As discussed in chapter two on planning, measurable goals and objectives need to be articulated for volunteer contributions at the start of the period under evaluation. If there is agreement on what you set out to do, it should be possible to ask whether goals were met. The key is to *measure outcomes*, not simply report activity. In *Measuring the Difference Volunteers Make: A Guide to Outcome Evaluation for Volunteer Program Managers*, editor Melissa Eystad explains,

> For years, accountability most often was centered on how funds were spent, who received volunteer services, how many people got services, how many volunteers provided services, what activities they participated in, how many hours volunteers contributed and how many volunteers continued with the program. These indicators measured processes and implementation procedures, but they did not focus on the impact of volunteer involvement on the primary clients volunteers were serving. They were not answering questions such as what difference the program made in the lives of participants and the community—questions that policy makers, taxpayers, elected officials, agency boards and philanthropic funders were asking . . . How we manage programs from the very beginning should be driven by what we want to happen as a result of our efforts. The focus is on the *purpose* of our voluntary efforts—on the desired outcomes—with less emphasis on process.[1]

Outcomes measurement is used to expand and explain quantitative data reports on activities and is increasingly the method of choice for assessing the impact of most nonprofit organization activities. There are many useful resources outlining the necessary steps.[2]

An evaluation of volunteer contributions should analyze performance in several areas:

1. The actual quantity and quality of the work done by volunteers—preferably in each assignment category

2. The accomplishments of the volunteer management team, including such overview questions as the demographic makeup of the volunteer corps, number and type of recruitment outreach efforts, and other activities

3. The type and degree of service provided to employees by volunteers, the volunteer office, or both

4. The difference volunteer involvement made to the organization's clientele

5. The benefits to the organization as a whole from volunteer involvement

Some of the questions that could be asked to assess the contribution of volunteers in a given period are similar to those that would be asked about the work of paid staff. In addition, formulate questions such as the following to identify the value of volunteers more clearly:

- Have our clients expressed any awareness of, appreciation for, or comments about volunteers here?

- What were we able to do more of this year than last because of the extra help from volunteers?

- What did volunteers free staff to do?

- What were we able to innovate or experiment with this year because volunteers offered or agreed to test something new?

- Did the involvement of volunteers allow us to offer enlarged or improved services to our clients?

- In which volunteer assignments did we have the most turnover, and why? Which assignments are the most popular with volunteers, and why?

- Has our public relations or image changed, and can we trace any of this change to the impact of volunteers?

- Is our volunteer corps representative of the community we serve?

- Have members of the paid staff visibly developed their supervisory skills as a result of working with volunteers?

- Are volunteers themselves satisfied with their work?

These kinds of questions will provide information immediately translatable into management decisions. The data gathered can be used to uncover training needs, recruitment strategies, service deserving recognition, and other things to do.

Retention

It is common to look for uniform, universal standards for volunteer involvement in order to compare one organization's situation against external benchmarks and thereby measure success. The best example is the question, "What's a successful retention rate for volunteers?" Well, obviously the answer is, "It depends."

Studying retention (how long volunteers remain with you) or attrition (how many volunteers leave over time) as something external to your organization implies that either is a characteristic of the volunteers themselves (or something in the air that infects everyone). There may be commonalities among certain types of volunteers, but high attrition is also likely to be a reaction to something going on *in that institution*. In which case, inter-agency comparisons would be useless.

It makes much more sense to compare attrition within your own facility, department to department or assignment to assignment. That has the potential to uncover which areas require redesigning, retraining, or some other action. Further, you cannot analyze the meaning of your "retention" data until you identify the following:

- What you need or expect as a minimum duration of volunteer service
- What amount of time the volunteer promised to commit when first interviewed

In other words, if you plan (wish) for, say, five years of service and volunteers leave earlier, the problem may not be attrition but unrealistic expectations! Or, if you never ask volunteers for an initial commitment of time (e.g., one year), then you have no idea if one person only intends to stay six weeks and another for six years. I generally advise using the following definition of *retention*:

Retention is when a volunteer remains with you for the period of time to which s/he committed when beginning service.

So retention is an *individual* measure. It may also be a recruitment goal, since you will need to bring on board volunteers who are willing and able to commit for whatever time you have determined is your minimum need.

It also matters *which* volunteers you retain. If you have a revolving door through which the newest or most well-trained volunteers leave faster than you can replace them, while longtime volunteers sit entrenched in roles that have lost their priority, you have a problem. On the other hand, if you actively recruit college students for a summer program and they all complete their assignment and leave for school in the fall, they honored their commitment to you even though the data will show a group of volunteers leaving all at once.

Retention is a useful measure of volunteer satisfaction in that unhappy or bored volunteers will simply leave. Therefore, low rates of unplanned attrition can be interpreted as a positive indicator and vice versa. But retention by itself is usually not useful in determining whether volunteers have contributed anything of value to the organization, its clientele, or its staff. In the same vein, the volunteer you award a twenty-five-year pin has certainly been devoted, but whether her/his service has been *effective* or meaningful must be assessed by criteria other than duration.

Universal Standards

The quest for "tell me what's standard for all volunteers" emerges over and over. In workshops, online discussion forums, and informal conversations, it is common to hear questions such as, What should I put in a volunteer manual? What should I ask in a volunteer screening interview? Is there a standard volunteer satisfaction survey? A good test when formulating a question about volunteers is to substitute *volunteer* with the word *employee* and consider if the same question would be asked in relation to paid staff. Trying to draw universal conclusions about what's best for volunteers, who can be doing such wildly unrelated things as mountain rescue and collating papers, is as hopeless as expecting to treat astronomers and plumbers alike just because both get paychecks.

There are no easy, off-the-shelf solutions to tasks that need to be analyzed agency by agency, but you should be confident in your ability to develop the best approach or materials for your setting. Rather than looking for external validation of the way you engage volunteers, determine the measures that matter most to you.

First, look inside your organization:

- Are there units that seem to be more successful with volunteers than others? Study why.

- Do volunteers of certain ages or with certain backgrounds seem more successful in different assignments? Which and why?

- Compare data from this year to past years and analyze changes up or down.

- Compare what has *not* worked in the past year to what has been successful and try to find commonalities and differences in approach.

- Continuously find ways to get feedback from volunteers— newcomers, long-timers, those from different backgrounds, and so on.

There are times when looking outside your organization for comparison is sensible, but be targeted in your search to understand why something you are assessing is particularly problematic (or even why it seems to work so well):

- Is this something related to our specific *type of setting or service* (e.g., nursing home, school) and therefore might the experience of any organization doing the same work be helpful to us?

- Is this related to the *type of assignment* volunteers fulfill (e.g., blogger, mentor to teenagers) and therefore might any organization, regardless of type, that asks volunteers to do similar assignments be helpful to us?

- Is this something that might be related to *our geographic location* (e.g., outbreak of an epidemic, local newspaper not covering volunteer issues) and therefore other organizations in our community might also have relevant experience with this?

- Is this related to the *types of volunteers* we have (e.g., university students, seniors over age seventy-five, homemakers) and therefore we can learn something from any setting that utilizes these same populations?

Don't forget that sometimes you can learn more from a place that is totally different from you on the surface than from a "competitor" doing what you do. Because you are different, you will have less preconceived notions about how things ought to be done and may be pleasantly surprised at what you can adapt.

Intangible Quality

One of the problems in evaluating volunteer achievement is that certain types of volunteer assignments require services that are described in terms of their quality rather than their quantity. Indeed, the titles given to some of these assignments reflect the inherent "how-can-we-ever-measure-this?" aspect of the work: "friendly" visitor, Big "Brother," victim "support" counselor. In reality, it is quite possible to determine some identifiable benchmarks of achievement, regardless of the assignment. Such indicators may be a bit subjective and anecdotal, but both the recipient and the giver of service should be able to point to successes such as the client makes a point of asking the volunteer's advice on something; the teenager goes to school regularly for two months; the patient's family identifies an increase in morale.

It is equally difficult to evaluate the efforts of salaried staff on services designed to affect the "quality of life" for recipients. Accountability and evaluation are nevertheless sought after by all types of agencies, so the challenge of finding ways to assess the impact of volunteer efforts may have implications for other service evaluation as well.

Periodically, think of ways that you can get the opinion of your clients as to whether they feel volunteers have been helpful. What kinds of information do you try to get during exit interviews or when ending a service? Can a question about volunteers be routinely included? If the feedback is positive, be sure to share it with all volunteers, perhaps at a recognition event.

Comparing Paid and Volunteer Staff

There is one danger worth mentioning. Be cautious of drawing comparisons between the work of volunteers and that of employees. As you are already aware, this book recommends making sure that the position descriptions of volunteers differ tangibly from those of employees. If you follow this advice, it will always be clear that you are evaluating each group separately, based on the different assignments they are each handling.

However, we have also already identified one major reason volunteers are threatening to salaried staff: the fear that, if volunteers do well, it will raise questions about the role played by employees. When reporting the results of any evaluation, therefore, it is helpful to praise the good work of both groups—and to indicate areas of weakness or need for improvement of both groups.

At times, there are reasons to do some comparing between the service provided solely by paid staff and the service provided by a combination of effort by employees and volunteers. This is important if you are trying, for example, to measure the impact of one-to-one volunteers assisting juvenile probationers. One way to do the measuring would be to compare the rate of recidivism of probationers without an adult volunteer friend to those with a volunteer. While this is a very reasonable evaluation approach, recognize that it could imply something about the abilities of the various probation officers, too. It is an excellent example of how the way you present findings in a final evaluation report can help or hurt volunteer-employee relationships.

Ongoing Assessment: Reports on Volunteer Participation

Apart from an annual or periodic evaluation of the entire volunteer engagement effort, you should be looking for indicators all year-round for whether volunteers are being effective—and whether your organization is providing the most supportive working environment for volunteers.

This means requiring reports from the director of volunteer involvement with the same frequency as you require them from other department heads, probably monthly. The data in these reports will be compiled not only from statistics being maintained in the volunteer office but also from reports submitted to the director of volunteer involvement by the various departments in which volunteers operate. You can also ask each department to include the accomplishments of volunteers in their unit directly to you within their monthly report (this is another way to demonstrate that you are interested).

Among the things to look for in regular reports are such data as the rate of turnover in specific assignment categories, accomplishments of short-term versus long-term volunteers, and assignments that have been vacant for an unusually long time. The data may alert you to trouble spots. If turnover seems to occur monthly in a particular unit, perhaps there is a problem with the supervisory staff or the physical environment there.

As with all data, the numbers alone do not tell the whole story. Some statistics reflect normal variables in the operation of a volunteer component, such as anticipated high rates of turnover in a particular month (such as students leaving when semesters end). Vacancies may demonstrate the careful screening being done by the director of volunteer involvement, who is willing to allow vacancies for a time rather than to fill a slot with inappropriate volunteers. See if the report includes information on recruitment efforts focused on the unfilled assignment categories and if the number of screening interviews of applicants is higher than the number of new volunteers actually brought on board.

The director of volunteer involvement also has the responsibility of giving you information about volunteers that is useful to you in your work as executive. At any given time, you should know the answers to the following questions:

- What is the "profile" of the volunteers in your facility? Specifically, do you know
  - the range of ages represented?
  - the percentage of men and women?
  - their racial distribution?
  - their occupations or professions?
  - the neighborhoods they represent?
- *Exactly* what do volunteers do?
- Do they perform these roles successfully? (If so, by what criteria?)
- Which units in the agency have not created roles for volunteers? Why not?
- Where is there the highest turnover of volunteers, and why?

- How many public relations and community contacts does the volunteer involvement department make weekly, with which organizations or individuals, and with what results?
- What suggestions or observations are being made by volunteers that might be useful to agency management?

If the director of volunteer involvement is not already supplying you with this type of data, ask for it. Think about how much more useful such data are than the so-called bottom-line figure of "how many volunteers do we have?"

Volunteer Satisfaction Surveys

It has become popular to survey volunteers about their degree of satisfaction with their work for the organization. This seems like a valuable thing to assess, but unfortunately, this type of evaluation too often is misapplied as an indicator of "success" of the organization's volunteer engagement. All that a volunteer satisfaction survey reports is, well, satisfaction. It can confuse satisfaction with effectiveness, in that volunteers might enjoy their service or like their colleagues, but have a false impression of whether their time and effort is really accomplishing anything.

Some volunteers (perhaps long-timers) may love their time in the agency because it feels comfortable and social. If new volunteers quickly leave out of frustration at being underutilized, who remains each year to complete the satisfaction survey, and can you trust the results? Or, at a time of change, whether it's something tangible (such as learning to use new computer software) or something mission related (such as adding a new type of client service), volunteers may, in fact, respond negatively to questions about their satisfaction levels.

As already mentioned, organizations tend to look for a *standardized* volunteer satisfaction survey form—and find templates that they use without tailoring it to their specific situation. This is usually bad practice. As always, ask yourself whether you would use a generic form with employees. If not, take the time to ask volunteers the sorts of questions most important to your organization.

Go ahead and use such surveys if you wish, but only in addition to more important assessments of what volunteers feel they accomplish and how they might contribute even more. After all, dissatisfied volunteers will not stay around long enough to complete your questionnaire!

Evaluating the Director of Volunteer Involvement

Though it is reasonably obvious, it does not hurt to point out that the evaluation of volunteer impact is not the same thing as an evaluation of the person who leads volunteer engagement for your organization. You are justified in assessing the competence and achievements of the director of volunteer involvement by examining the way in which volunteer engagement is managed, but the achievements of the *volunteers* themselves are not necessarily the reflection—nor the fault—of the leader of their efforts.

A great deal depends on your expectations of what the position of director of volunteer involvement means to your agency. If you set your sights low and only want volunteer participation "maintained," then you do not need much in the way of creativity or vision from the designated leader. If you recognize the potential of this component of your service delivery, you will want the leader to be a full participatory member of your administrative team.

Leland Kaiser, an authority in hospital management, has an interesting point of view about what an executive should expect from any department head. He challenges CEOs to require every department head to report annually on the major trends and issues affecting his/her area of specialty and how the institution should respond. Kaiser's point is that leadership involves not only day-to-day management but also continuing education about developments in the outside world that will impact on your operations.[3]

You should hold the director of volunteer involvement responsible for keeping informed about volunteerism in general. S/he is, as already indicated, your in-house expert on volunteers. Is s/he truly aware of what is happening with citizen participation in other settings? Can s/he express long-range goals for volunteer engagement and predict changes that will occur in the future? Is s/he aware of trends in your organization's specific field (health care, recreation, child welfare, etc.) and how these might affect your needs for volunteer involvement in the future?

Assessing Your Volunteer Management Practices

It is hard to evaluate the director of volunteer involvement in a vacuum, however. So periodically, you might conduct an internal operations assessment using a tool such as the one I provide in the *Volunteer Management Audit*. This is

> a tool for analyzing the effectiveness of an organization's approach to and procedures for involving volunteers. It is an assessment of the current status of the organization's volunteer management effort, specifically designed to examine the internal management practices of an organization—the standards necessary to support volunteers regardless of setting. It is above all a *discussion starter*.[4]

The audit process allows teams of stakeholders to complete a "scorecard" on which they compare your current ways of working with volunteers against best practices of the field.

The United Kingdom has a national process available to create "quality standards" for different fields of work. The Investing in Volunteers (IiV) Standard[5] was piloted in 1998 and is fully operational today. It enables organizations to comprehensively review their volunteer management procedures and publicly demonstrate their commitment to volunteering. There is also a related standard for corporations wishing to assess their employee volunteering efforts. On the IiV Web site, Margaret McKay, chief executive of the charity CHILDREN 1st, explains why the assessment process is important: "[We are] committed to involving volunteers in all aspects of our work. Investing in Volunteers provides a valuable framework that has helped us to develop best practice and ensure that we provide well thought through volunteering opportunities benefiting volunteers and the work of our Charity."

Individual Volunteer Performance Assessments

Yes, it is legitimate and reasonable to evaluate the individual performance of volunteers—provided that volunteers know in advance that there will be periodic assessment, that it is done equitably for all volunteers, and that it is based on having told each volunteer what was expected from him/her in the first place (the position description). The evaluation should be a two-way process, also allowing the volunteer the chance to give feedback on the support received from the organization and even to elicit suggestions for improved operations. This is not only fair but can be quite revealing. For example, consider how much you can learn from asking a volunteer questions such as the following:

- Have you found your position description to be an accurate representation of the work actually required? If not, how might it be improved?

- What do you identify as your most important contribution, to whom, and why?

- Have you wished for more training, supervisory time, supplies, or anything else that would support future success?

- If you could change one thing for the better—in any aspect of the organization—what might that be?

Inviting such input from volunteers is a powerful way to show appreciation for their efforts and caring.

It is more than semantics to call the volunteer performance assessment a "progress report" or "future action plan." This sounds less judgmental and emphasizes moving forward rather than simply looking back. In this way, the mutual assessment process can remotivate everyone.

Making Changes

As with any program evaluation, it is only worth the effort if you are willing to analyze the results of the assessment and develop plans to implement necessary changes. If done correctly, an evaluation will point out areas of strength as well as of weakness in volunteer engagement, since improvement might come simply from doing more of what has been done right in the past. Of course, evaluation does uncover what is not going well, but this can be turned into a positive:

> The reason some administrators do not report their measurement results is often due to the identification of a significant problem area. Although distressing to everyone involved, the simple truth is that mistakes and oversights cannot be rectified if they are not known. The discovery of areas for improvement should be considered a gift—albeit a strange one—in that the organization can now problem-solve around, and correct the error. Errors do not become performance errors unless they are revealed and then ignored, or handled ineffectually.[6]

Assessment of the value of volunteer participation must then be meshed with your planning for the whole organization. Are volunteers still doing the most important things? Will there be changes of any sort that will have an impact on volunteers, and how? What should the next year's goals and objectives be for volunteer engagement?

From the volunteer management perspective, the importance of evaluation is to assure that volunteers are assigned to work that genuinely requires their attention. Otherwise, volunteer effort is wasted on activities that are not useful. There is too much to be done to permit that.

To implement ideas in this chapter, see . . .

Leading the Way to Successful Volunteer Involvement: Practical Tools for Busy Executives by Betty B. Stallings with Susan J. Ellis (Philadelphia: Energize, Inc., 2010).

Idea stimulators, worksheets, step-by-step guides, and more in the following section:

- Section 10: "Monitoring, Evaluating and Improving Volunteer Involvement"

Notes

1. Melissa Eystad, ed., *Measuring the Difference Volunteers Make: A Guide to Outcome Evaluation for Volunteer Program Managers* (St. Paul: Minnesota Department of Human Services, 1997), 5. This book is out of print but available as a free electronic document at http://www.energizeinc.com/download/Measuring_the_Difference2003.pdf.

2. See, for example, the Urban Institute, "Key Steps in Outcome Management," Series on Outcome Management for Nonprofit Organizations, http://www.urban.org/UploadedPDF/310776_KeySteps.pdf; and Carter McNamara, "Basic Guide to Outcomes-Based Evaluation for Nonprofit Organizations with Very Limited Resources," Free Management Library, http://managementhelp.org/evaluatn/outcomes.htm.

3. I first heard Leland Kaiser make these points when he and I cotrained at a workshop for nonprofit executives in Pittsburgh in 1984 and several times again when we were both faculty with the Estes Park Institute in the 1980s.

4. Susan J. Ellis, *Volunteer Management Audit* (Philadelphia: Energize, Inc., 2003), 1–2.

5. Investing in Volunteers, http://iiv.investinginvolunteers.org.uk/. Also from the United Kingdom is the *Volunteering Impact Assessment Toolkit*, published by Volunteering England in 2004.

6. Christine Burych, Alison Caird, Joanne Fine Schwebel, Michael Fliess, and Heather Hardie, *A Balanced Scorecard for Volunteer Programs: A Measurement Tool for Demonstrating and Measuring the Impact and Outcomes of Volunteer Contributions* (Toronto: Published by the authors with the support of the Ontario Hospital Report Research Collaborative, 2009), 51.

11

The Financial Value of Volunteer Contributions

Evaluating volunteer effectiveness provides you with information help-ful in your administrative responsibilities. But so far we have only dis-cussed the evaluation of volunteer activities, not the assessment of the financial value of volunteer involvement. This chapter presents meth-ods available to you as executive for becoming more aware of the real cost of operating your organization.

The information in this chapter changed greatly between the first and second editions of this book and has evolved again in the last dozen years. The accounting profession, the government, and even the public have become more involved in presenting and assessing the financial sit-uation of nonprofit organizations. While most of the attention is focused on other accounting questions, volunteers are increasingly understood as a resource with economic value. In the preface to their 2007 book, *What Counts: Social Accounting for Nonprofits and Cooperatives*, authors Laurie Mook, Jack Quarter, and Betty Jane Richmond state,

The accounting statements used for organizations in the social economy are identical to those applied to businesses oriented to generating profits for their owners. However, accounting statements for nonprofits and cooperatives miss an important feature of their activities—these are organizations with a social mission and, as such, their social impact is a vital part of their performance story. In addition, nonprofits rely in varying degrees on volunteers, yet ironically the value of this service normally is excluded from accounting statements. In other words, for organizations with a social mission conventional accounting misses critical aspects of their operations.[1]

The rules have changed, and the ideas presented here twenty years ago as innovative and even challenging to the accounting profession are now becoming "generally accepted accounting principles." There has been progress but with continuing controversy over whether and how best to account for volunteer services.

Almost all nonprofit organizations receive in-kind contributions and the donation of services of a board of directors and other volunteers. Office space, printing and copying, video production, and a variety of other in-kind services are often donated to nonprofits. All these are of great importance to program services, and all have a monetary value. Unfortunately, most nonprofits ignore such contributions on their financial statements—both those for internal use and those for external dissemination. In order for you to know how much it *really* costs to run your organization, a cost equivalency should be placed on volunteer time and in-kind contributions. These are as valuable as cash contributions.

Generally, volunteers have simply not been mentioned on nonprofit agency financial reports. This omission tends to devalue their services. To report that it cost $7,200 to winterize ten homebound elderly peoples' homes without mentioning the $4,000 *worth* of volunteer services or the $2,000 *worth* of donated supplies risks the reader forming some false conclusions about the actual cost of the service. From a management perspective, never having to "account" for the contributions of volunteers can result in wasting volunteer effort or in discounting its cost to the volunteer and its value to the organization.

The premise of this chapter can be summed up in the following formula:

Cash expenses + the marketplace equivalency of
contributed time and materials = the true cost of service.

Whether you adopt any of the accounting techniques presented here, you may well want to consider how you can be certain that you (and your board or other decision makers) base your planning on the most accurate picture of your resource expenditures. Further, managers tend to spend time managing what is measured. So making an effort to calculate the finances of volunteers' participation validates the importance of putting time and effort into working with them.

As with chapter nine on legal issues, some of the information in this chapter on accounting and tax reporting will be relevant only in the United States. But the principles are still universal, and many countries have similar financial reporting requirements. As always, the best advice is to talk to your organization's accountants for the most relevant rules and requirements.

Why Compute Your True Costs?

You may be thinking, "I'm not sure we want to know the full cost of our program . . . We certainly don't want anyone else to compare how much our program really costs versus another program's operations." Maybe you don't—but you, as the administrator, and your board of directors should be aware of the full costs of operating.

Clearly, there are some philosophic issues at stake here. For example, some might argue that almost all nonprofits involve volunteers as an inherent part of their operations. Such donated services are therefore assumed, and there is no need to keep track of their monetary value. Furthermore, if people are willing to volunteer their time to an organization, should a cash equivalency of that time be measured? Or is the volunteering itself proof of the value of the program? The argument includes the belief that it is hard to keep records anyway and the expense of doing so cannot be justified by the benefits of keeping track of the monetary worth of volunteers' hours.

Another issue relates to the bottom line. Profit-making organizations have the bottom line of whether they make a profit or not. Sales measure whether the public thinks the company is making a desired product or providing a worthwhile service. Should nonprofits be treated differently? If a social good is being provided, should cost be considered?

We could also ask whether one nonprofit should be compared to another based on how much money each spends to provide its services. Should an alcohol rehabilitation program be compared to another alcohol rehabilitation program on any basis other than the effectiveness of their programs?

An additional problem inherent in keeping track of volunteer services is that valuing donated time and materials and including them in your financial statements will increase the apparent size of the organization. Will this be seen as an attempt to inflate the figures to make the agency look bigger than it is? Might it affect how some grant makers compute your overhead allowance? Will it make the agency appear "rich"? Will such conclusions make potential donors think you do not need their money?

None of these questions has an easy answer, but there are strong arguments in favor of keeping track of your donated time and materials.

Your board of directors and funding sources, both current and potential, are interested in what your resources are and how you use them—and donated time and materials are very significant resources. Properly presented, inclusion of donated time and materials in your financial statements may impress potential funders with the degree of support demonstrated by the community—and with your managerial sophistication at recognizing the value of such support. Funding sources may see the monetary equivalency of volunteer service as leverage for their money. The funder's cash contribution to your program has the potential to generate two, five, or twenty times its worth through volunteer time and in-kind materials. You can best make this point by keeping records of donated time and materials and putting a monetary assessment on them.

Certain donors and government grant-making agencies will accept volunteer time as in-kind "matching funds" on grant applications. Again, you will need to be able to document any monetary value you place on such contributed services.

There are internal management reasons for wanting to keep records on volunteers, too. You need to be able to recognize and thank volunteers. It is much more meaningful to thank someone for 105 hours, or for five hours a week for ten weeks, than for "all your time." (Even more important is acknowledging specific results and end products of the contributed time.)

It is therefore essential to keep records of volunteer time and determine a monetary equivalency for that time, at least for internal purposes. You may, initially, decide not to record the figure in your public accounting records. At a minimum, making a start at assessing the contributions of volunteers should give you and your board a more significant and valid picture of the cost of human effort you expend in delivering services. As presented in chapter three, your organization is incurring costs to facilitate the work of volunteers, both to purchase tangible equipment and supplies and in staff time. Calculating the financial equivalency of volunteer services therefore shows the revenue and support gained from these expenses.

Return on Investment

Most administrators are justifiably concerned with measuring the cost-effectiveness of agency projects—whether the funds and staff time expended are commensurate with the extent of the service provided. Cost effectiveness, or ROI (return on investment), is easy to prove for volunteer involvement. The actual cost of salarying the program staff, paying for supplies, and other expenses is money that leverages many more multiples of hours of volunteer service than that same money could have "paid" for hours of employee time. (However, this argument is only valid if the evaluation of the quality of volunteer service concludes that something meaningful was produced!)

Costs versus Value

When I was writing the first edition of this book, I kept trying to put various caveats into this chapter in an attempt to caution against the natural tendency to apply the old "money talks" philosophy to assessing volunteer contributions financially. In response, the accountant who was providing the accounting information finally challenged me with the question, "Do you *really* want to include this chapter in the book?" Since I did indeed feel it was important to discuss monetary evaluation, I accepted the inevitable.

What always troubled me was the blurring of the lines between what it would cost in cash to hire staff to do what volunteers do versus the *value* of what volunteers do beyond money. Linda L. Graff, in her excellent 2005 book, *Best of All: The Quick Reference Guide To Effective Volunteer Involvement*, provides an articulate statement of the issues:

> There has been a strong movement to assess "the value of volunteer time" or the "value of volunteer work" using the wage replacement approach. Briefly, this methodology involves multiplying the number of volunteer hours by an average hourly pay rate based on what an employee might be paid to do the same work. The resulting total

is reported as the "value" of the work done by volunteers. It is not. The resulting figure is quite simply what the organization did not pay to have the work done. That is very different from what the work is actually worth. Consider how you might go about answering these questions:

- What is a park worth?

- What is a police department worth?

To answer either of these questions, one would not take the number of hours worked by the park workers/police officers, multiply their hours by their average wage and claim that to be the worth of the park or the police department. It is clear that that calculation is what it costs to generate the value of the park/police department, not its actual value.[2]

Graff further argues that "the wage replacement method of calculating the value of volunteering actually serves to mask [and underestimate] the real value of volunteer involvement."[3] She points out that volunteering provides multiple benefits to the organization, its clientele, the volunteer personally, and the community as a whole—benefits that cannot be reduced simply to the cost of replacing the service.

The more complex but infinitely more honest approach involves the identification of real outcomes of the work, calculating the full costs of achieving those outcomes, and then asking the question: is this a good investment of our resources? Consider:

... If it costs an organization $300 to place a volunteer tutor with an illiterate adult student for a year and it takes an average of three years to teach an adult student to read at a functional level, is that a good investment? If the student is then successful in getting a better job, does not go on welfare, does not end up homeless . . . , is the volunteer literacy program worth what it costs?

[This] number ... illustrates how a different way of thinking about the value of volunteer work more honestly represents the true worth of volunteer involvement, and more appropriately honours the real contributions that volunteers make. If you decide to use the wage replacement approach in your program statistics, be certain to be very clear about what the resulting figure represents, which is not the actual "value" of volunteering, but rather, what the organization has not paid in wages.

Describing the outcomes of volunteer efforts and contrasting those against the actual costs of outcome generation is a more promising approach and may very well become the new best practice in volunteer program management in the near future. At minimum, it is more accurate and more respectful.[4]

Keeping Track of Donated Time

How do you keep track of donated time? The method is very similar to how you keep track of time for which you pay: by using time sheets or electronic sign-in systems.[5] It is also important, for accounting purposes, to have all staff members (paid and unpaid) allocate their recorded time, at least by each major program or service category: management and general administration, and fundraising. This information is needed to prepare your financial statements and the report to the federal government (Form 990), both of which require that expenses be broken out into these categories (at a minimum).

Once you have recorded accumulated volunteer hours, you can calculate their value by multiplying hours by an appropriate hourly rate for each activity performed. One of the objections often raised about keeping track of volunteer hours is that it is difficult, if not impossible, to get volunteers in all categories to keep an accurate record of the time they contribute. This may be true, but the solution is to aim for recording as much of the time as possible, not to ignore recording some because you cannot record all. You can begin to apply the following valuation system to whatever number of hours you have gathered for volunteer service.

Determining Marketplace Wage Equivalency

To generate the most useful data, take the time to assess volunteer time financially as fairly as possible. Do not fall into the common trap of using the minimum wage or the national median wage as a basis for your computation. The vast majority of volunteer assignments are worth a great deal more than minimum wage and probably more than the median, too.

One other trap is to confuse the wage replacement cost of the service provided by volunteers with the earning power of the people who are doing the volunteering. If someone earns his/her living as a lawyer, teacher, or doctor and volunteers to write a brief, teach classes, or do blood tests for your organization—serving in what is a pro bono capacity—then you are justified to estimate the cash value of those donated services at the hourly rate normally charged by that volunteer professionally. But if that same lawyer, teacher, or doctor volunteers to paint your recreation hall, drive clients to a picnic, or play chess with residents—the cash value of such volunteer work has nothing to do with her/his regular earning power. You must assess each volunteer assignment based on what it would cost you to purchase that type of work in the marketplace.

The best system for determining what is called "the true dollar value of volunteer services" was developed by G. Neil Karn while he served as director of the Virginia Department of Volunteerism.[6] Here are his key points:

1. It is possible to find an equivalent paid job category for every volunteer assignment, even if it means a little creativity and searching. Each volunteer assignment should be given its own monetary equivalency, without trying to find an average rate for all volunteer work.

2. The cost of paying an employee includes fringe benefits that raise the total value of the "annual employee compensation package" considerably.

3. We routinely pay employees for hours they do not work, while we credit volunteers only for hours they actually put in.

4. Volunteers should be "credited" with the cash equivalent of the hourly amount an employee would earn for actual hours worked.

The illustration on the next page shows the way to compute a legitimate marketplace-based wage equivalent of volunteer services using the Karn method.

By using the volunteer position description for each assignment, it is possible to compare the tasks given to volunteers to those listed in the job descriptions for employees somewhere. This may require some research to identify paid job classifications. The local offices of the United States' and your state's Department of Labor (and equivalent bodies in other countries) maintain useful listings of job categories and pay scales in your geographic region. Some of the actual equivalent job categories in Virginia that Karn uses as examples are as follows:

TRUE DOLLAR VALUE OF VOLUNTEER TIME WORKSHEET

Volunteer Job Title: _____

  I. Equivalent Salaried Job Classification
      *(Based on a comparison of the tasks and responsibilities described
      in the volunteer position description with those of an equivalent
      employee.)*
      Equivalent Salaried Job Title: _____

  II. Annual Salary for Equivalent Salaried Classification: $_____

 III. Value of Benefits Package:
          FICA $ _____
          Health Insurance   _____
          Life Insurance   _____
          Workers Compensation Insurance   _____
          Retirement   _____
          Other Benefits: _____   _____
                     Total Value of Benefits: $_____

 IV. Annual Salary + Benefits Package =
      TOTAL ANNUAL COMPENSATION PACKAGE: $_____

  V. Established Annual Work Hours for
      Agency: ___ hours/week × 52 weeks =   _____ hours

 VI. Hours Paid but Not Worked Annually:
      Annual Leave   _____ hours
      Paid Holidays   _____
      Paid Sick Leave   _____
          Total Hours Paid/Not Worked: _____

 VII. Established Annual Hours - Hours
      Paid but Not Worked =
      ACTUAL WORK HOURS ANNUALLY: _____ hours

VIII. **TOTAL ANNUAL COMPENSATION PACKAGE ÷
      ACTUAL WORK HOURS ANNUALLY =**

      **TRUE DOLLAR VALUE OF EACH
      HOUR OF VOLUNTEER TIME IN
      THIS JOB DESCRIPTION:** $_____

Volunteer Assignment	Equivalent Paid Classification
Criminal justice one-to-one visitor	Probation and parole officer trainee
Volunteer member of a conference planning committee	Special events coordinator
Little League coach	Playground supervisor
Little League official	Recreation specialist
Big Brother/Sister	Outreach worker
Board member	Executive director

For some volunteer positions, the equivalent paid classification will be more obvious. For example, a volunteer assigned to help with mass mailings and photocopying would be equivalent to an entry-level clerk or secretary position. A volunteer writing your newsletter would be equivalent to a public relations specialist or editor.

Also, the qualifications of each volunteer may be an important factor in measuring the cost of volunteer service. If someone comes to you with experience in the type of assignment s/he will carry, that volunteer's wage equivalent should be calculated as higher than a trainee level. Similarly, if a volunteer has been with your organization for several years, that person's equivalent wage would be higher than a new volunteer's or new employee's wage.

Once you have identified the equivalent paid classification and its annual salary, you next must add the value of a typical benefits package: federal insurance contributions (FICA), retirement, insurance, and other benefits. The total cost of the benefits package and the salary equals the "Annual Compensation Package" for an employee in that position.

Now compute how many hours a year your organization has established as expected work hours. For example, forty hours per week times fifty-two weeks per year equals 2,080 hours per year. Using this as a base, add up the hours for which employees are paid but do not work. This includes annual leave (vacation), paid holidays, paid sick leave, and paid personal leave. For many organizations, this can total over two hundred hours per year.

Now subtract this from the total number of work hours per year to arrive at "Actual Work Hours Annually." By dividing the Actual Work Hours Annually into the Annual Compensation Package, you arrive at the "True Hourly Value." It is *this* hourly rate that should be used in determining the marketplace-based wage equivalent of volunteer service. And, as Karn says, this figure should be presented unapologetically!

A number of administrators have questioned this high dollar figure because volunteers are rarely, if ever, full-time workers and so would not qualify for a benefits package. Karn answers this objection by pointing out three economic realities in the paid workforce. First, organizations commonly pay hourly or part-time workers at a higher hourly rate than full-time workers because part-timers do not receive benefits. Similarly, help hired through a temporary employment agency also costs more per hour, to cover both the agency's profit margin and some benefits paid. So if you prefer using what it would cost to hire temporary employees as the measure of volunteer economic worth, you would still wind up with an amount higher than the equivalent of the base salary of a full-time employee for each hour served. Finally, organizations pay premium prices for the time of a consultant with technical expertise, which is another way of looking at many volunteer services.[7]

The good news is that the best computer software programs designed to manage volunteer program data allow you to enter a wage equivalency for each position description and then automatically calculate totals for each assignment and for all volunteers. You must do the work up front to determine the marketplace equivalent, but then you can let technology take over!

Other Valuation Options

The Karn method of calculating the finances of volunteer time remains the most highly regarded. But because it is time consuming to implement initially, some agencies have developed simpler ways of arriving at the wage replacement costs of volunteer time. For example, it is possible to take the total annual agency budget for wages and benefits and divide it by the number of hours worked by employees on the payroll. This provides an average hourly wage for your agency, which can be used to estimate the replacement costs for volunteer time. This method acknowledges that volunteers do a variety of tasks, comparable to various levels of staff, and adds in the amount spent on benefits.

Your state's Department of Labor (or its equivalent in another country) may keep regional statistics on salaries for the general categories of staff in your agency. This allows you to use labor costs in your own area rather than a national aggregate. Always remember to add in benefits packages, for which the Department of Labor can also supply statewide average percentages.

Since 1980, the organization Independent Sector has calculated an estimated dollar value of volunteer time for the United States. In 2009, they set this value at $20.25 per hour for 2008.[8] While this figure is widely used as a national standard, it is not accurate for every type of volunteer involvement, sometimes over-valuing and other times under-valuing the cash replacement cost of volunteer contributions.

Whatever method you use, do everything possible to avoid relying on the minimum wage as the standard wage replacement cost of volunteer time.

Remember the points made in chapter three about fundraising for volunteer engagement. Volunteers frequently spend money to give their time to your organization, without asking for (or being able to get) reimbursement. Yet this is rarely seen—or counted—as a financial donation. Costs may be incurred for transportation, uniforms, or other special clothing, and even for supplies the volunteers use as they give service (e.g., buying arts and crafts materials for a class). Capturing and reporting this monetary information also adds to the understanding of what volunteers contribute to your organization in total.

Finally, when was the last time you compared your list of money donors to your list of time donors? Is there a correlation between volunteers and donors, and what is it? As said before, volunteers frequently also give money to the organization they care enough about to support with their time. Conversely, donors who come in person as well as write checks tend to be more committed for the long term.

Your Financial Records

Let's discuss how to record the cash equivalency amount of volunteer service in your agency's internal financial reports. It is really not different from how you record the salaries of paid staff. The information that follows has been written, revised, and reviewed by professional accountants.[9] The accounting practices described here are based on American law and guidelines; please seek expert guidance as to what is acceptable financial reporting in other countries.

Social Accounting

In the last decade, attention has been paid to "social accounting" and its practical applications are evolving. Mook, Quarter, and Richmond define the term as "a systematic analysis of the effects of an organization on its communities of interest or stakeholders, with stakeholder input as part of the data that are analyzed for the accounting statement."[10] This involves the consideration of a broader set of variables than are typically included in conventional accounting and far more *stakeholders* than a business's financial shareholders:

> [T]here are fundamental differences between social organizations and profit-oriented businesses that should be enshrined in the accounting practices that are applied to them. First, while the primary targets of a business's financial statements are the investors and creditors, the primary targets of a social organization's reporting are members, funders, clients, and the community (Richmond 1999). Second, the main objective of accountability for social organizations is not profit maximization but stewardship (or trusteeship), quality, and social impact. Social organizations should be evaluated on the extent to which they are achieving their social objectives and contributing to the community. If an organization's services are not transacted in the market, creative methods must be established for evaluating the services and including them in accounting statements. Third, social organizations in general rely heavily either on volunteer labor or on social labor in the form of the contributions of members.[11]

Also driving the examination of the limitations of financial accounting is the growth of the "knowledge-based economy," in which intellectual capital and other knowledge-based assets must be identified (rarely "counted"), valued, and assessed in new ways.

Despite the relative rigidity of current accounting practices and such reporting documents as the Form 990 (even after its revision for 2008), demonstrating the impact of the services of volunteers and members in nonprofit organizations may receive greater attention in coming years. Keep asking your accountants!

Colleen Kelly made an interesting comment in a margin note to me when reviewing this manuscript. She said that another reason business accounting doesn't work in nonprofits is because generally accepted accounting principles (GAAP) "consider all the people (salaries) a *liability*, not an *asset*. We say people are your largest asset! The accountants say 'no,' though many businesses will argue with them on this one, too."

Your Internal Financial Reports

You, other members of management, and your board need to have financial information for budget and decision-making purposes that reflects the total cost of all the people who work on behalf of your agency. The total cost of your paid staff comes directly from your payroll records, and the marketplace-based wage equivalent of volunteer services can be estimated using the Karn method previously described or a simpler one. The replacement cost of volunteer services would appear as both expense and contribution revenue. True, it has no impact on your bottom line, but it does enable you to show internal financial reports that provide a more complete picture of your organization's programs and supporting activities.

As already advised in chapter one, no matter what, never use the phrase, "Volunteers *save* us money." This statement implies that you had resources you did not need to spend because volunteers are free. A better and more accurate way to make the same point would be to say, "Volunteers *extend our budget* beyond anything we would otherwise be able to afford."

Your External Financial Statements

The Financial Accounting Standards Board (FASB), the profession's most important rule-making group in the United States, recognizes that "differences between nonbusiness organizations and business enterprises arise principally in the way they obtain resources."[12] As a result of those differences, FASB has issued several rules that pertain to nonprofits. The American Institute of Certified Public Accountants (AICPA) has issued two industry guides to help accountants and auditors implement the requirements of these rules.[13]

One of the most important rules under FASB guidance requires nonprofits to report certain contributions received from donors, including volunteer services. Here are rules dealing with contributed services:

> Contributions of services shall be recognized [at fair value] if the services received (a) create or enhance nonfinancial assets or (b) require specialized skills, are provided by individuals possessing those skills, and would typically need to be purchased if not provided by donation. Services requiring specialized skills are provided by accountants, architects, carpenters, doctors, electricians, lawyers, nurses, plumbers, teachers, and other professionals and craftsmen. Contributed services

and promises to give services that do not meet the above criteria shall not be recognized.[14]

Contributions of services that create or enhance nonfinancial assets may be measured by referring to either the fair value of the services received or the fair value of the asset or of the asset enhancement resulting from the services.[15]

A major uncertainty about the existence of value may indicate that an item received or given should not be recognized.[16]

These rules mean that your agency may need to include the value of certain volunteer services in its external financial statements. The services that meet the criteria described above must be recorded as revenues or gains in the year in which your agency receives the services. At the same time, the services are recorded either as expenses (if they provide no future benefit) or as part of long-term assets (if they create or enhance assets such as buildings, inventory, and equipment).

Under the FASB rules, not all volunteer services must be recorded. A volunteer whom you train to be a tour guide, for example, does not necessarily have "specialized skills" as defined above. However, the time of a lawyer who contributes free legal service or a carpenter who builds new storage space may have to be included in your financial statements. Of course, advocates of social accounting would argue that, for many organizations, omitting mention of the contributions of all volunteers and members (or relegating them simply to a footnote to the financial statements) may greatly misrepresent your total assets.

Let's consider three other examples of how the FASB rules currently apply. We are including these here to assist you in presenting the concepts in this chapter to your accountants.

- Nonprofit A begins to construct a new facility to house its programs. It incurs a total cost of $75,000 to acquire land and to obtain necessary permits. A local contractor volunteers to contribute the materials and to build the facility for Nonprofit A. Upon completion, the facility (including the land) is estimated to have an appraised value of $125,000. Nonprofit A must record contributed services revenue of $50,000 because the contractor's services create a nonfinancial asset, the new facility, with a value of $50,000. The facility should be recorded as an asset of $50,000.

- Nonprofit B employs both paid and unpaid teachers. The unpaid teachers volunteer their services because they are members of a religious order. Both types of teachers have the same duties, responsibilities, and teaching qualifications. Nonprofit B should include both contributed services revenue and salaries expense for the services contributed by the unpaid teachers. Teaching requires special skills; the unpaid teachers have those skills, which would have been purchased by Nonprofit B had the unpaid teachers not contributed their time. To estimate the value of the unpaid teachers' time, Nonprofit B could use either the Karn method or the salaries of paid teachers with similar qualifications, experience, and duties.

- One of the members of Nonprofit C's board of trustees is an accountant who has served for many years. The accountant has occasionally provided routine business advice to management and the board but refers all substantive questions to the organization's CPA firm. Nonprofit C should not include the fair value of the board member's services in its financial statements. Those services do not require specialized skills because the board member did not answer any complex questions requiring an accountant's specialized skills.

Even if contributed services are recorded in the external financial statements, the FASB requires that information about contributed services be included *in the notes* to those statements. This additional requirement is as follows:

> An entity that receives contributed services shall describe the programs or activities for which those services were used, including the nature and extent of contributed services received for the period and the amount recognized as revenues for the period. Entities are encouraged to disclose the fair value of contributed services received but not recognized as revenues if that is practicable.[17]

This means that you should include descriptive information in your external financial statements about the types of contributed services your agency receives. That information should help the readers of your statements understand the nature of your programs and supporting activities in addition to the extent to which you depend on contributed services. What follows are two examples of notes to financial statements that discuss volunteer services.

Example 1

No amounts have been reflected in the financial statements for donated services. The United Way pays for most services requiring specific expertise. However, many individuals volunteer their time and perform a variety of tasks that assist the United Way with specific assistance programs, campaign solicitations, and various committee assignments. The United Way receives more than 12,000 volunteer hours per year.[18]

Example 2

The organization recognizes contribution revenue for certain services at the fair value of those services. Those services include the following items:

	20X1	20X0
Home outreach program:		
Salaries:		
Social work interns—261 and 315 hours at $12 per hour	$3,132	$3,780
Registered nurse—200 and 220 hours at $15 per hour	3,000	3,300
Total salaries	6,132	7,080
Management and general:		
Accounting services	10,000	19,000
Total contributed services	$ 16,132	$ 26,080

In addition, approximately 80,000 hours, for which no value has been assigned, were volunteered by tutors in the home outreach program.[19]

Both of these notes meet the FASB's minimum requirements. But which better conveys the importance of the agency's volunteers to financial statement readers? As previously demonstrated, it is possible to measure, on an objective, verifiable basis, the value of contributed services. It requires the agency to keep records. This may be a difficult job, particularly at first, but it can be done.

You will need an information system that can do the following:

- Distinguish between contributed services that must be recorded in the financial statements under FASB rules and those that cannot be recorded

- Capture information describing the programs and supporting activities for which volunteer services are used

- Develop numerical information to be used to estimate the wage equivalency of those services (The Karn method described earlier is an example of such information.)

Too many nonprofits have not kept accurate records of volunteer time and have made only a minimal attempt to assign a cash figure to such time. In the past, accountants accepted this without questioning the validity of the omission or suggesting possible approaches to documenting monetary values because accounting rules did not require disclosure of contributed services. Work with your CPA, and use the methods suggested in this chapter to estimate how one of your organization's most valuable resources—volunteer time—affects your bottom line.

Sample Statement of Activities

On the next page is an example of how contributed services and contributions of other resources might appear in an agency's statement of activities under FASB guidance on preparing financial statements of a not-for-profit organization.

Other types of social accounting reporting, particularly a proposed "Expanded Value Added Statement," can be found in great detail in the book *What Counts: Social Accounting for Nonprofits and Cooperatives*, by Mook, Quarter, and Richmond.

The Internal Revenue Service

The Internal Revenue Service (IRS) completely revised Form 990 for American nonprofit organizations to report on their financial activities, with the first filings in 2009 for fiscal year 2008. Despite the universal presence of volunteers in the nation's nonprofits, the IRS continues to minimize their importance to the bottom line, with clear instructions that the amount reported for donated services and materials may not be included as part of the organization's "support" or "expense." This

Newtown Agency
Statement of Activities
Year Ended June 30, 20X6

	Unrestricted	Temporarily Restricted	Permanently Restricted	Total
Revenues, gains, and other support:				
Contributions: (See note A)				
Cash	$XXX	XX	XX	XXX
In-kind	X			X
Promises to give	XX	XX	XX	XXX
Volunteer services	XX			XX
Total contributions	XXXX	XXX	XXX	XXXXX
Fees	XXX			XXX
Other income	X			X
Total	XXXXX	XXX	XXX	XXXXXX
Expenses and losses:				
Program A	XXXX			XXXX
Program B	XXXX			XXXX
Management & general	XX			XX
Fundraising	XX			XX
Other expenses and losses	X			X
Total	XXXXX			XXXXX
Changes in net assets	XX	XXX	XXX	XXX
Net assets at beginning of year	XXX	XXX	XXX	XXXX
Net assets at end of year	XXX	XXX	XXX	XXXX

perpetuates the concept that only transactions involving cash should be used in measuring the financial results of a nonprofit organization.

In Part I, line 6, of Form 990, the organization is required to provide the number of volunteers, full and part time, who provided services during the reporting year. It is hard to know what a simple head count of volunteers means to the IRS or donors, but even this minimal requirement is immediately undercut. In their instructions to Form 990, the IRS gives those organizations that either do not track the information or provide it elsewhere, such as in their annual report, the option of providing "a reasonable estimate . . . and [they] may use any reasonable basis for this estimate." But, volunteer engagement is rarely that simple:

> At first, entering the total number of volunteers may appear to be relatively simple. However, when you consider what the IRS is trying to communicate to a third party looking at your Form 990, perhaps to compare it with other not-for-profits, it becomes a more difficult task.
>
> For example, a small not-for-profit has three full time employees, and also has a program which relies on volunteers. There are two volunteers that come in three days a week for the entire year. Those two volunteers donated almost 2,500 hours. On the other hand, a large not-for-profit has a large staff and 500 individuals that donate 5 hours of their time for the whole year. Those 500 people donated 2,500 hours just like the individuals at the small not-for-profit.
>
> Now think about your original answer. Would you still record your not-for-profit's total volunteer numbers the same way? Also, is it fair to the small not-for-profit and their volunteers?[20]

There is, however, the option to disclose more information about the number of volunteers reported on the first page of Form 990 by using Schedule O, where "organizations may, but are not required to, provide an explanation . . . as to how this number was determined, as well as the types of services or benefits provided by their volunteers."[21] Further, they can report "the amount of any donated services . . . it received or used in conjunction with a specific program service, on the lines for the narrative description of the appropriate program service":[22]

> In all, if you can describe how you track the total number of volunteers, or calculate an estimate that is based on reasonable assumptions, and are willing to document the processes that you used to determine the number on Schedule O, along with types of services that the volunteers provided, you have presented meaningful information to those who review your Form 990.[23]

As always, readers outside the United States will need to research relevant tax code and reporting requirements in their countries.

Tax Issues

American volunteers should be informed that they can take certain deductions on their federal income tax returns for some of the expenses incurred in their volunteer work. These contributions are all included as cash contributions on Schedule A for the volunteer's personal income tax return (Form 1040).

This means certain unreimbursed, out-of-pocket costs such as auto mileage;[24] parking; tolls; train, bus, or cab fares; travel expenses, lodging, and meals for overnight trips; uniforms; telephone bills; office supplies; and so on. Also, expenses spent on the service user are deductible. For example, a Big Sister who takes her Little Sister to the zoo may deduct the admission price for her Little Sister—but not for herself.

Other items that are not deductible include the value of time donated (at any hourly rate), child care expenses, and meals (unless the volunteer is away overnight).

Your organization may, of course, reimburse volunteers for any expenses they incur on your behalf. Such reimbursement is not considered income to them for tax purposes. Be aware, however, that if you give volunteers a predetermined "allowance" for expenses without documentation of actual costs incurred, any excess over actual reimbursement may indeed become taxable income to the volunteer.

It makes sense that, if volunteers spend money for you and are not reimbursed, they have made a financial contribution to your organization. If you ask your volunteers to keep track of the items on which they spend money and give you a copy of their listing, there are benefits to both of you. You help them to keep records of possible federal income tax deductions they might otherwise overlook, and you have documentation for recording these amounts as contributions to your organization.

The Value of Personal Services

As already mentioned briefly, the value of personal service given to a charitable organization is not deductible by an individual volunteer as a contribution. This is true whether the volunteer is self-employed or works for a company. In many cases, companies allow employees to do charitable work on company time, while on salary. This would usually be deductible by the company as an operating salary expense but not as a contribution, unless the amount becomes significant enough to warrant other treatment.

Sometimes an individual will suggest giving your organization an invoice for hours worked and then donating the fee back to the agency. This sounds fine, but upon closer examination has no benefit to either party and, in fact, can cause a tax liability to the individual volunteer. The volunteer in this transaction would need to record the invoice as "income" but would also have the contribution "expense"—and the net result would be zero. But some taxes are based on gross receipts (billings), so the volunteer would be taxed on the value of the invoice, even if later donating the money back. Also, a corporation might have a loss and therefore not be able to deduct the contribution in the year it was made. In neither case is much gained.

However, some volunteers (those who are contributing their professional services) may want to prepare an invoice, giving a dollar amount for the services rendered, but marked with some appropriate wording such as "cancelled—contributed time." This invoice, needing no payment from the organization, provides a basis for the amount to be recorded as donated services in the financial statements. Legally, the volunteers do not have to record the cancelled invoice on their financial records, but the invoice gives them some documentation of their time.

Sometimes individuals or organizations provide services (or goods) to nonprofits at a discount price. At the time of invoicing, you should request that the bill show the full fair market value of the services (or goods), as well as the discount. In this way, you establish a more accurate base for future budgeting and fundraising. Of course, the discount may have to be recorded on your financial statements as a contribution.

Stipends

Be careful about whether or how you give cash to volunteers, both to protect your organization from violating employment law and to avoid income tax repercussions for volunteers themselves.

Avoid uniform "reimbursement" payments of a fixed sum each week or month to cover vague expenses. Request receipts from volunteers, and maintain documentation that monies paid do not exceed costs. Similarly, while a small recognition gift to volunteers is usually appropriate, a gift of cash rarely is. Also, a very expensive or valuable gift may be questioned by taxing authorities as a form of income.

Most importantly, do not give volunteers a set amount of money that you call a "stipend" and from which you do not deduct payroll taxes. There are rules about this, and you are urged to get expert advice before acting on the misguided reasoning that "it's only a small amount in light of so much volunteered time." There may be situations in which some monetary recompense can be offered legally, but most often it causes more complications than benefits.

It's Up to You

As executive director, you must have a complete understanding of the financial aspects of your agency. The procedures described in this chapter will help you achieve this goal—and give you a starting point for discussing the issues in more depth with your financial officers and accountants. Only with a total picture of your organization's resources and how they are used can you adequately explain them to your board and potential funders. This knowledge is also needed to manage your organization on a day-to-day basis.

To implement ideas in this chapter, see . . .

Leading the Way to Successful Volunteer Involvement: Practical Tools for Busy Executives by Betty B. Stallings with Susan J. Ellis (Philadelphia: Energize, Inc., 2010).

Idea stimulators, worksheets, step-by-step guides, and more in the following section:

- Section 3: "Budgeting for and Funding Volunteer Involvement"

Notes

1. Laurie Mook, Jack Quarter, and Betty Jane Richmond, *What Counts: Social Accounting for Nonprofits and Cooperatives*, 2nd ed. (London: Sigel, 2007), xxix.
2. Linda L. Graff, *Best of All: The Quick Reference Guide To Effective Volunteer Involvement* (Dundas, Ontario, Canada: Linda Graff and Associates, 2005), 20–22.

3. Ibid.

4. Ibid.

5. For more information on how to develop a volunteer tracking system, see Susan J. Ellis and Katherine Noyes Campbell, *Proof Positive: Developing Significant Recordkeeping Systems* (Philadelphia: Energize, Inc., 2003).

6. G. Neil Karn, "The True Dollar Value of Volunteers," *The Journal of Volunteer Administration* 1, no. 2 (Winter 1982–83): 1–17; and 1, no. 3 (Spring 1983): 1–19.

7. G. Neil Karn, "Addendum to 'Money Talks,'" *The Journal of Volunteer Administration* 3, no. 1 (Fall 1984): 12–13.

8. Independent Sector, "Value of Volunteer Time," http://www.independent sector.org/programs/research/volunteer_time.html.

9. Acknowledgment is given to John Paul Dalsimer, CPA, who contributed to the original version of this chapter in the first edition. His work was revised in the second edition by Alan S. Glazer, CPA, PhD, professor of business administration at Franklin & Marshall College in Lancaster, Pennsylvania. For this third edition, review and updates were provided by Janine Bovatsek, CPA, of Beucler, Kelly & Irwin, Ltd., in Wayne, Pennsylvania.

10. Mook, Quarter, and Richmond, *What Counts*, 2.

11. Ibid., 6–7.

12. FASB, Statement of Financial Accounting Concepts No. 4, Objectives of Financial Reporting by Nonbusiness Organizations, 1980, para.15.

13. AICPA, *Audit and Accounting Guide, Not-for-Profit Organizations* (1996, rev. 2009) and Audits of Health-Care Organizations (1996, rev. 2008).

14. FASB ASC 958-605-25-16.

15. FASB ASC 958-605-30-10.

16. FASB ASC 958-605-25-4.

17. FASB ASC 958-605-50-1.

18. FASB, Results of the Field Test of the Proposed Standards for Financial Statements of Not-for-Profit Organizations and Accounting for Contributions, 1994, 85.

19. AICPA, *Audit and Accounting Guide*, para. 5.133.

20. Brett Hubert, staff accountant, Henry & Horne, LLP, "The NEW Form 990, Part I, Line 6," Nonprofit GPS, http://www.hhcpa.com/blogs/non-profit-accounting-services-blog/2009/01/06/the-new-form-990-part-i-line-6/.

21. Bruce R. Hopkins, Douglas Anning, Virginia Gross, and Thomas Schenkelberg, *The New Form 900: Law, Policy, and Preparation* (Hoboken, NJ: Wiley, 2009), 8.

22. Ibid., 25

23. Hubert, "The NEW Form 990, Part I, Line 6."

24. As of 2010, the IRS permits taxpayers who itemize deductions to calculate unreimbursed charitable driving costs at $0.14 per mile (as compared to the current business mileage deduction of $.55 per mile). This amount has been unchanged since raised from $0.12 by the Taxpayer Relief Act of 1997.

12

Executive Role
Checklist

Appendix A provides you with a "Volunteer Involvement Task Outline," a summary of the work responsibilities that make up the job description of a director of volunteer involvement. But, as we have been discussing throughout this book, that staff member cannot be effective if top management does not demonstrate institutional and personal support of volunteers on a continuous basis.

Inherent to mission success and the best public relations is making sure your organization is volunteer friendly and that the experience every volunteer has is first rate. This is as much an executive responsibility as assuring quality client service and satisfied employees.

Here are the major elements of volunteer management, described briefly. I have not gone into detail about what the daily tasks are in each area because that is what you should expect your director of volunteer involvement to focus on. Instead, I have developed a set of specific responsibilities in each area that do require your executive leadership and authority. Some have been mentioned already in previous chapters but are summarized here as well to give you the complete picture.

You can use this as a checklist to assess your present level of participation and to set goals for your future involvement in assuring the success of volunteers in contributing to your organization's important work.

1. Planning and Resource Allocation

Planning is the key to success in all administrative responsibilities, and volunteer engagement is no exception. Planning for volunteers involves the need to determine exactly why volunteers are wanted, exactly what volunteers are expected to do, what resources will be necessary to support the work of volunteers, who will be designated to lead the volunteer effort, who will provide training and ongoing supervision of volunteers, and what preparation these key people will need.

Executive Role

❑ Develop mission-focused goals and objectives and then the necessary policies and procedures for volunteer involvement. Write and disseminate a statement of philosophy regarding volunteers in your organization.

❑ Place the subject of volunteers and community involvement on the agenda of staff meetings regularly and on the agenda of board meetings at least annually.

❑ Staff your volunteer engagement effort appropriately, and hold the leader of volunteers to high standards.

❑ Assure that the director of volunteer involvement answers to the most logical administrator. Make yourself accessible if and when special questions needing decision-making authority arise concerning the involvement of volunteers organization-wide.

❑ Budget funds and allocate other resources appropriately. Recognize the financial value of volunteer service as an important contribution to your organization.

❑ Seek adequate funding for volunteer engagement, and include requests for money to support volunteers in grant applications for any project or program that proposes volunteer participation.

❑ Make sure that all employees are trained to work effectively with volunteers and participate in identifying categories of work for volunteers.

❏ Assure that good risk management practices are implemented to keep volunteers, staff, and recipients of services as safe as possible. Work with legal counsel and insurance agents to find ways to support volunteers, not limit their involvement because of worst-case-scenario fears of risk.

❏ Include the director of volunteer involvement in future planning for the organization.

❏ Allow volunteers to experiment for you by testing new ideas that may later be fundable.

2. Designing Volunteer Work

To assure effective involvement of volunteers, define the work to be done as specifically as possible. Clarify volunteer positions in writing. Develop a wide variety of volunteer assignments so as to attract diverse people with many skills and available schedules. Consider roles for individuals and groups; those who want an ongoing commitment; and those seeking short-term or one-time projects, service that can be done on-site, in the field, or online; and other variations.

Executive Role

❏ Make sure every unit and every administrative level in the organization submits requests for volunteers. Investigate if you see pockets of refusal to consider volunteer participation.

❏ Ask for innovative engagement of volunteers in a wide variety of ways, including as consultants, in virtual assignments, in groups, on call, and more.

❏ Uphold the director of volunteer involvement when s/he says no to an inappropriate request for volunteers.

❏ Develop position descriptions for volunteers to assist you directly, to model your personal acceptance of volunteer talents.

❏ Insist that volunteer position descriptions be put in writing.

❏ Challenge everyone to be as creative as possible in tapping the expertise and talents of your community.

3. Recruitment and Public Relations

Public relations is what makes an organization visible to the public. It is necessary to have visibility and a good image so that people will be attracted to your organization to volunteer. *Recruitment* is the process of inviting people to give their time and energy to your organization. The best recruitment is targeted to the audiences most likely to have the skills and interests to match available volunteer position descriptions.

Executive Role

❑ Be sure that volunteer participation (and therefore the opportunity to apply to become a volunteer) is mentioned in the organization's descriptive materials, on your Web site, in annual reports, on membership application forms, and other public relations vehicles.

❑ Direct the information technology (IT) staff to provide links to volunteer opportunities throughout the organization's Web site; maintain an up-to-date, online list of vacancies needing new volunteers; and offer a way for someone interested to apply or at least send a message directly from the Web site.

❑ Direct the public relations or marketing staff to partner with the director of volunteer involvement in planning promotional campaigns to benefit volunteer recruitment as well as other goals.

❑ Keep the director of volunteer involvement informed of your speaking schedule, and distribute volunteer recruitment materials whenever you distribute other agency literature.

❑ Invite the director of volunteer involvement to accompany you to community events at which volunteer recruitment might be possible.

❑ Make the most of volunteers as representatives of and advocates for your organization.

4. Screening and Selection

Many supervision and management problems can be prevented by effective initial interviewing of prospective volunteers. The screening (including screening out, if necessary) and selection process surfaces the expectations of the applicant and allows the director of volunteer involvement to explain the standards of the organization. Also, each new volunteer should be matched to the most appropriate assignment. Screening includes complying with legal requirements such as doing background checks on prospective volunteers who will work with vulnerable clients.

Executive Role

- ❑ Back up the director of volunteer involvement's right to screen out inappropriate candidates and also the right of unit staff to determine if a particular candidate is right for the volunteer position or not.

- ❑ Keep the director of volunteer involvement informed of requirements for background checks, health screening, or other legal procedures. Budget for expenses incurred in fulfilling such requirements.

- ❑ Assure that any and all people who help your organization without going on the payroll undergo the same interviewing and screening process and are registered with the volunteer office, regardless of who recruits them, to whom they are related, who will supervise their work, or how influential they are. This includes student interns, holiday helpers, expert advisors contributing their time on a pro bono basis, and others.

- ❑ While every member of the staff is welcome to seek out prospective volunteers, allow no one to bring a volunteer on board without processing them through the volunteer office—including unpaid student interns and pro bono volunteers working at a management level.

- ❑ Tell the personnel department not to send rejected job applicants to the volunteer office with the suggestion that volunteering is an alternative to employment with you (unless they are really appropriate candidates to be good volunteers).

- ❑ Apply the same hiring procedures and standards to volunteers as to employees, particularly avoiding discrimination and welcoming diversity.

5. Orientation and Training

Orientation is the overview of the total organization necessary for every new volunteer, regardless of specific assignment. It places the work into context and allows for consistent introduction of policies, procedures, rights, and responsibilities. *Training* is individualized and should vary with the demands of each specific volunteer position description and the background each volunteer brings to the organization. There is the need for initial, start-up training, plus the need for ongoing, in-service training. Much training is really the giving of good instructions and is often integrated into the overall supervision plan.

Executive Role

❏ Participate in the welcoming of new volunteers (either in person each time, through videotape, or by a letter of greeting).

❏ Review the content of the orientation to be sure it represents the organization as you wish it to.

❏ Assure that all volunteers receive training appropriate to their needs, position descriptions, and individual knowledge level.

❏ Recognize that it will take staff time to train volunteers and adjust workload demands accordingly.

❏ Develop a training plan for volunteers assigned directly to you.

❏ Include volunteers whenever possible in in-service or continuing education training opportunities available to employees.

❏ Budget for the director of volunteer involvement to attend professional development conferences and seminars and to take along leadership volunteers when appropriate.

6. Volunteer-Employee Relations

The interrelationship of volunteers and paid staff is the single biggest pitfall to success, unless steps are taken early to encourage teamwork. There are numerous reasons why employees are threatened by volunteers or why volunteers may be resistant to working well with employees. This is a human relations issue, and staff development training on this topic is vital. Clarification of roles and commitment from top administration are critical aspects to success in this area.

Executive Role

☐ Provide training for employees on the subject of working successfully with volunteers.

☐ Monitor the degree of acceptance of volunteers by the paid staff, paying special attention to the attitudes of middle managers. Provide positive and negative sanctions for working or not working well with volunteers.

☐ Include questions on agency employment application forms and in applicant job interviews about past experience working with volunteers and being a volunteer.

☐ Include the expectation of effective teamwork with volunteers in the job description of any staff member who will be working with volunteers.

☐ Approach specific interpersonal problems between members of staff and particular volunteers objectively. Do not tip the scales in favor of the employee before hearing all the facts, and be open to deciding that either may be in the right.

☐ Negotiate with labor union leaders as an advocate for volunteers.

☐ Clarify the roles and interrelationships of the volunteer department with the public relations staff, personnel, or human resources department; the development office; staff responsible for special events; and any other unit with responsibilities related to involvement of volunteers.

7. Supervising and Partnering with Volunteers

As with paid staff, volunteer staff need support from those in a position to see the total picture and who know what work needs to be done. This may require the paid staff to supervise volunteers in the traditional sense or to partner with an expert volunteering consultation time—serving as a point of contact or liaison. For volunteers, a key aspect of supervision is access to someone in charge during the actual time the volunteer is on duty or when the volunteer who is working independently in the field needs a question answered.

Executive Role

- ❏ Again, recognize that it will take staff time to supervise volunteers well.
- ❏ Clarify that volunteers are the responsibility of all staff members—and that volunteers do not "belong" to the director of volunteer involvement.
- ❏ When interviewing new hires, ask questions about their past training and experience in working with volunteers. Stress that they will be expected to partner with volunteers in your organization. If they are not skilled in this responsibility when hired, assure they receive training.
- ❏ Include volunteers on the organizational chart under each unit in which they are active.
- ❏ Reserve time to supervise volunteers assigned directly to you.
- ❏ Clarify lines of responsibility between the organization and any independently organized volunteer advocacy, support, or fundraising group such as an auxiliary. Be accessible to the officers of such groups, and make sure they are kept informed about agency plans.
- ❏ Apply the principles of effective volunteer management in your work with the board of directors.

8. Coordination

By definition, volunteers are part-time staff. Your organization may have volunteers who work once a year or regularly on schedules ranging from one afternoon a week to four days a week, mornings and evenings, alternate Sundays, and so on. Add to this the diversity of the people who volunteer (all ages, backgrounds, physical conditions, academic degrees), and you end up with an amazing logistical challenge to coordinate all the details of scheduling and assigning.

Executive Role

- ❑ Recognize the unique nature of the volunteer scheduling pattern (diverse, part-time hours), and make sure the organization can respond. For example, assure that everyone recognizes the importance of taking messages when the director of volunteer involvement is unavailable, or keep evening reception desk staff informed about volunteer projects under way in the evenings.

- ❑ Assign adequate staff leadership to volunteer engagement. At a minimum, designate evening, night, or weekend supervisors responsible for supporting volunteers in the absence of the director of volunteer involvement.

- ❑ Require that every department, major function, or separate physical location designate someone to serve as liaison between that department, unit, or branch and the volunteer office.

- ❑ Assure that there is communication and coordination among the volunteer office and other departments, particularly public relations, marketing, development, and special events.

9. Recordkeeping and Reporting

If volunteers are important to the work of the organization, then it is important to know what volunteers are doing. Such documentation assists in recruitment, training, recognition, and fundraising. For purposes of insurance and to back up the income tax deduction claims of volunteers, recordkeeping by the agency is also vital. Once records are kept, they are of little meaning if they are not reported. Reports of the cumulative achievements of volunteers should be shared routinely with the volunteers themselves, as well as with other top managers, the board, and funding sources.

Executive Role

- ❑ Require useful reports about volunteer involvement, and expect to see these regularly even if you do not directly supervise the director of volunteer involvement.

❏ Ask for narrative information about volunteer activities, not simply "bottom line" totals of the numbers of volunteers on board.

❏ Read and respond to volunteer involvement reports when submitted.

❏ Purchase computer software designed for the special needs of volunteer management, and insist that the agency's IT department work with the director of volunteer involvement to make existing software do what is necessary to manage volunteers better (or recommend purchasing software that will).

❏ Make sure each department submits forms and other necessary data about volunteers to the volunteer office in a timely and complete fashion.

❏ Look for (and ask for) mention of volunteer activities in the reports of other department heads or staff members.

❏ Include data on volunteer participation in reports you make to the board or to funders. Also include such data in agency annual reports.

❏ Integrate the databases of time donors and money donors so that they all can be compared and acknowledged for the full extent of their support and invited to be active on both lists.

10. Evaluation

It is sinful to waste the time of a volunteer. Therefore, it is imperative to evaluate regularly the impact of services performed by volunteers and whether those services are still necessary. Along with program evaluation, it is helpful to conduct individual performance reviews with volunteers so as to maintain their motivation, troubleshoot potential problem areas, and adjust assignments as necessary.

Executive Role

❏ Articulate outcome measures for volunteer participation that are aligned with the work of the entire organization. Set measurable goals and objectives.

❑ Insist on performance that meets high standards—hold volunteers accountable for meeting goals and being productive, just as you do employees.

❑ Include assessment of volunteer involvement in any evaluation of the overall organization.

❑ Evaluate the director of volunteer involvement on his/her ability to implement a volunteer engagement strategy that taps a wide variety of community resources and responds to current trends in volunteerism.

❑ Evaluate paid staff on the criterion of how well they have worked with volunteers during the period being assessed.

❑ Ask volunteers for their perspective, opinions, and suggestions on the operational effectiveness of the organization.

11. Recognition

Recognition is one way we "pay" volunteers for their efforts, but it has many nuances. If there is an annual banquet but no daily support, recognition is given "with forked tongue"! While formalized, annual thank-you events are worthwhile, informal, continuous recognition is more important. This includes everything from simple courtesy to including volunteers in staff meetings and decision making. It is also a part of recognition to offer constructive criticism, since such feedback implies a belief that the volunteer can do even better work.

We sometimes confuse "recognition" with "appreciation." These are not the same thing and do not always go together. Their common denominator is *acknowledgment*. Perhaps the sincerest form of recognition is to see one's ideas put into action. Both employees and volunteers want to see that they make a difference. The annual volunteer recognition event is not an end; it's a *beginning* to the next year. Volunteers—and paid staff—should leave remotivated and recommitted. As executive, this is also your opportunity to articulate and reaffirm your vision for the importance and potential of volunteer involvement.

Executive Role

❑ Be visible to volunteers year-round, and take time to interact with them occasionally in an informal manner.

❑ Participate in formal recognition events, whether as a speaker, in signing certificates, or by simply taking part. Write your own speeches, and show how informed you are about the work volunteers are doing. Stay for the whole event.

❑ Encourage board members to attend volunteer recognition events, both because they, too, deserve thanks for their contributed efforts and to show that they value the volunteer services of others.

❑ Periodically share updates on new developments, future plans, and other news with the corps of volunteers— especially actions that will affect them.

❑ Provide tangible recognition to employees who have been successful in working with volunteers.

12. Volunteer Input

Too many organizations want help, not *input*. Volunteers bring a different perspective from employees or clients. This point of view may result from being less vested in the professional process, from being younger or older, or from simply having the distance that a part-time schedule allows. Volunteers are in a position to observe the organization and can take more risks in criticizing or speaking out. Develop ways to let their perspective be heard, or volunteers will either cause friction or leave. Also, actively seek practical and innovative ideas from volunteers.

Executive Role

❑ Develop channels for allowing volunteers to voice ideas and suggestions, including criticisms.

❑ Be open to considering volunteers' ideas. Respond to such ideas, even if you must explain why the suggestion cannot be implemented.

❑ Get volunteers to form collaborations between your organization and other community groups, especially if there are obstacles that might confront paid staff, such as restrictions on areas of jurisdiction.

❑ Maximize the special, unique benefits of volunteers on a day-to-day basis: use volunteers as a sounding board, and ask them to give you honest reactions to plans; tap their knowledge of the community.

❑ Schedule time for members of administration to meet volunteers individually and in small groups as a "think tank" (which is also a very meaningful form of recognition).

❑ Be accessible to meeting with volunteers personally when appropriate.

❑ Make sure that any evaluation of the organization or its programs includes the surveying of volunteers.

❑ Tap frontline volunteers to serve on agency planning committees, advisory groups, and board subcommittees.

13. Volunteers as Supporters

Volunteers are a powerful corps of supporters—if you make use of their perspectives and influence. But they do not produce "good public relations" or "community representation" to and from the organization spontaneously. In order for volunteers to be effective as public relations agents, they need accurate information. Keep volunteers informed regularly about new services, changes in personnel, and issues impacting your organization. Find specific ways for volunteers to become external messengers about your work.

Executive Role

❑ Periodically, give each volunteer three agency brochures and ask him/her to give them to someone who might benefit from knowing about your services.

❑ Ask volunteers to write to funders, legislators, or the newspaper about what they have learned about your organization or cause while doing volunteer work with you. Or suggest they include their volunteer experiences in a blog or other social networking forum.

❑ Select a work project that requires many hands, and ask each volunteer to bring one friend or relative for three hours to help accomplish the task. The project is an end unto itself, will make all who participate feel good, and does more to publicize your usefulness to the community than speeches do.

❑ Consider whether periodic meetings to inform volunteers about your plans for the future might not yield positive results.

❑ Add volunteers to your communication distribution list, even to in-house memos, to increase their ability to speak accurately on your behalf.

A Last Word about Your Role

Underlying everything in the checklist presented in this chapter is your role in *setting the tone* for volunteer involvement. Your personal support and enthusiasm (or lack of it) will be obvious to volunteers and employees alike. Your willingness to allocate organization resources to and time on your own schedule for volunteers validates that community participants are indeed part of the personnel team.

You also provide *leadership* in making volunteer involvement integral to the work of your organization. You can put the subject of volunteers "on the agenda," finding opportunities to ask, "Are we doing the best job of tapping volunteer skills in this area?" Including the director of volunteer involvement and, when appropriate, representative volunteers themselves on such committees as quality assurance or long-range planning sends a positive message to everyone—and gives you valuable input.

To implement ideas in this chapter, see . . .

Leading the Way to Successful Volunteer Involvement: Practical Tools for Busy Executives by Betty B. Stallings with Susan J. Ellis (Philadelphia: Energize, Inc., 2010).

Each of the ten sections closes with an "Executive Self-Assessment," a checklist allowing you to consider your role in each area in greater depth.

Conclusion

Historically, volunteers were the pioneers, the innovators who recognized existing community needs and found ways to meet them. Almost every institution and profession we take for granted today owes its initial establishment to the efforts of citizens who chose to become involved in a cause. Such pioneering continues to be a part of the volunteer picture today. The organization you head may well be able to name the key volunteers who filed your incorporation papers and made up your first board. Some of them may even still be around to see the fruits of their early labor.

In 1986, I noted that the previous decade had seen volunteers institute hospice programs, services to victims of abuse, and projects looking ahead to space colonization—just to name a few. By the second edition ten years later, volunteers had been instrumental in founding innumerable services to people with AIDS, programs to help "crack babies," and previously inconceivable forms of virtual interaction on the Internet. By 2010, we have seen volunteers rally in response to acts of terrorism and the destruction of natural disasters, take up the cause of global warming, and create online charter schools. New frontiers continue to emerge.

The media in the 1980s gravitated toward labels such as "the Me Generation" or "self-involved Yuppies." The 1990s brought dismay over the negativity of "Generation X" and the disillusionment of the middle class. Economic crisis is in the headlines as the first decade of the new century ends, caused in large part by those who placed personal gain over the common good. Volunteering is the antithesis of such negative images. All the studies and polls prove that vast numbers of Americans (and people in other countries) do become involved in their communities. In fact, volunteering is so pervasive that we tend to take it for granted. And, as discussed throughout this book, there are many exciting new sources of people seeking ways to serve, whatever vocabulary they may use to identify themselves. Volunteerism has truly become "community resource mobilization."

Legislative and economic changes continue to create uncertainty about the future of many nonprofit organizations and government services. Volunteering has been tossed into the limelight, often for the wrong reasons. The question is not whether volunteers can fill budget gaps but whether organizations are truly prepared to utilize volunteers in teamwork with paid staff.

The common wisdom that "people are our greatest asset" resonates in all settings but especially when volunteers are involved. The most effective executives in the future will learn to lead, not manage—to bring out the best in employees and volunteers. "People raising" comes before fundraising.

From the Top Down presents executives with the challenge of tapping community resources to the maximum. Volunteers cannot fully and successfully contribute to an organization unless they receive visibility and management attention. You have the authority and power necessary to set the tone for volunteer involvement in your organization—your vision and commitment will provide leadership for paid and volunteer staff alike.

Appendix A

Volunteer Involvement Task Outline

The following is an outline of the major functions and responsibilities necessary to lead an organization's volunteer engagement strategy and shows the scope of the job of the director of volunteer involvement. Therefore, you can use it as a framework from which to write a job description for the position of leader of volunteers in your organization.

I. Planning and Administration

A. *With top management*, provide support to accomplish the following:

1. Articulate a vision for volunteer involvement in the organization, including determining who will be considered a "volunteer" and therefore administered by the volunteer office.

2. Develop long-term goals and objectives for the maximum impact of volunteers.

3. Set policies and procedures.

4. Develop risk management strategies.

B. Determine annual goals, objectives, and strategies.

C. Propose and manage the budget and other support needs for volunteer engagement.

D. Advocate for the inclusion of volunteers in all organization plans.

E. Create and manage a comprehensive recordkeeping system both to track data about volunteers and descriptive details about their activities.

F. Assure that all employees are prepared to work effectively with volunteers.

G. Develop and work with an advisory or steering committee focused on volunteer involvement planning.

H. Coordinate activities with other department heads whenever activities overlap, especially those staff responsible for development and fundraising, marketing, special events, Internet technology, and client services.

I. Provide the organization with information on current trends and issues in volunteerism, with suggestions as to how to react to or adopt new approaches to volunteer involvement.

II. Volunteer Work Design

A. Assess and analyze the needs of the organization's clientele, staff, and the public to determine highest priority roles for volunteers to fill.

B. With the staff who will work directly with volunteers, design volunteer assignments that contribute meaningful work and are attractive to potential volunteers.

C. Develop new projects and activities for a wide variety of volunteers, including group service, one-time and episodic tasks, online assignments, pro bono and highly skilled roles, and so on.

D. Assure that position descriptions are written for all volunteer roles, and maintain an updated archive of all such descriptions.

E. Model effective volunteer management by creating leadership and support assignments for volunteers to assist in running the volunteer program.

III.   Recruitment

A. Keep track of all vacancies in volunteer positions and needs for additional help.

B. With Internet technology staff, develop an area on the organization's Web site that highlights volunteer involvement and keep the information current.

C. Plan targeted volunteer recruitment strategies, including making use of the growing variety of online resources.

D. Develop recruitment and media relations materials.

E. Handle public speaking and personal contacts; maintain such relationships on behalf of the organization.

F. Manage ongoing recruitment efforts.

IV.   Interviewing and Screening

A. Prepare application forms and procedures for conducting any required background and reference checks on applicants.

B. Conduct initial interviews, and schedule second interviews with staff who will work directly with any candidates.

C. Determine which candidates are best, and appropriately refuse those who do not qualify.

D. Match accepted volunteers to the assignment to which they are most suited.

E. Facilitate group volunteer involvement by interviewing the leader, liaison, or contact person of each source of group effort.

V.   Orientation and Training

A. Develop and run an orientation program for all volunteers, regardless of assignment.

B. Offer staff development in how to work effectively with volunteers.

C. Assure that each supervisor or staff partner designs an appropriate training plan that supports each volunteer position description and is appropriate to each volunteer's skill level.

D. Develop in-service training opportunities for volunteers.

E. Prepare volunteer manuals and handbooks.

VI. Supervision and Liaison Support

A. Handle direct supervision of volunteers and employees working with the volunteer office.

B. Assure and support good supervision and partnering practices by those to whom volunteers are assigned, and help middle managers to provide oversight to volunteer supervision in their departments and units.

C. Be a liaison, available to all volunteers and employees as the next step in the chain of command or grievance procedure.

D. Assist in the individual volunteer performance assessment of volunteers.

VII. Ongoing Motivation and Recognition

A. Assure ongoing volunteer motivation by helping to create a welcoming work environment for both paid and volunteer staff, including daily, informal appreciation of service contributed.

B. Arrange for opportunities for volunteers to give feedback and input into organizational planning; create a feedback loop that encourages constructive criticism and creative thinking.

C. Communicate, communicate, communicate. Represent the plans and decisions of the organization to the volunteers and, in turn, provide a voice for the volunteer perspective to be expressed to organization leaders.

D. Plan and conduct formal and annual recognition activities.

E. Provide recognition to paid staff who partner effectively with volunteers.

F. Develop ways for interested volunteers to advance in responsibility and assignment challenges.

VIII. Evaluating Impact

A. Conduct regular evaluations of volunteer involvement, both as part of any organization-wide assessment and to focus independently on questions important to volunteer engagement.

B. Assess ongoing progress in all volunteer projects, activities, and program components.

IX. Recordkeeping and Reporting

A. Assure that data gathering protocols are followed throughout the organization so that information is available on the contributions of volunteers.

B. Write monthly reports on current volunteer services; bring highpoints and concerns to the attention of top management.

C. Compile an annual report to give an overview of the year's ongoing and special accomplishments, including a profile of that year's volunteers (their diversity and backgrounds, as well as their number).

D. Share reports with all stakeholders such as other department heads and especially with volunteers themselves.

E. Periodically present information on volunteer involvement to the board of directors.

F. With the development office, compare the list of financial donors to the list of volunteers (time donors), and invite people from each list to consider also becoming involved in the other.

X. Other Responsibilities (as applicable to each organization)

A. Be a liaison to any all-volunteer group supporting the organization, such as an auxiliary or friends group.

B. Participate in planning and running agency fundraising events, coordinating volunteer assistance.

C. Solicit in-kind donations to assist agency services.

D. Represent the organization at community functions; represent the organization to visiting community members.

E. Support the executive in board development, orientation, and recognition.

F. Organize any workplace volunteerism efforts in which the organization's employees provide service to the community at large.

G. Develop own professional skills, and remain current on developments in volunteerism.

Appendix B

Volunteerism Resources

Volunteerism continues to grow as a distinct management discipline. This means that the skills of developing and managing volunteers are being codified so that newcomers to this responsibility can learn from the experience of their predecessors.

It should be noted that *volunteerism* is connected to but different from *voluntarism*, and these two words are often confused. *Voluntarism* refers to all voluntary activities in a society (in the United States, that includes religion) and covers issues of concern to voluntary, not-for-profit agencies. *Volunteerism*, on the other hand, refers to anything involving *volunteers* and *volunteering*, regardless of setting. Government agencies, which are not part of the "voluntary sector," may indeed be included under the umbrella of *volunteerism* when it comes to volunteers active in schools, libraries, courts, parks and recreation, and all other such public services.

In most geographic areas, it is increasingly possible to obtain some training in volunteer management, either through a formal institution of higher learning (though still usually for continuing education, not academic, credit) and through workshops sponsored by a wide array of organizations. Books, journals, Web sites, and online learning on volunteerism are available. There are also full conferences for leaders of volunteer involvement throughout North America and around the world, some with a general reach to any type of service and setting, others focused on specific fields.

As executive, you should expect your director of volunteer involvement to become familiar with such resources and to become active in relevant professional associations. It is important to encourage this leader of volunteers to seek out colleagues in volunteerism generically, as well as those in settings similar to yours. Many of the approaches and techniques successfully utilized in other types of organizations can be applied with equal success in any setting.

If you do not already have a director of volunteer involvement, you may need to become familiar with volunteerism resources yourself or help the staff member you have designated to work with volunteers as a part-time responsibility to make use of such resources. Leadership-level volunteers themselves may also benefit from such training and information.

Here are some of the most commonly available sources through which to seek information on successful volunteer engagement strategies.

Online Sources of Information

Neither the first nor second edition of this book could have included a section about resources available on the World Wide Web, as the Web did not exist until 1991 and most volunteerism practitioners were slow to get involved with the new technology. How things have changed! One of the biggest complaints directors of volunteer involvement used to have was isolation—often being the only person in their setting responsible for the success of volunteers and therefore having no one with whom to discuss issues knowledgeably. It's dramatically different today, particular for anyone who can at least read the English language.

Enter the words "volunteer management" into any online search engine, and you'll get thousands of results. And the Web sites will be all over the world, too. In fact, the problem really is more how to cull the wheat from the chaff to find the most useful material. To that end, start your research at one of the "portal" Web sites listed below that collect and categorize the material for you, as well as continuously add new resources.

- **Energize, Inc.** (http://www.energizeinc.com). My company, Energize, Inc., offers the largest Web site in the world focused exclusively on information for *leaders* of volunteers in any setting. With over one thousand free site pages, we provide an extensive online library and annotated list of links, directories of volunteer-related resources around the globe, visitor-contributed quotes and stories, and much more. We also have a job bank through which you are invited to advertise any job opening for a position directly responsible for some sort of volunteer project—at no cost to you.

- **Idealist** (http://www.idealist.org). Idealist (a program of Action Without Borders) is an international multilingual (English, French, and Spanish) site that serves people who wish to volunteer, agencies seeking volunteers, and people seeking jobs in either human resources or volunteer management. In 2007, in partnership with Energize, they opened the Volunteer Management Resource Center (http://www .idealist.org/vmrc) to provide targeted information on the position of volunteer program manager.

- **National Service Resource Center** (http://www.national serviceresources.org). The National Service Resource Center, administered by ETR Associates, is the knowledge management training and technical assistance provider to the Corporation for National and Community Service (commonly referred to in field as "the Corporation"). Some of its resources are for the use of federally funded service programs such as AmeriCorps and RSVP. But much of the site is publicly accessible and free. Two other useful Corporation sites are Volunteering in America (http://www.volunteering inamerica.gov), which provides the most recent statistics about volunteering in interactive form, and the National Service-Learning Clearinghouse (http://www.servicelearn ing.org).

- **Volunteering England** (http://www.volunteering.org.uk). The Web site of Volunteering England offers a good deal of excellent information on topics as diverse as corporate employee volunteering, engaging a diverse volunteer force, and more, including downloadable guides on specific subjects.

- **ServiceLeader** (http://www.serviceleader.org). ServiceLeader is a project of the RGK Center for Philanthropy and Community Service at the Lyndon B. Johnson School of Public Affairs of the University of Texas at Austin. It offers a range of practical and research information about volunteer management.

- **World Volunteer Web** (http://www.worldvolunteerweb .org). ServiceLeader United Nations Volunteers (UNV) runs World Volunteer Web, a truly international site providing volunteer-related news and information from every country in the United Nations (UN). It is a great starting point to find more in-depth resources in different countries.

- **The Center for Association Leadership** (http://www .asaecenter.org). The Center for Association Leadership from the American Society of Association Executives is one go-to source for leaders of membership associations, including professional societies, trade associations, and others who get their work done predominantly through the volunteer participation of their members. The site offers many knowledge resources.

- **BoardSource** (http://www.boardsource.org). BoardSource is focused exclusively on developing effective nonprofit boards of directors.

- **The Taproot Foundation** (http://www.taprootfoundation .org). The Taproot Foundation is a leader in supporting corporate employee volunteering and pro bono service.

The Web is an ever-changing environment, and URLs can disappear overnight. The sites above have a track record of stability and consistent quality, but there are literally hundreds of wonderful volunteerism sites in cyberspace, especially if you are searching for information on specific topics. The overall goal of http://www.energizeinc.com is to find, collect, and refer visitors to what's currently available. So you can always use us as a starting point.

Volunteer Opportunity Registries

Hardly imaginable a decade ago, one of the important resources today for volunteer engagement is the growing number of online sites where volunteer opportunities can be posted—in a wide array of countries. The largest of these in the United States are http://www.Volunteer Match.org and http://www.Idealist.org, but there are many more, some narrowly focused on certain types of service or types of volunteers. A number of "aggregator" sites such as http://www.Serve.gov and http://www.AllforGood.org search the largest databases and provide information from all of them to users. Several sites also offer online training and other services for both or either volunteers themselves and project managers. Energize maintains a list of all such sites around the world at http://www.energizeinc.com/prof/volop.html.

Online Discussion Forums

Just as every other profession, volunteer management has evolved ways for practitioners to exchange information and support online. Many listservs or online discussion boards exist, but three are the most established and are open to leaders of volunteers from any type of setting. CyberVPM was first and stands for "cyberspace volunteer program managers." Then came UKVPMs and OzVPM, serving the United Kingdom and Australasia, respectively. As it happens, all three are hosted by Yahoo Groups, and those who already have a Yahoo account can sign on directly from within that site. Otherwise, for any or all three, one can join by *sending a blank e-mail* to the following e-mail addresses:

- cybervpm-subscribe@yahoogroups.com
- UKVPMs-subscribe@yahoogroups.com
- OzVPM-subscribe@yahoogroups.com

For a list of other electronic discussion groups related to volunteering, see http://www.energizeinc.com/prof/listserv.html.

Blogs

Note, as well, that blogs (and, increasingly, microblogs) concerning volunteer issues are proliferating and provide a new source of valuable collegial exchange. Again, Energize maintains an updated listing of the field's blogs at http://www.energizeinc.com/prof/blogs.html.

Associations and Resource Providers

There is an infrastructure supporting effective volunteer management in many countries. The United States, Canada, Australia, and the United Kingdom are highly organized, with both professional associations and agencies providing resources to the volunteer field at local, regional, and national levels. However, there is a growing infrastructure in places such as Japan, Singapore, Israel, New Zealand, and across Europe.

For the purposes of this appendix, I am going to explain these groups as they operate in the United States. This will give non-American readers a framework within which to identify resources available in their countries.

At the Local Level

Volunteer Centers, HandsOn Affiliates, and Other Volunteer Clearinghouses

Volunteer centers (the one in your community may have a variation on the name) are local advocates for community service and clearinghouses for information on volunteer opportunities. Organizations seeking volunteers can "register" their needs, while members of the public can contact the volunteer center to discover what volunteer assignments are available (though increasingly they are being directed to online directories and matching sites). There are active volunteer centers around the world.

Different volunteer centers engage in different projects. Today, most maintain an online database of volunteer opportunities, either independently or as part of a national database fed by many volunteer centers. Other centers actually interview potential volunteers and try to individualize the assistance in finding the right volunteer activity. Many centers organize community-wide events for National Volunteer Week or International Volunteer Day or coordinate collaborative recruitment efforts such as shopping mall fairs. The larger volunteer centers also maintain libraries of materials on volunteer program development. Those that are part of their local United Way, however, may be limited in what they actively support beyond human service agencies or may be distracted during campaign time.

In 2008, the national organization representing volunteer centers, Points of Light Foundation, merged with an organization focusing on single days of service, called HandsOn Network (see the section on national resources for more on what is now called HandsOn Network

Generated by Points of Light Institute). Each existing volunteer center has been given the chance to become an official HandsOn affiliate, but it is too soon to know how many will rename themselves; so you might discover your community now has a "HandsOn Center" or, the 2009 name of choice, simply "Action Center." Some of the older affiliates still carry the original name of "[City] Cares," as in New York Cares, Philadelphia Cares, and so on.

HandsOn affiliates all recruit volunteers interested in episodic volunteering. To that end, each HandsOn affiliate produces a monthly calendar of volunteer opportunities from which their members can choose one, none, or several to do that month. The volunteer's identity is as a HandsOn volunteer, providing services to different community agencies all the time.

If your community has a volunteer center or HandsOn affiliate, by all means get on its postal or e-mail list. This should assure you of receiving information about local training workshops, conferences, or meetings focused on volunteerism.

There are other volunteer clearinghouses, as well. Colleges and universities that encourage their students to volunteer or require some form of community service before graduation often create a campus office to help students find placement sites. Campus centers welcome receiving information on what types of volunteering are available and often can help find students with particular skills and interests.

Similarly, large corporations that want to help their employees to volunteer (usually on the employee's own time) also maintain a database of information on agencies interested in finding volunteers. At a minimum, these companies will help to disseminate information on volunteer opportunities

Directors of Volunteers in Agencies (DOVIAs)

Whether or not your community has a volunteer center, it may have what has come to be called, generically, a DOVIA. This stands for Directors of Volunteers in Agencies and is simply an association of people who have the responsibility for leading volunteer engagement in their organizations. Many different names are out there, from Volunteer Coordinators Roundtable to Association for Volunteer Administrators.

DOVIAs usually meet regularly several times a year and operate as self-help professional groups. They plan their meetings to provide a mixture of collegial interaction (often the main benefit of attending)

and provision of information. There is usually a speaker who addresses the group about some aspect of volunteer management.

The more established DOVIAs sponsor periodic workshops in which nationally known trainers may be invited to present. Newsletters and other forms of resource exchange are also common. All costs for these activities are covered through very reasonable membership dues or registration fees. Often, the local volunteer center offers some staff support for the DOVIA in its community.

Corporate Volunteer Councils and Special Affinity Groups

In large cities, there may also be a Corporate Volunteer Council (CVC), again under a range of names, possibly using the words "workplace" or "employee" volunteering. These are associations of the people charged with running their for-profit company's employee volunteer effort. CVCs are like specialized DOVIAs, providing education and support to their members. Some develop collaborative projects to pool the efforts of their employees. In some cities, the local volunteer center also staffs the CVC.

All the local resources described so far support volunteering *generically*, regardless of the setting. But some fields have evolved their own organizations and associations, which may be totally independent in one city or may be national with state and local chapters. For example, directors of volunteer services in hospitals have a well-established network, as do hospices, with membership limited to health care settings only. On the other hand, when there is a large enough concentration of cultural arts institutions in a city, it's common for each of their directors of volunteer involvement to meet together in an organized but largely informal way.

Whether or not someone joins a CVC or other special affinity group, there is still the need to join the generic infrastructure to get the "big picture" of volunteerism as a whole.

At the State Level

State Offices and Commissions

As a result of 1993 federal legislation, almost all states established governor-appointed "Commissions on National Service" to administer programs funded by the Corporation for National and Community Service (see the section on national-level resources). These commissions were superimposed onto an existing, less uniform system of state-level government offices charged with coordinating volunteerism.

Previously, state-level bureaus had names such as State Office on Voluntary Citizen Participation, Governor's Office on Volunteerism, and the like, and operated under mandates ranging as widely as their names. All attempted to be statewide clearinghouses of information about citizen involvement. In some ways, these state offices functioned as volunteer centers for a wider geographic area.

In the last decade, many former state offices have merged with—or been subsumed under—their state commissions. In a few states, both still operate as separate entities. When they are combined, 95 percent of the staff's focus is on supporting state-level, federally funded programs. So community volunteering rarely gets much attention beyond the occasional Governor's Proclamation during National Volunteer Week. On the other hand, in 2008, California became the first state with a cabinet-level position of "Secretary of Service and Volunteering," and in 2009, New York City named a "Chief Service Officer" to the mayor's cabinet, too. This may indicate new initiatives in the future.

Get on the mailing list of your state office or commission. The good state offices sponsor statewide conferences for volunteer leaders and publish informational newsletters.

State Associations

Just as there are local DOVIAs that bring together volunteer management practitioners, there are also state associations. There are about twenty-five state associations, many of them weak but at least a half dozen are quite vibrant. They run statewide conferences and provide other resources to their members. Note that local DOVIAs are not "chapters" of their state association, and membership can be held in both or either.

On the other hand, special affinity groups usually do have a state-level association with local chapters.

At the National Level

On the national level, there are several organizations devoted to furthering volunteerism generally, as well as some focused on one or another specific field of volunteer activity. What follows are some of the major generic organizations.

- **Corporation for National and Community Service** (http://www.nationalservice.gov). First formed in 1971 as ACTION (capitalized but not an acronym), this is the federal agency focused on volunteering. The name was changed to the Corporation for National and Community Service (the Corporation) by the Clinton administration in 1993. They state their mission in "What We Do" on their Web site as follows:

  > The Corporation provides grants and training and technical assistance to developing and expanding volunteer organizations. In addition, the Corporation explores, develops, and models effective approaches for using volunteers to meet the nation's human needs and conducts and disseminates research that helps develop and cultivate knowledge that will enhance the overall effectiveness of national and community service programs.[1]

  The largest programs they fund or administer are AmeriCorps, which still includes VISTA as a distinct program; the National Senior Service Corps, which includes RSVP, Foster Grandparents, and Senior Companions; and Learn & Serve America.

  The 2009 Edward M. Kennedy Serve America Act has expanded the number of AmeriCorps members and mandates the formation of several new "Corps" for special groups and causes, including military veterans.

  Annually, the Corporation holds a National Conference on Volunteering and Service (see http://www.volunteeringandservice.org) in conjunction with the Points of Light Institute.

- **HandsOn Network Generated by the Points of Light Institute** (http://www.handsonnetwork.org and http://www.pointsoflight.org). HandsOn Network Generated by the Points of Light Institute (HON/POLI) is the official name selected during the 2008 merger between the former Points of Light *Foundation* and HandsOn Network. As of the writing of this book, the projects and services of the merged organization are still evolving, as is the division of labor between what the institute will do and what HandsOn will do. They have inherited a number of projects, such as managing National Volunteer Week (usually the third week of April;

logos and materials can be downloaded each year at http://
www.handsonnetwork.org/programs/more/nvw) and partnering on the National Conference on Volunteering and Service. Along with its network of local affiliates, HON/POLI
also works with corporate partners and provides online
training for volunteer leaders (i.e., volunteers who serve as
team leaders for local HandsOn projects).

- **Association for Research on Nonprofit Organizations and
  Voluntary Action** (http://www.arnova.org). Self-described
  on their Web site home page as an "interdisciplinary community of people dedicated to fostering through research
  and education, the creation, application and dissemination
  of knowledge on nonprofit organizations, philanthropy, civil
  society and voluntary action," Association for Research on
  Nonprofit Organizations and Voluntary Action (ARNOVA)
  members are predominantly academics. They produce the
  scholarly journal *Nonprofit and Voluntary Sector Quarterly*
  and hold an annual international conference. They have an
  active listserv (ARNOVA-L), open to anyone interested.

- **Association of Leaders in Volunteer Engagement** (http://
  www.volunteeralive.org). Incorporated in 2009, the Association of Leaders in Volunteer Engagement (AL!VE) is the new
  national professional association for volunteer resource
  managers in the United States. Its mission, as stated on its
  Web site under "Mission, Vision, & Values," is "to enhance
  and sustain the spirit of volunteering in America by fostering collaboration and networking, promoting professional
  development, and providing advocacy for leaders in community engagement." AL!VE supersedes the former Association
  for Volunteer Administration (AVA), which closed its doors
  in 2006.

- **Council on Certification in Volunteer Administration**
  (http://www.cvacert.org). Practitioners with at least three
  years of experience in the field of volunteer resources
  management can earn the credential CVA (Certified in Volunteer Administration) through this unique, international,
  performance-based program. Originally developed decades

ago by the AVA, the CVA program is now sponsored by the Council for Certification in Volunteer Administration.

- **National Associations for Volunteer Program Managers in Specialized Settings**. There are many professional societies for affinity groups, including the Association for Healthcare Volunteer Resource Professionals (AHVRP), the American Association of Museum Volunteers (AAMV), the National Association of Volunteer Programs in Local Government (NAVPLG), and more. Energize maintains a list of such associations at http://www.energizeinc.com/prof/orgspec.html.

At the International Level

- **United Nations Volunteers** (http://www.unv.org). United Nations Volunteers (UNV) is the United Nations (UN) organization that contributes to peace and development through volunteerism worldwide. Based in Bonn, Germany, and active in 140 countries, UNV's main focus is full-time, stipended service by people from one country going to another (the Peace Corps is the UNV affiliate for the United States). In 2001, when the UN declared the "International Year of Volunteers," UNV was designated as its coordinating body, which propelled it into an advocacy role for the field of volunteerism. That was when it launched the Web site http://www.worldvolunteerweb.org and began producing research and other resources. UNV also coordinates International Volunteer Day, held annually on December 5 since 1985.

- **International Association for Volunteer Effort** (http://www.iave.org). The International Association for Volunteer Effort (IAVE) was founded in 1970 by a group of volunteers from around the world who saw volunteering as a means of making connections across countries and cultures. It has grown into a global network of volunteers, volunteer organizations, national representatives, and volunteer centers, with members in over seventy countries and in all world regions. The majority of IAVE members are in developing countries. IAVE holds a biannual world conference and various regional conferences at rotating host locations.

Other Resource Providers in the Field

Risk Management and Insurance Resources

- **The Nonprofit Risk Management Center** (http://www.nonprofitrisk.org) has produced pioneering books on volunteer risk-related subjects. The center offers a variety of online tutorials, including a volunteer risk management self-assessment tool, produces an electronic newsletter, and answers risk and insurance questions.

- **Linda Graff and Associates, Inc.** (http://www.lindagraff.ca). Linda Graff is the author of several key books on policies, risk management, and other volunteer-related issues (see the bibliography in the next section). The Web site offers both practical advice and "Linda's Musings." One valuable tool is "The Short Course On Screening Protocol Design" (http://www.lindagraff.ca/Past%20Musings/TheShortCourse.html).

- **Volunteers Insurance Service** (http://www.cimaworld.com/htdocs/volunteers.cfm). While there are insurance policies to indemnify the volunteers who serve on boards of directors and special riders to cover special event volunteers, it is less clear who insures the majority of frontline volunteers (see chapter nine on risk management and liability). One long-standing insurance program developed to cover the unique needs of a volunteer project by providing excess accident and liability insurance is Volunteers Insurance Service, which is underwritten by The CIMA Companies, Inc.

Volunteer Tracking Software

There are quite a number of software companies now offering either dedicated volunteer management programs or volunteer management "add-ons" to fundraising, special events, and other software programs. The most extensive, nonevaluative list of who is producing such software has been compiled by Jayne Cravens and can be found at her site, Coyote Communications, http://www.coyotecommunications.com/tech/volmanage.html.

Academics, Researchers, and Consultants

The last component of volunteerism infrastructure is the people who are knowledge generators and trainers for the field. These can be university-based academics, some of whom work within one of the institutions with a center for philanthropy or with the Cooperative Extension Service. They can be research staff in any number of nonprofit, corporate, or government organizations large enough to do research and publish meaningful reports, such as the Urban Institute; Independent Sector; Deloitte, LLP; and the American Red Cross. And they can be private consulting firms (like Energize). In the United States, the private consulting firms produce the most focused materials targeting volunteer management practices.

Training and Education in Volunteer Management

For Directors of Volunteer Involvement

Leaders of volunteer involvement have a growing selection of professional conferences and workshops from which to choose throughout the year, in many locations. There are also ongoing and periodic volunteer management academic courses, certificate programs, and institutes offered by various colleges and universities, some of which offer distance-learning online. Energize maintains an international listing of regularly scheduled learning opportunities as well as a calendar of conferences and events on our Web site at http://www.energizeinc.com/prof-1.html. Also be sure to check with your local HandsOn affiliate, DOVIA, or state association to learn what might be offered close to home.

For Staff Who Work with Volunteers

Another critical need in professional education is developing the skills of frontline staff expected to partner with volunteers daily. These staff may be trained in any number of professions but not in the skills of working with volunteers. To meet this need, Energize offers two popular resources so that you can teach paid staff the fundamentals of working with volunteers in *your* setting:

- *Training Busy Staff to Succeed with Volunteers: The 55-Minute Training Series* by Betty Stallings provides twelve training modules designed for delivery in fifty-five minutes of staff time. Each electronic module comes with a complete PowerPoint presentation; a timed script for the trainer highlighting "4 Key Concepts" on each topic; suggestions for expandable group activities; handout masters ready to duplicate, including a workshop evaluation form; and more. The complete set of modules can be purchased by individual organizations, and there are a number of limited- and unlimited-use licensing arrangements available for national organizations wishing to obtain the curriculum for their entire network. For more information, go to http://www .energizeinc.com/store/4-109-E-1.

- *Everyone Ready®* is a professional development program in volunteer management delivered via online seminars, electronic self-instruction guides, interactive discussion boards, and other online resources—available to each member organization's entire network of paid and volunteer staff, 24/7 year-round. A new featured topic is presented each month, on a thirty-six-month cycle. The higher the membership level, the greater the access to *Everyone Ready®* resources and additional tools for each learner. Learn more at http://www.energizeinc.com/everyoneready.

Bibliography

Periodicals

Many publications produced for the nonprofit field, public administration, or association management occasionally offer articles on volunteer topics. The following publications, however, are fully focused on volunteering and contain articles of sufficient length to qualify as more than e-newsletters. Several are produced in both printed and electronic form, but online editions are increasingly the norm.

- *e-Volunteerism: The Electronic Journal of the Volunteer Community*, http://www.e-volunteerism.com
- *International Journal of Volunteer Administration (IJOVA)*, http://www.ijova.org
- *SALT* (out of Singapore), http://www.nvpc.org.sg/
- *Service Enquiry* (out of South Africa), http://www.service -enquiry.org.za

- *Volunteer Management Review* (Charity Channel), http://www.charitychannel.com/articles/article-categories/volunteer-management-review.aspx
- *Volunteering: The Magazine* (UK), http://www.volunteering.org.uk/News/volunteeringmagazine/

Books

There has been a steady increase in the number of publications related to volunteer management. While the following list is by no means intended to be all inclusive or even comprehensive, it is a starting point for those learning more about the principles and practices of volunteer management.

The Energize Online Bookstore, supported by its *Volunteer Management Book Blog*, offers the largest selection of titles to the field, most in electronic form. Titles marked with an asterisk can be purchased at http://www.energizeinc.com/bookstore.

Campbell, Katherine Noyes, and Susan J. Ellis. *The (Help!) I-Don't-Have-Enough-Time Guide to Volunteer Management.* Philadelphia: Energize, Inc., 2004.*

Connors, Tracy Daniel, ed. *The Volunteer Management Handbook.* New York: John Wiley & Sons, 1995.

Cravens, Jayne, and Susan J. Ellis. *The Virtual Volunteering Guidebook: How to Apply the Principles of Real-World Volunteer Management to Online Service.* Palo Alto, CA: Impact Online, 2000. Available for free download at http://www.energizeinc.com/download/vvguide.pdf. A revised edition is in production and expected to be available in late 2010.

Ellis, Susan J. *Volunteer Management Audit.* Philadelphia: Energize, Inc., 2003.*

————. *The Volunteer (and Membership Development) Recruitment Book.* 3rd ed. Philadelphia: Energize, Inc., 2002.*

Ellis, Susan J., and Katherine H. Campbell. *By the People: A History of Americans as Volunteers.* 3rd ed. Philadelphia: Energize, Inc., 2005.*

Ellis, Susan J., Anne Weisbord, and Katherine H. Noyes. *Children as Volunteers: Preparing for Community Service.* Philadelphia: Energize, Inc., 2003.*

Graff, Linda L. *Best of All: The Quick Reference Guide To Effective Volunteer Involvement.* Dundas, Ontario, Canada: Linda Graff and Associates, 2005.

————. *Better Safe . . . Risk Management in Volunteer Programs & Community Service.* Dundas, Ontario, Canada: Linda Graff and Associates, 2003.*

————. *Beyond Police Checks: The Definitive Volunteer & Employee Screening Guidebook.* Dundas, Ontario, Canada: Linda Graff and Associates, 1999.*

————. *By Definition: Policies for Volunteer Programs.* 2nd ed. Dundas, Ontario, Canada: Linda Graff and Associates, 1997.*

Institute for Volunteering Research. *Volunteering Impact Assessment Toolkit.* London: Volunteering England, 2004.

Lee, Jarene Frances, with Julia M. Catagnus. *What We Learned (the Hard Way) about Supervising Volunteers: An Action Guide to Making Your Job Easier.* Philadelphia: Energize, Inc., 1999.*

McCurley, Steve, and Rick Lynch. *Volunteer Management: Mobilizing All the Resources of the Community.* 2nd ed. Kemptville, Ontario, Canada: Johnstone Training and Consultation, 2006.*

———. *Keeping Volunteers: A Guide to Retention.* Olympia, WA: Fat Cat, 2005.*

McCurley, Steve, and Sue Vineyard. *Handling Problem Volunteers: Real Solutions.* Downers Grove, IL: Heritage Arts, 1998.*

Mook, Laurie, Jack Quarter, and Betty Jane Richmond. *What Counts: Social Accounting for Nonprofits and Cooperatives.* London: Sigel, 2007.*

Noble, Joy, Louise Rogers, and Andy Fryar. *Volunteer Program Management: An Essential Guide.* 3rd ed. Adelaide, South Australia, Australia: Volunteering South Australia and Northern Territory, 2010.*

Nonprofit Risk Management Center. *No Surprises: Harmonizing Risk and Reward in Volunteer Management.* 5th ed. Washington, DC: 2009.

Ramrayka, Liza. *Employee Volunteering: The Guide.* London: Volunteering England, 2001.

Rehnborg, Sarah Jane and others. *Strategic Volunteer Engagement: A Guide for Nonprofit and Public Sector Leaders.* Austin, TX: RGK Center for Philanthropy and Community Service, the LBJ School of Public Affairs, the University of Texas at Austin, 2009.

Scheier, Ivan H. *Building Staff/Volunteer Relations.* Philadelphia: Energize, Inc., 2003.*

Stallings, Betty B. *Training Busy Staff to Succeed with Volunteers: The 55-Minute Training Series.* Philadelphia: Energize, Inc., 2007.*

———. *12 Key Actions of Volunteer Program Champions: CEOs Who Lead the Way.* Philadelphia: Energize, Inc., 2005.*

Stallings, Betty B., with Susan J. Ellis. *Leading the Way to Successful Volunteer Involvement: Practical Tips for Busy Executives.* Philadelphia: Energize, Inc., 2010.*

Volunteer Vancouver. *A People Lens: 101 Ways to Move Your Organization Forward.* Vancouver, British Columbia, Canada: Volunteer Vancouver, 2009.*

Index

About the Author

Susan J. Ellis

Susan J. Ellis is president of Energize, Inc., an international training, consulting, and publishing firm that specializes in volunteerism. She founded the Philadelphia-based company in 1977 and since that time has assisted clients throughout North America, Europe, Asia, Latin America, Israel, and Australasia to create or strengthen their volunteer corps.

Sought after as a trainer and presenter, Susan has motivated and taught audiences around the globe in small groups and at major conferences. She is the author or coauthor of twelve books, including *The Volunteer Recruitment (and Membership Development) Book* and *By the People: A History of Americans as Volunteers*. She has written more than ninety articles on volunteer management for dozens of publications and writes the national bimonthly column "On Volunteers," for *The NonProfit Times* (since 1990). From 1981 to 1987, she was editor-in-chief of *The Journal of Volunteer Administration*.

Energize's comprehensive Web site has won international recognition as a premier resource for volunteer program leaders (http://www.energizeinc.com). In 2000, she and Steve McCurley launched the field's first online journal, *e-Volunteerism: The Electronic Journal of the Volunteer Community* (http://www.e-volunteerism.com), for which she continues to serve as editor. Energize also offers *Everyone Ready®*, an online volunteer management training program for organizations and individuals (http://www.energizeinc.com/everyoneready), for which Susan serves as the dean of faculty.

Susan has a strong commitment to the value of volunteer involvement and to leading the volunteer community toward its maximum impact and recognition. She is a dynamic spokesperson for volunteerism and an active volunteer in a variety of professional associations and community groups.